D0376108

LANDMARK LAW CASES

AMERICAN SOCIETY

Peter Charles Hoffer

N. E. H. Hull

Series Editors

CAROLYN N. LONG

Mapp v. Ohio

Guarding against Unreasonable

Searches and Seizures

UNIVERSITY PRESS OF KANSAS

Published by the University Press of Kansas (Lawrence, Kansas 66045), which was
organized by the Kansas Board of Regents and is operated and funded by Emporia
State University, Fort Hays State University, Kansas State University, Pittsburg State
University, the University of Kansas, and Wichita State University

Library of Congress Cataloging-in-Publication Data

Long, Carolyn Nestor.
Mapp v. Ohio : guarding against unreasonable searches and seizures /
Carolyn N. Long.
p. cm. — (Landmark law cases & American society)
Includes bibliographical references and index.
ISBN 0-7006-1440-0 (cloth : alk. paper) — ISBN 0-7006-1441-9 (pbk. :
alk. paper)   1. Mapp, Dollree—Trials, litigation, etc.   2. Searches
and seizures—United States.   3. Exclusionary rule (Evidence)—United
States.   I. Title: Mapp versus Ohio.   II. Title.   III. Series.
KF224.M213L66 2006
345.730522—dc22   2006000286

British Library Cataloguing-in-Publication Data is available.

Printed in the United States of America

10 9 8 7 6 5 4 3 2 1

The exclusionary rule seems a bit jerry-built — like a roller coaster track constructed while the roller coaster sped along. Each new piece of track was attached hastily and imperfectly to the one before it, just in time to prevent the roller coaster from crashing, but without the opportunity to measure the curves and dips preceding it, or to contemplate the twists and turns that inevitably lay ahead.

—Justice Potter Stewart, discussing *Mapp v. Ohio* and the exclusionary rule

CONTENTS

In casebooks of law and constitutional textbooks they are just names — Griswold, Gideon, Mapp, Escobedo, Miranda — part of the "caption" or label on U.S. Supreme Court criminal rights cases. In fact, they were real people whose basic rights the Court vindicated when no one else would. Sometimes they were petty criminals, sometimes innocent men and women whom the police regarded as the usual suspects. As the stories fade from the newspapers and the precedents the cases set are replaced by other cases, the legal and constitutional historian becomes the last custodian of the drama, suspense, and humanity of the people behind the names.

Dollree Mapp's story is one of those that might have been lost, save for the remarkable detective work of scholar Carolyn Long. Using written police and legal sources and interviews with the principals, Long tells Mapp's story from the moment the police burst into her Cleveland, Ohio, home without a search warrant, seeking evidence of a crime they could not find, and then arresting her for an entirely different offense. That they were white and she was black played a part in their conduct, conduct that was condoned by the criminal and appeals courts in Ohio. What happened when the American Civil Liberties Union and Mapp's own counsel sought relief from the federal courts turns what was too common a story of police misconduct into a unique tale of courage and vindication.

Long has a sympathetic ear for all the participants in the story, bringing them to life. But this is not mere journalism. The crucial meaning and scope of the Fourth Amendment protection against illegal search and seizure, and its application in *Mapp v. Ohio* to the states, constitute the other thread in Long's tapestry. She traces the Fourth Amendment from its English beginnings, through the adoption of the Fourteenth Amendment, to the high court in the 1950s, and then beyond. Around the same time police were breaking into Mapp's home, Chief Justice Earl Warren's Court was working a revolution in procedural guarantees to go along with its strong civil rights record. In *Mapp* those two strands of cases came together. The decision to exclude wrongfully obtained evidence in state criminal prosecutions, "the poisoned fruit" of illegal searches, was a draconian measure, but one made necessary by some police forces' persistent violation of the rights of minorities.

Long assesses the impact of *Mapp* on the conduct of the police and the outcome of criminal cases, as well as on the Court itself. Critics of the case then and later insisted that it hamstrung police forces in their war against crime. In Congress and the media, some began to demand justices who were not "soft on crime." Certainly the case, taken with others in the "Warren Court revolution," created a backlash whose consequences we still feel. We will not reveal Long's conclusions on that matter, but they make a superb conclusion to a compelling book.

One of the most rewarding parts of writing this book was that it introduced me to Ms. Dollree Mapp, who graciously invited me into her home to share her thoughts on this landmark Supreme Court decision. We met on several occasions in 2004 and 2005, and it was a pleasure speaking with her in detail about her life. She was very candid about her experiences with the law and circumspect about this decision's impact on constitutional rights for all Americans. Carl Delau provided a phone interview in 2004, which also aided my research. Because many others who played a role in *Mapp v. Ohio* are no longer with us, these interviews provided an important firsthand account of the case as it moved through the system.

I am deeply indebted to my old high school and college friend Steven Leek, who offered much needed advice about the manuscript. He saw it in its roughest form and offered excellent suggestions for improvements. Steven was generous with his time and kind, yet firm, in his review. It was also a joy to recount the old days in Brookings, Oregon. Also helpful was Sha Hinds-Glick, a former student and friend who was able to track down some Ohio state court records to aid my research of *Mapp*'s travels through the state criminal justice system.

I am also very appreciative of the kind assistance of Mike Widener, the Archivist/Rare Books Librarian at the Tarlton Law Library at the University of Texas School of Law in Austin. He aided me in my review of Justice Tom C. Clark's private papers, which provide an inside look at the Supreme Court's deliberations in *Mapp*.

I am especially thankful to the reviewers and editors who provided constructive criticism on the book proposal and manuscript. I was extremely fortunate to benefit from excellent advice from reviewers when this project was at the proposal stage. Professor Joshua Dressler, the Frank R. Strong Chair in Law at Ohio State University's College of Law, and Professor David Bodenhamer, Director of the Polis Center, contributed very thorough and helpful comments that helped shape this project, and Series Editor Peter Charles Hoffer provided an excellent critique of the draft manuscript. His suggestions improved the manuscript significantly. I am also thankful that he and

N.E.H. Hull agreed to include this book in the fine Landmark Law Cases and American Society series. I count Michael Briggs, the editor in chief of the University Press of Kansas, as a good friend and mentor who has done a fine job encouraging and tolerating me over the years. His thoughtful direction improved this project, and our conversations about our shared interests in politics, literature, and film provided much-needed breaks.

Thanks, as always, to my kind colleagues in the Department of Political Science at Washington State University; in particular, my mentor and friend Lance T. Leloup, as well as Nicholas Lovrich and Cornell Clayton. Each offered their encouragement and direction, which are always appreciated. Thanks as well to the crew in Vancouver, including Amy Wharton, Paul Thiers, Mark Stephan, Laurie Drapela, and Dana Lee Baker.

Last but never least, I would like to thank my family for their support and patience during the writing of this book, including my father, John Hedding, and his wife, Gail, and my numerous siblings, Bob Hedding, John and Kama Hedding, Steve and Cydney Nestor, and Dawn Nestor. But most of all, I am blessed with the support of my husband, Kevin, and the special gift he gave us this year, young Tennyson Lynne. For that reason, this book is dedicated to him.

Prologue

One has to wonder why the Cleveland police decided to go after Ms. Dollree Mapp. They could not have found a more formidable foe. Today, more than forty years after the incident that would lead to the landmark *Mapp v. Ohio* decision, Ms. Mapp can easily intimidate even the most confident person. At age eighty-two she is still slender and fit from a vegetarian diet and a fitness routine that includes walks around her neighborhood three times a week. She remains quite beautiful, with high cheekbones, wide brown eyes, and a quick smile. But underneath that visage is a steely personality; a confident, articulate woman who locks you in her gaze and tells it like it is. She commands respect from her audience. It is quite evident that Ms. Mapp is not one to suffer fools. She makes no apologies to anyone and takes full responsibility for the life she has led. When asked about her personal philosophy, she says, "Everything happens for a reason. I am comfortable with the choices I have made in my life, and I'm not embarrassed about anything I've done. I have lived my life as I see fit."

Dollree Mapp was born on Halloween in Austin, Texas, in 1924. She is of mixed race; her father, Sam, was a Cherokee Indian, and her mother, Marian, African American. The fourth of six children, Mapp stood out among her siblings with her confident nature and sure sense of self. Her strong will was evident at a young age. "I was an assertive child . . . a determined child," she says. "My parents knew I was strong-willed." She enjoyed a good relationship with her parents but "gave my mother fits." Mapp's father, a cattleman, and her mother, a schoolteacher, "kept close watch" on her. "They knew I wasn't meek. That I had a mind of my own." Even as a youngster she told her parents that she "wanted to live my life my way." When she was ten they allowed her to move to Cleveland, Ohio, where she lived with an aunt.

In school, Mapp was a bright student, interested in a variety of subjects and popular with the boys. By age fifteen she found herself pregnant and later had her only child, her "angel," Barbara. She continued going to school but left at an early age. She would go out in the evening, socializing with friends at nightclubs, and was soon a familiar fixture on the Cleveland boxing scene. It was there that she met and began dating Cleveland boxing great Jimmy Bivins, who was regarded as one of the best light-heavyweight and heavyweight boxers of his time. During his career he defeated eight world champion boxers and was ranked in the top ten in one division or another from 1940 to 1953. In 1942 he was rated the number one contender in both the light-heavyweight and the heavyweight division.

Mapp and Bivins married, but he was a less than model husband. It was an abusive relationship, and Mapp soon realized the marriage was a mistake. She explains, "I had a girlfriend who was beaten by her husband three times a day. I would never take that. I always told myself, I'm not taken a beating from no man." Mapp found herself with two choices, only one of which viable. "I had to leave him or kill him, and I wasn't ready to kill him," she says. She left the marriage and lived for a short time with a friend from school, Dorothy Miller, and her daughter, Margaret. Mapp makes a conscience effort to avoid talking about her ex-husband. "He was a nonentity," she notes noncommittally, reflecting his unimportance in her life. After the divorce Mapp went back to school to study fashion design. She also took art and drafting classes and contemplated where life would take her.

Despite the divorce, Mapp still socialized in Cleveland's boxing circles and met people such as Donald King, who lived with his wife down the street from her Milverton home. "We were acquaintances," she says, "we had similar friends." At one time she was engaged to Archie Moore, the former light-heavyweight world boxing champion. Speaking with Mapp, one gets the impression that it was she, and not these world-class athletes, who had the upper hand in these relationships. She readily admits that some of the people she associated with were likely involved in some "shady" business but insists that she was not. And, although she describes herself as a bit of a loner, a person who values her privacy, she recalls how much she enjoyed the company of her friends. "I was a black woman living on her own in a white neighborhood," she explains, "and there was racial tension in the city." This tension was exacerbated by the Cleveland police Bureau of Special Investigation. "They thought they controlled the town," Mapp recalls. The experience left her guarded and suspicious of authority. However, it would also shape her into the person she is today: an intelligent, proud woman who likes who she is and is comfortable with the choices she has made in her life.

———

This story begins with an early morning police search of Ms. Dollree Mapp's home in Cleveland, Ohio. Police, acting on an anonymous tip and pretending to have a warrant, burst into Mapp's home, which they searched for several hours. The search yielded material the police officers considered obscene, and Mapp was arrested for violating the state antiobscenity statute. As the case moved through the state legal system, the constitutionality of the law prohibiting the possession of obscenity was questioned, an issue that eventually attracted the attention of the U.S. Supreme Court. However, shortly after the Court's conference deliberations, a slim majority turned its focus away from the constitutionality of the state law and toward the appropriateness of the police conduct and the question of whether illegally obtained evidence should be excluded from state criminal trials. As a result, this case about the "woman with the dirty books" was transformed from an obscenity case to one about Fourth Amendment protection from illegal searches and seizures. The Court's decision in *Mapp v. Ohio* imposed the exclusionary rule on more than half the states in the union, thereby ensuring that unlawfully seized evidence would be excluded from state criminal trials. The decision significantly altered police conduct and helped ensure that every American's right against unreasonable searches and seizures was protected under the Constitution. And, it sparked the Warren Court's criminal due process revolution, which some have characterized as "the second Constitutional Convention."

This book follows the story of *Mapp v. Ohio* chronologically. The first half offers a detailed look at the case as it moved through the state and federal courts. Chapter 1 begins with the illegal search and seizure of evidence from Ms. Dollree Mapp's home, which led to her arrest and introduction into the Ohio state criminal justice system, and details the case's disposition in the state courts. Chapter 2 provides a brief history of the Fourth Amendment and the origins of the federal exclusionary rule. This chapter also reviews the state of exclusionary rule jurisprudence prior to *Mapp v. Ohio*. The next two chapters examine the Supreme Court's consideration of this landmark decision; chapter 3 details Mapp's appeal and oral arguments before the Court, and chapter 4 describes the Court's deliberations and the circulation of opinions.

The second half of the book captures *Mapp*'s effect. Chapter 5 explores the public reaction and the arguments in favor of and in opposition to the exclusionary rule as a mechanism for ensuring protection against unreasonable searches and seizures. This chapter also reviews *Mapp*'s implementation and examines whether states complied with the Supreme Court's mandate. Chapter 6 presents the empirical research on the exclusionary rule and its influence on police behavior and the disposition of cases in state criminal trials. Chapter 7 looks more broadly at *Mapp* as part of the Warren Court's criminal due process revolution. This chapter also reviews several significant Fourth Amendment decisions handed down during Warren's tenure. Analysis of how these decisions were later used by the Burger and Rehnquist Courts to undermine and limit the exclusionary rule is provided in chapter 8, which also covers the political effort to address *Mapp v. Ohio*. It ends with an observation about the implications of new judicial federalism on the future of the exclusionary rule debate. The epilogue provides an update on Ms. Dollree Mapp, whose court battle paved the way for this landmark decision.

familiar with the address — the home belonged to Ms. Dollree Mapp, whom he would later describe as "a foxy girl" with "a swagger about her that was just as calm as can be and just as jibe as can be and just as flippant as can be." The description was not meant as a compliment. Delau believed Mapp, whom he describes as an "arch enemy," was connected to Cleveland's organized crime. He characterized her as a "top figure as a pickup person of numbers wagers" and knew she associated with people involved in illegal gambling.

Delau, accompanied by officers Thomas J. Dever and Michael J. Haney, went to Mapp's home to investigate the tip. When they arrived around 1:30 that afternoon, they noticed Ogletree's car parked outside of the house. Believing the bombing suspect was still inside, Delau recalls that they "sat there and waited for a long time." Weary of the waiting game, he eventually turned to Dever and Haney and said, "Well, how would it look if we made an inquiry. They might just say, 'Hiya, come right in.'" However, he admits, "I knew Dollree Mapp, and I figured it would be a little different than that."

The plainclothes officers approached the home and rang the bell at the side door. Mapp was upstairs in her second-floor apartment when she heard the bell. She leaned out the upstairs window and asked the men what they wanted. Delau told her they wanted to "come in and take a look around." But when Mapp asked why, he refused to give her any information. She told the police that she would not let them in until she called her lawyer. Delau and the patrolmen continued to ring the bell and insist on entry into the house. Frustrated, Mapp closed the window and phoned her attorney, A. L. Kearns, to ask for advice. Unable to reach him, she was transferred to Walter L. Greene, a young attorney who had recently joined Kearns's firm, where his father, Irwin, was a partner. Greene told Mapp, "If they can produce a warrant, and show you the warrant, let you read it to see it is in proper order, then let them in." His advice was based on his reading of the Ohio state constitution. He informed Mapp that law enforcement officers were required to procure a search warrant based "upon probable cause, supported by oath or affirmation, particularly describing the place to be searched and things to be seized."

Mapp returned to the window and asked the police if they had a warrant. When they admitted that they did not, Mapp told them that she would not let them in without one. Sergeant Delau was frustrated by

Mapp's resistance. He explains, "You have to have had contact with her to understand her. She was a cunning, daring, and audacious person." Moreover, he had conducted hundreds of searches without a warrant and did not believe they were required under Ohio law. His interpretation of the law was technically incorrect; the Ohio Constitution required searches to be conducted with a warrant. At this point in history, however, law enforcement officers in approximately half the states in the union, including Ohio, routinely conducted searches without warrants. There was little reason not to because illegally seized evidence could still be admitted in criminal trials.

But Mapp understood the law and knew she did not have to let the police into her home, so she was defiant. She told Delau to have his boss, Lieutenant Thomas Cooley, call her to discuss the situation. The officers then returned to the car, drove approximately one block away, and contacted Cooley. The lieutenant phoned Mapp and explained to her that the police needed to speak with her and search the house. Mapp told him the same thing she told Delau — that she would not allow the police into her home without a warrant. She hung up the phone and looked out her window. She was startled to see the three officers still watching the house. Not knowing what to do, she called Greene again. "She was terrified," says the lawyer, "and asked that I come out."

Greene arrived at Mapp's home around 4:30, just in time to see several additional police cars, a paddy wagon, and he estimates between ten and fifteen police officers, half in uniform, surrounding the home. "It was something out of the movies or TV," he notes. "There were the black-and-whites with their flashing lights and cops all around. Neighbors from all up and down the street had gathered on the sidewalk across from Dolly Mapp's house, curious about what was happening." Greene found Delau, Haney, and Dever attempting to enter through the side door. He asked them if they had a search warrant, stating that if they did, it was not necessary to force their way into the home. "Just show it to Ms. Mapp," he told the officers. As he confronted them, Lieutenant Thomas White from Central Police Station, sent by Lieutenant Cooley, arrived on the scene. According to Greene, Delau turned to him and said now they had a warrant. But, he adds, "they refused to show it to anybody. I never did see a warrant." Greene then saw Delau use an instrument to pry open the outer screen door and break a pane of glass to gain entry into Mapp's home. As the officers barged into the home, the lawyer attempted to follow them to consult with his client, but he was denied access.

When Mapp heard the glass break, she descended the stairwell at the same time Lieutenant White and Sergeant Delau, with officers Dever and Haney behind them, ascended the stairs. Standing a few steps above White, Mapp confronted him, exclaiming, "I want to see the search warrant." Holding up a piece of paper, White replied, "Here is the search warrant. You can't see it." Mapp then grabbed the paper and put it down the front of her dress. One of the officers said, "What are we going to do now?" after which Delau replied, "I'm going down after it." Startled, Mapp told him, "No you are not!" But, she said, "he went down anyway." There was a struggle with Delau attempting to retrieve the paper and Mapp yelling at Delau to "take your hand out of my dress!" Delau characterized Mapp as "quite belligerent" as he recovered the paper. He said that "she did tussle and fight. . . . And I said, 'Dollree, don't do that. You come with me while we search.' Once we were in, she was going to be hostile to us. All the time she was playing games with us and talking cute, defying us, and threatening us. . . . And she was going to be real nasty. And I think she took a swing at one of the uniformed men if I'm not mistaken. . . . She was, in a sense, resisting, so she was handcuffed . . . to one of the uniformed men."

Handcuffed, Mapp was led upstairs, where she sat on the bed with a uniformed officer standing over her while Haney and Dever searched her room. At the same time, several other police officers entered the downstairs apartment, which Mapp had rented to a boarder, Minerva Fitzpatrick Lockheart. It was there that they found Virgil Ogletree, who was arrested and led outside.

With Ogletree in custody, the police conducted a wide-ranging search of Mapp's home. Delau and Haney looked through every drawer and chest in her bedroom and every other room in her apartment. Dever searched the basement, and several other officers searched Lockheart's downstairs apartment. Mapp recalls that at one point she was handcuffed to a banister on the stairwell so the officer watching her could join the search.

Outside, Greene repeatedly tried to gain entry to the house. He was concerned about his client. He remembers "a great deal of commotion and loud talk" and that he heard Mapp "call out several times." While outside, Greene, who frequently carried a small camera with him, tried to capture the incident on film. "I tried to take pictures of the people as they were being taken away, but . . . I guess in the excitement I didn't pull the film through; they didn't come out." He recalls that his attempt to photograph the scene was not welcomed by the police.

After the search, Sergeant Delau and officers Haney and Dever converged in the hallway next to the handcuffed Mapp to review the fruits of their labor. Dever produced a trunk of policy paraphernalia he said he found in the basement, and Delau and Haney revealed that their search of Mapp's bedroom yielded material they believed to be obscene. They presented four books, *London Stage Affairs*, *Affairs of a Troubadour*, *Memoirs of a Hotel Man*, and *Little Darlings*, they said had been found in a dresser drawer, along with an unloaded gun, a nude pencil sketch, and several photos found in a suitcase. Mapp watched the officers as they looked over the material. She remembers that "they seemed to enjoy them immensely." She insisted that the material was in a bag in the basement and that it belonged to a former boarder. Unconvinced, the police arrested Ms. Dollree Mapp. She was placed in the back of a patrol car with Sergeant Carl Delau and driven to the station.

———

Carl Delau was born in August 1918 in Cleveland, Ohio, the fifth of eight children born to German parents, who had emigrated from Poland several years earlier. He served in the Ohio National Guard after graduating from high school and was later called to active duty in the U.S. Army, where he served for five years during World War II. He joined the Cleveland police department on January 1, 1946, as a temporary police officer and was hired full-time that summer. He quickly distinguished himself and in November 1949 was selected to serve as a member of the Cleveland police's Bureau of Special Investigation. The unit, which was empowered to investigate vice crimes throughout the city, was led by Lieutenant Thomas Cooley, who reported directly to the police chief. An imposing man at six foot two and 180 pounds, Delau was good at his job and was soon promoted to the position of sergeant. According to Delau, the bureau was very successful in controlling vice crimes in the city. "After putting a severe crimp in the illegal horse wagering, we were assigned to work on the numbers racket due to complaints of police payoffs, car bombings and other violence." It was his work on the numbers racket that brought him into contact with Ms. Dollree Mapp. Delau contends that "she was a top figure as a pickup person of numbers wagers from the various writers. Our three-man squad arrested her several times and had other conversations with her."

In Cleveland, as in many large cities, professional gambling was thought to be connected to organized crime, and because there had been an increase in violence, the police were making a concerted effort to clean up the problem. "Number" or "policy" games were forms of a daily lottery where bettors would select a three-digit or series of three-digit numbers, and winners were paid at a rate between 200 and 1,000 to 1. The bets placed were often small, from ten cents to a dollar, which meant the game was predominantly played by people in the lower socioeconomic class. Because in Cleveland these were usually people of color, this meant that the police, who were overwhelmingly white, would frequently target African Americans during their investigations. As a result, there was an undercurrent of racial tension in the city as the Bureau of Special Investigation vice squad aggressively followed leads, and, as described by Delau, "swept clean" the "back alleys of the numbers game." The problem was exacerbated by the fact that the unit would frequently search suspects and their property without a warrant. As Delau explained, "We [made] hundreds of searches of houses a year and use[d] a warrant maybe only two times. We didn't think we needed one."

Delau's unit used a variety of strategies to crack down on the numbers racket. Sometimes its members would intimidate suspects or harass them in an effort to discourage illegal gambling, or they would make arrests knowing they were unlikely to result in prosecution. Because many of the crimes associated with the numbers game were misdemeanors punishable only by a small fine or limited jail time, arrests for purposes other than conviction were common. For example, offenders might be arrested and jailed for a short period to interrupt the illegal activity, or as a form of punishment as offenders were forced to spend money on legal representation and endure the inconvenience of the criminal justice process. Searches in order to seize contraband and gaming paraphernalia to get it off the streets were also common. The Bureau of Special Investigation would also arrest small-time players in the numbers game in an effort to gather information on those higher in the policy syndicate.

Delau and his unit were doing their best to combat vice in Cleveland. He declares, "We were a well-trained, innovative, aggressive squad, working to curtail the numbers racket, to which we caused much harm." However, to Mapp and others in the African American community, local law enforcement consistently and purposefully harassed them. And, they did so knowing they themselves were violating the law. As one observer noted, "The white police officers who invaded Dollree Mapp's home did so with confidence that they would not be called to task for violating her fundamental rights by entering her home without a warrant."

Nor was this police behavior unusual at this time in our country's history. Many metropolitan areas struggled with vice crimes, and because they occurred mostly in minority communities, this meant that white police and people of color would be in frequent contact. The problem, as evidenced by Mapp's case, was that police misconduct was so common that it was seen as legitimate. Reflecting on police tactics during this period, one scholar explained, "The illegal entry of Mapp's house by the police was nothing extraordinary; it was an everyday fact of life for blacks and other racial minorities. Police throughout America were part of the machinery of keeping blacks 'in their place,' ignoring constitutional guarantees against unreasonable arrests and searches and those that barred the use of 'third-degree' tactics when questioning suspects. The Constitution played little role in the relationship between blacks and the police, and the black population had little power at the time to seek redress through the political process."

After her arrest, Mapp was taken to the Cleveland municipal police station, where she was questioned by Delau. Mapp was outraged over the search and the manner of her arrest and was less than cooperative with police. She felt the all-white unit had targeted her and invented the story about the anonymous tip as a ruse to harass her. But Delau and the Bureau of Special Investigation believed their actions were justified. They had gone to Mapp's home to investigate a bombing and during their investigation had uncovered evidence of criminal activity. Moreover, Mapp was known to associate with people involved in illegal gambling, and they believed her arrest might lead to others, especially given a possible connection to racketeers "shaking down" people like King. According to Delau, they were just doing their job. Illegal gambling was a serious problem in Cleveland, and the unit was charged with cracking down on those violating the law.

Delau questioned Mapp about any knowledge she might have about the bombing at Donald King's home. He found her "very evasive in her answers" and believed she was "not making an effort to be helpful to the police." According to the sergeant, although Mapp admitted that she knew King and other clearinghouse figures, including a man she was currently dating, she "could give no help relative to the bombing of King's home." Mapp was also asked about the policy paraphernalia and obscene material found at her home. She denied they belonged to her and repeated her earlier claim that they belonged to Morris Jones, a boarder who had moved away five weeks earlier. However, based on the interview and the clearinghouse material found in her home, the police had sufficient evidence to charge Mapp with possession of gambling paraphernalia, a misdemeanor. They decided to hold her overnight in hopes that time behind bars would make her more forthcoming in the morning.

Virgil Ogletree was questioned separately by Delau. Ogletree, who owned Friendly Service Dry Cleaners, told the sergeant he had arrived at Mapp's home several minutes before the police to pick up some clothing. He said he was at home at the time of the bombing of King's home and that he had no information about who may have committed the crime. Although Ogletree admitted to a previous arrest for a clearinghouse violation, he stated that he had no connection with an illegal gambling operation and that he was unaware of the policy paraphernalia in Mapp's home. After determining that he was not connected to the bombing or illegal gambling, police released Ogletree without charge.

In the police report filed the next day, Delau described how the officers had gone to Mapp's home based on the confidential tip that a suspect connected with the bombing was "confining himself to this address and that there also was a lot of clearinghouse evidence at this location." The report summarized the police action and search of the home, including Mapp's reluctance to admit police into the house without a search warrant and the officers' decision to wait outside the residence until a search warrant was brought to the scene by Lieutenant White. The report also addressed the issue of the search warrant—a matter that would later become central to this case. "With the warrant in our possession," Delau wrote in the report, "we then gained entrance via the side door and placed Mapp under arrest while they searched the premises." More than twenty years later, Delau would admit that the police did not in fact have a warrant to search the home but rather only had an affidavit for a warrant. Because he knew this at the time he wrote the report, Delau lied in the official police record. The lie would be repeated as the case moved through the state and federal courts.

After spending the evening in jail, Mapp awoke to a front-page story in the *Cleveland Plain Dealer,* "Policy House Closed after 3-Hour Siege: Police Break In, Arrest Former Mrs. Bivins," which described the raid of her home. Accompanying the story was a photograph of Delau next to the trunk of policy slips found in Mapp's basement. That morning Mapp appeared before the Cleveland Municipal Court, a court of limited jurisdiction that traditionally handles traffic violations and misdemeanor offenses. She was represented by A. L. Kearns, sixty-two, a seasoned litigator who had practiced law in Cleveland for more than four decades. Kearns persuaded the judge that his client was not responsible for the gambling material, and she was acquitted of the charges.

But Mapp's troubles were far from over. Over the weekend Officer Michael Haney prepared an affidavit charging her with possession of obscene pictures and books and secured a warrant for her arrest. It was a felony crime under section 2905.34 of the Ohio Revised Code, punishable by one to seven years in prison and a fine of up to $2,000. Mapp was rearrested on Monday and brought before the municipal court for arraignment. However, because the crime was a felony and outside the jurisdiction of his court, Judge Andrew Kovachy bound the case over for grand jury consideration. Mapp was released after posting bail of $2,500.

The grand jury for Cuyahoga County convened several months later, in September 1957, to consider the charges against Mapp. The prosecuting attorney, John Corrigan, presented the state's evidence. As is typical in grand jury proceedings, only the prosecution was present. The purpose of the grand jury hearing was to determine whether there was enough evidence to bring formal charges against Mapp. Corrigan told the grand jury about the search of Mapp's home and the seizure of the obscene material. Although the prosecuting attorney had the option of calling witnesses to testify on the state's behalf, none appeared.

After reviewing the information presented by Corrigan, a majority of the fifteen-person grand jury issued an indictment which stated that Mapp "unlawfully and knowingly had in her possession and under her control, certain lewd and lascivious Books, Pictures and Photographs, said Books, Pictures and Photographs being so indecent and immoral in their nature that the same would be offensive to the Court and improper to be placed upon the records thereof contrary to the form of the statute in such case made and provided, and against the peace and dignity of the State of Ohio." The indictment was stamped case number 68326, signed by the prosecuting attorney and filed with the court of common pleas. Several days later Mapp pled not guilty to the charge, requested a jury trial, and was released pending trial.

It would take nearly a year before the case was heard. During the interim, Mapp, always interested in new opportunities, took classes on fashion design, art, and drafting and worked part-time at an interior decorating shop. As time passed, Mapp's anger at the Cleveland police grew. She was outraged over the police's conduct and very critical of Delau's Bureau of Special Investigation. Mapp insisted that the police unfairly targeted her. "I think they were just nosy sons of a bitch," she says. "That squad was allowed to do whatever it wanted. These three cops thought they owned the world." She explains that she resisted letting them into the house because she did not trust them. "Of course I was nasty. And rightfully so. They came into my house for no reason."

To this day, Mapp believes that the officers were motivated, in part, by racism. "They were very prejudiced. Hitlers. They would target certain people in the community. They wanted me to rat on my friends." She adds that she also "feared them because I thought they might plant evidence." Mapp points to the extraordinary measures the police took to charge her with a crime as proof of their lack of partiality. She also remembers clearly, years later, how the police manhandled her during the search, cuffing her while they retrieved the paper they described as a warrant, and how they extensively searched every room and piece of furniture in her house — all ostensibly under the pretense of looking for someone with information about a bombing. "They searched the drawers, the kitchen cabinets, the closets, in the pills — I had some diet pills. I guess they were looking there for some man in the pill package. They went all over."

Adamant of her innocence, Mapp was determined to fight the obscenity charge. However, she also knew the process could be lengthy and potentially expensive. A single mother with a thirteen-year-old daughter and a modest income, Mapp found herself in an unenviable position. Fortunately, news of her predicament reached one of her friends who was sensitive to her situation. He gave her the funds to pay for her legal bills. "Without his help I never would have been able to fight the case at all," she says.

Mapp's trial on the obscenity charge was set for fall 1958. Prior to the hearing, Kearns spoke to Mapp about the possibility of plea-bargaining in an effort to avoid a trial, which could be unpredictable. He told her it would be difficult to avoid jail time, and asked her if she would accept a one-year sentence. "The idea infuriated me," Mapp recalls. "I refused to go to prison for something I didn't do." She rejected the plea outright. However, prior to the trial and without his client's approval, Kearns made an effort to settle the case. On July 31, 1958, he appeared before Judge Joseph A. Artl in the court of common pleas and proposed a possible plea agreement. Kearns told the judge that he might be able to persuade Mapp to change her plea to guilty if the judge could assure him that his client would receive only a fine. The plea would allow Mapp to avoid jail time, which would be difficult for the mother of a young teenager. However, the prosecuting attorney's office rejected the offer. Although the judge has the final say regarding whether a plea bargain will be approved, the defense and prosecuting attorneys must first be in agreement about the nature of the plea. After the state rejected Kearns's offer, the case was set for trial.

Ohio v. Mapp was heard in Courtroom Number 1 in the criminal branch of the court of common pleas in downtown Cleveland on September 3, 1958. Judge Donald F. Lybarger presided over the case. Mapp was represented by Kearns and was accompanied in court by Walter Greene and her friend Dolores Clark, both of whom were slated to appear as witnesses for the defense. The state of Ohio was represented by Gertrude Bauer Mahon, the assistant prosecuting attorney for Cuyahoga County. Mahon, fifty-four, had practiced law in Ohio for the past sixteen years. She was a pioneer for women in the legal profession, one of a small number of women who had graduated from law school in the early 1940s. With Mahon were Sergeant Delau and officer Haney, witnesses for the prosecution.

The first order of business was a motion to suppress the evidence that resulted from the search of Mapp's home on Milverton Road. Kearns had repeatedly asked the state to produce evidence of the warrant authorizing the search but was rebuffed. Convinced a warrant did not exist, Kearns argued that because the search of Mapp's home was illegal, the evidence used to arrest his client — the obscene material — had been unlawfully seized and should be suppressed, or excluded from trial. This "exclusionary rule" had been applied in federal criminal trials since 1914 when the U.S. Supreme Court ruled in *Weeks v. United States* that illegally obtained evidence must be excluded from federal criminal trials as a requirement of the Fourth Amendment to the Constitution. However, in 1949 the Supreme Court ruled in *Wolf v. Colorado* that the exclusionary rule applied only to federal criminal proceedings. The ruling left it up to each state to determine whether the rule was appropriate to enforce the dictates of the Fourth Amendment to the U.S. Constitution or a similar provision under the state constitution. At the time of Mapp's trial, approximately half of the states in the country used an exclusionary rule similar to the one applied in federal criminal prosecutions under *Weeks*. The other half of the states, including Ohio, had not adopted the rule.

Kearns knew that his motion to suppress the evidence in Mapp's case would be an uphill battle. This was because in 1936 the Ohio Supreme Court ruled, in *State v. Lindway*, that illegally seized evidence could still be admitted in state criminal trials because the Fourth Amendment to the U.S. Constitution did not apply to the states. Victims of an illegal search did have redress, however. The state supreme court added that "an officer of the law who makes a search and seizure in a dwelling or other premises without a warrant or with an illegal warrant in contravention of Section 14, Article I of the Constitution of Ohio is a trespasser and amenable to an action for such trespass."

Despite the *Lindway* precedent, Kearns argued that exclusion of illegally seized evidence was appropriate under state law and the state constitution. To support his reasoning, Kearns first noted that state law required warrants for police searches under section 2905.35 of the Ohio Revised Code, which requires that a magistrate or judge "shall issue warrants to search such house or place upon written complaint, supported by oath or affirmation." State law also included a "particularity" clause; under section 2933.24 of the code, a search warrant must "particularly describe the things to be searched for." Both statutes were enacted in October 1955 and were a reflection of article I, section 14, of the Ohio state constitution, which forbade issuance of search warrants except "upon probable cause, supported by oath or affirmation, particularly describing the place to be searched and things to be seized." Kearns argued that because "the state of Ohio did not have a search warrant setting forth the items that are mentioned in this indictment, and which the state of Ohio intends to use as evidence in this case against this defendant," the search was illegal.

Illustrating that the search of Mapp's home was illegal was the easy part of the argument; the more difficult part was getting around *Lindway*, which allowed illegally seized evidence to be admitted in an Ohio state criminal trial. Kearns took a stab in the dark. He argued that passage of the two statutes in 1955, almost twenty years after the *Lindway* decision, illustrated the state legislature's intention to strictly enforce the state constitution's warrant requirement. In essence, Kearns suggested that the statutes requiring a warrant and a warrant specifically noting items to be searched for made the *Lindway* precedent moot.

Gertrude Mahon, representing the prosecution, was asked by Judge Lybarger whether there was a search warrant. She replied, "Yes, your honor, a search warrant was issued." Mahon added that the others "obtained this evidence as a result of it." Kearns tried to press the issue by adding that if such a warrant existed, it did not fulfill the "particularity" requirement under state law, but he was unsuccessful in his attempt to persuade Judge Lybarger to suppress the illegally seized evidence. The judge overruled Kearns's motion based on *Lindway*, and the illegally seized evidence was admitted.

The trial of *Ohio v. Mapp* began moments later with the two attorneys offering brief opening remarks. Mahon, representing the state, described the police as lawfully conducting a legitimate search which yielded probative evidence that Mapp was knowingly in possession of obscene materials in violation of state law; Kearns portrayed the police as overzealous and abusive, illegally searching Mapp's private residence while at the same time denying her access to her attorney. Kearns also hinted at Mapp's defense — that she was not "in possession" of the obscene material found during the search.

Officer Haney was the first witness called on behalf of the prosecution. A member of the Cleveland police force for more than twelve years and of the department's Bureau of Special Investigation for a substantial portion of that time, Haney played an instrumental role in the search of Mapp's home. He testified that the defendant let the officers into her home voluntarily, whereupon they conducted a search over two and a half to three hours that produced the obscene books in a dresser in Mapp's room and the "vulgar" pencil drawing and a photograph album in a suitcase by the bed. "In removing them," he told the court, "Ms. Mapp saw them and said, 'Better not look at those; they might excite you.'" Haney also confirmed that he was present when Delau found the obscene books in a chest of drawers in the bedroom. The items were admitted into evidence as the state's exhibits 1 through 13. Mahon sat down, confident she had established that police found obscene materials in the defendant's possession during a legitimate search of her home.

It was up to Kearns to challenge that impression. During his cross-examination of Haney, Kearns asked the patrolman a series of pointed questions regarding the location of the obscene material. In an attempt to confuse him, Kearns suggested that the seized material could have been located in other parts of Mapp's apartment or the basement, and that the material had actually been found among the belongings of Morris Jones, her former boarder. Kearns also tried to cast doubt on Haney's claim that he witnessed Delau finding material in the bedroom dresser. However, the officer, unflappable, refused to change his story. Kearns used the final few minutes of his cross-examination to challenge the legitimacy of the police search. Although Judge Lybarger ruled prior to the onset of the trial that the evidence seized in the case was admissible, even if unlawfully obtained, Kearns wanted to cast doubt on the integrity of the officers' actions. His examination of officer Haney concluded with this exchange:

"Where is that search warrant?" Kearns asked.

"I don't know," Haney replied.

"Do you have it here?" Kearns continued.

"I don't have it here."

"Would you tell the jury who has it?"

"I can't tell the jury who has it; no, sir."

"And you were one of the investigating officers in the investigation by the police department?"

"Yes."

"But you can't tell us where the search warrant is?"

"No, I cannot."

"Or what it recites?"

"No."

"You yourself did not obtain the search warrant, did you, officer?"

"No, I did not."

"Do you know who did?"

"I was told Lieutenant White obtained it."

Sergeant Delau, the lead officer in the search and arrest of Ms. Mapp, was the second witness called on behalf of the state. Like officer Haney, Delau had been a member of the Cleveland police force for more than a dozen years. Delau corroborated Haney's testimony regarding the police search and the location of the obscene material in the defendant's bedroom. He testified that both he and officer Dever searched the basement of Mapp's home, where Dever found the policy paraphernalia in a foot locker. In regard to the purported search warrant, Delau insisted that Lieutenant White arrived on the scene with a proper warrant to search the home, as he described in the police report. Because we now know that Delau was aware that the warrant did not exist, it was at this point in the trial that he committed perjury. He did, however, candidly describe how Mapp grabbed the paper police described as a search warrant and "concealed it on her person" and how he "recovered the warrant." Also significant was the fact that Delau contradicted Haney's testimony that Mapp let them into the house voluntarily. Instead, he admitted that the police "did pry the screen door" open in order to enter her home. After Delau's testimony, the court adjourned for lunch.

When court resumed, Kearns questioned Sergeant Delau. He used the officer's admission that he had broken into Mapp's home as an opportunity to highlight the inappropriateness of the police activity. His questions during cross-examination focused on the number of officers engaged in the search, whether there was a valid warrant to conduct the search, and the possibility that the material was found outside of Mapp's room. However, aside from obtaining Delau's admission that the police broke into Mapp's home, rather than Haney's version that Mapp "voluntarily welcomed" them, Kearns made little headway with the confident sergeant.

It was now time for the defense. Kearns's strategy was to use the testimony of Walter Greene, his associate, to present a different perspective of the police officers' conduct during the search, including the fact that the Cleveland police denied him access to his client. He planned to use the testimony of Dolores Clark and Mapp to establish that the defendant was not in possession of the obscene material found in her home.

Greene was the first witness for the defense. When asked about the purported search warrant, Greene testified that he was never given the opportunity to see it. Greene stated that he heard Mapp call out several times during the search and explained how he was denied access to his client despite repeated requests. He described how the police stopped him from entering Mapp's home and how he "walked from door to door, yelled in, [and] asked the inspector to let me in to observe what was going on. Either I got no answer, or if I got an answer I wasn't going to be admitted." On cross-examination, Mahon tried to undermine Greene's testimony by suggesting that he was lying to help his employer. She also verified that he had full access to his client at the police station.

Dolores Clark, Mapp's friend "off and on" for more than thirteen years, testified how the material found in the home belonged to a former boarder, Morris Jones. She testified that she visited Mapp several months prior to the police search to help her pack up Jones's belongings, which they placed in a box and put in the basement. According to Clark, included among Jones's personal effects were some "dirty books and some pictures" in a brown paper bag. Clark recalled that Mapp said, "Look at what filthy stuff men read." She described that "we laughed it off, put it in the bag and put it with the man's stuff, and took it down to the basement."

The final witness to appear before the court was Dollree Mapp, who presented her version of the police activity at her home. She explained to the jury that she grabbed the purported search warrant because "Mr. Greene told me I should see it and read it." Mapp testified how the police officer "grabbed me, twisted my hand . . . and it was hurting. I yelled, I pleaded with him to turn me loose." She also described how she was handcuffed and placed on her bed while the officers "were all over the place" searching her home.

When asked about the obscene books found in her home, Mapp insisted that officer Haney had entered her room after searching the basement holding a brown paper bag containing the four books. According to the defendant, Haney asked her, "Does this belong to you?" And Mapp told the court, "I asked him not to look at it, it might embarrass him. He asked me again if it belonged to me. I said, 'No.' He said, 'Oh, yes, that's the kind of trash you read.'" She testified that the material belonged to Morris Jones, her former boarder, and corroborated Clark's account of how they had packed up the books and stored them in the basement. Mapp also stated that the suitcase in her room, where Haney allegedly found the gun, obscene pencil drawing, and several photographs, also contained Jones's belongings, including some papers from a beauty school where he was a student, a cosmetology book with his name on it, and some men's clothing — all confirmation that the material belonged to him. Kearns's direct examination ended with Mapp repeating that she had never been in possession of the obscene materials but had merely stored them for her boarder.

Gertrude Mahon intensely cross-examined Mapp's account of the events, especially her claim she had packed up Jones's belongings and placed them in the basement. There was a series of quick exchanges between the assistant prosecuting attorney and Mapp as Mahon attempted to get the defendant to admit that the seized materials belonged to her, but Mapp adamantly stuck to her story. After her testimony, the court adjourned for the day.

The next morning, Kearns and Mahon gave brief closing remarks, and the prosecution and the defense rested their cases. Judge Lybarger gave the jury instructions to guide their deliberations; it took him twenty minutes to review the jury instructions — the same amount of time the jury took deliberating the case before it returned the verdict of guilty. Several days later Mapp received a sentence of one to seven years in the Ohio Reformatory for Women, and a fine between $200 and $2,000.

Mapp was shocked. The obscene material did not belong to her, and now she was facing a seven-year prison sentence. Moreover, the material was found after the Cleveland police forced their way into her home, manhandled her, and illegally searched every inch of her home while she sat handcuffed to her bed. She was surprised the jury believed the police's account of the events, especially because Delau contradicted Haney's testimony that the search was voluntary. Delau, on the other hand, was delighted. He stated that Mahon "did a very commendable job" and that John Corrigan, the county prosecutor overseeing the case, "was just about the best person anyone could find for this position. Honest and fearless." He was convinced his Bureau of Special Investigation was just doing its job when it found the policy paraphernalia in Mapp's home, and that the discovery of the obscene materials was the fortunate consequence of a legitimate search.

Mapp and her attorneys were convinced the police did not have a search warrant and that the search, and therefore the seizure of the material, was unlawful. Based on their suspicions and outraged at the police misconduct, they agreed to appeal the verdict.

—————

On September 6, Kearns filed a motion for a new trial. The motion, a single page long, outlined what the attorney believed were several errors, as well as two brief constitutional arguments. Among the errors were the judge's decision to overrule his motion to suppress evidence obtained in the search and the admission of the evidence over his objection. Kearns also suggested that the Ohio antiobscenity statute was unconstitutional and that his defendant's right to due process of law was violated because of the nature of the police search. Motions for new trials are rarely granted, and this case would be no different. Lybarger was unpersuaded by Kearns's description of the errors he may have made while presiding over Mapp's criminal trial, and the motion was denied. However, Kearns's work on the petition would provide a foundation for future appeals.

The first step for appellate review would be the Court of Appeals for the Eighth District in Ohio. To start the appeals process, Kearns filed a "Notice of Appeal," which was followed by a more formal legal brief two months later. The brief outlined the facts of the case and the basis for the appeal.

{ *Chapter 1* }

An experienced trial and appellate lawyer, Kearns had written many legal briefs before. This one began with a review of the circumstances that led to Mapp's arrest. Kearns's strategy was to highlight the severity of his client's sentence in light of the circumstances that led to her arrest. It was a provocative introduction: "One would expect that this record would show a seizure by police in a store dedicated to profit regardless of the illegal nature of its merchandise, with window displays to lure the buyers. On the contrary the police operation was the result of other aims." Kearns stated how the police were involved in the search "to find some man for questioning as to a bombing, which some unknown said might be at the address," and not to find obscene material. He then described how police "forced" their way into Mapp's private residence based on a "claim of a search warrant, never allowed to be seen, let alone read by the defendant, shown to her attorneys, or produced in Court by the police." It was, he insisted, an illegal search.

Kearns next introduced three major arguments, which he suggested provided adequate justification for reversal on appeal. The first argument was that the trial court erred in ruling that Mapp had "possession or control" of the obscene material. He repeated his client's claim that the material belonged to a former boarder and cited several cases where state and federal courts had ruled that liquor left behind by former tenants did not constitute "possession" under the law. The second argument was that the trial judge's jury instruction that "one who deposits articles in a place of concealment may still be deemed to have them in his possession" prejudiced the jury in its decision making and led to his client's conviction. Rather, he argued, Mapp had at most "a mere superficial possession (in the loosest sense), and not the substantial act of a real possessor for a guilty purpose." To support the third argument, that Mapp's seven-year sentence violated the state constitution, Kearns argued that "it could not have been the intent of the Legislature that a woman in the position of the defendant should be sent to the penitentiary for seven years" for her failure "to destroy the articles of her roomer." This extreme sentence, he explained, violated article I, section 9, of the Ohio state constitution, similar to the Eighth Amendment of the U.S. Constitution, that "excessive bail shall not be required; nor excessive fines imposed; nor cruel and unusual punishments inflicted." To support his argument, Kearns cited several similar state and federal decisions in which courts declared such severe sentences unconstitutional.

The state's response brief, written by Mahon, supported the trial court decision. It repeated the state's claim that the search of Mapp's home was legal, that the defendant was "in possession" of the obscene material, and that she was appropriately convicted under proper jury instructions. Mahon also responded to the defense argument that Mapp's sentence was "cruel and unusual," noting that "the sentence of the court was a general one, and not fixed or limited in duration."

The Court of Appeals for the Eighth District handed down its decision on March 28, 1959. The decision affirming the ruling of the court of common pleas was a single paragraph long. "Upon review of the entire case," wrote Joy Seth Hurd, the presiding judge, "we find no error prejudicial to the rights of the defendant." The court chose not to address Kearns's argument that Mapp's sentence was "cruel and unusual," finding that "the question of punishment is within the exclusive jurisdiction of the trial court."

Mapp and Kearns were displeased but hardly surprised that the appellate court upheld the decision of the trial court. Generally, more than 80 percent of cases appealed to the next level court are affirmed. The short length of the decision was also common. Mapp and her attorneys knew their arguments would receive greater attention before the Ohio Supreme Court.

Kearns filed a motion to appeal the court of appeals decision to the Ohio Supreme Court one month later and, after receiving an extension from the court to work on his legal brief, submitted it on May 27, 1959. It would be Mapp's last appeal in the state judicial system. It was at this point that Kearns decided to change his strategy. Although the brief repeated the "assignments of error" argued in the court of appeals, it also included two major constitutional arguments: that the Ohio obscenity statute was unconstitutional, and that the state of Ohio denied Mapp due process of law by convicting her with illegally seized evidence.

Kearns's first argument was that the Ohio antiobscenity statute violated the First and Fourteenth Amendments because it was written vaguely and lacked standards governing what is considered obscene. He also characterized the Ohio statute as "rare in the United States" because other antiobscenity statutes, including the previous Ohio law and similar state laws, were directed at sellers, publishers, or exhibitors of obscenity, who usually received only a fine for violating the law. For good measure, Kearns also threw in a brief equal protection challenge, suggesting that the statute violated the equal protection clause of the Fourteenth Amendment because it empowered the prosecutor or grand jury with the discretion to make an act of possession either a felony with a sentence of up to seven years or a misdemeanor subject only to a fine.

Kearns's second argument was that Mapp's Fourth and Fourteenth Amendment due process rights were violated because the police conduct in the case "portray[ed] a shocking disregard of human rights" and that the evidence seized in the case should therefore be suppressed. To support this constitutional challenge, he cited the Supreme Court ruling *Rochin v. California* (1952), where it declared that police conduct that "shocked the conscience" was unconstitutional, and evidence seized as a result of such conduct be excluded from trial. In *Rochin* the Court reversed a conviction for morphine possession after police pumped the defendant's stomach to retrieve the capsules, behavior it characterized as offending "even hardened sensibilities." Kearns hoped *Rochin* would give the Ohio Supreme Court reason to exclude the evidence in Mapp's case.

Mahon and Corrigan filed a "motion to dismiss as a matter of right" on June 11, 1959. The basis of their motion was that there was "no debatable constitutional question" presented in the defense's appeal. The brief quickly repeated how the state's charge was supported by evidence because of Mapp's possession of the obscene material, and how the jury instructions and deliberations were proper. In response to the defense's new argument regarding the constitutionality of the Ohio statute, the state replied that the law was "sufficiently definite" in its description of what constituted obscene material. Moreover, the attorneys added, the jury instructions helped clarify any ambiguity in the law. The brief equal protection challenge regarding sentencing was addressed with their contention that "variance in the penalty of legislation relating to the same offense" was appropriate so juries could properly punish individuals for knowing violation of the law. The argument regarding the defense's request to exclude the seized evidence because the police conduct "shocked the conscience" was dismissed by the prosecution as inapplicable because the case at hand did not involve a "physical examination of the defendant" as occurred in *Rochin*. The state also cast the blame on Mapp, adding, "If anything . . . it was the defendant whose conduct was shocking, not that of the police. She showed a shocking disregard of the law."

On October 12, 1959, Kearns filed a "brief of defendant-appellant in reply and opposing motion to dismiss." He repeated his earlier claims and also responded to the state's salvo that it was Mapp, not the police, who displayed "shocking" conduct:

> The appellant's statement that Dollree Mapp showed a shocking disregard of the law is far fetched. What a remark! — against a mother of a 13 year old child, alone, we find twelve policemen, breaking into her home, manhandling her, who find nothing to arrest her for, and started out with no charge against her, and after they look through the basement of a two family dwelling, they groundlessly charge her — not with a crime under the obscene literature statute — but for allegedly possessing lottery material. She is discharged in police court, for she was proved to have nothing to do with it.

It was also at this point that Kearns and Mahon learned they were not the only participants in Mapp's case. On October 24, 1959, Fred J. Livingstone of the Ohio Civil Liberties Union (OCLU) asked the Ohio Supreme Court for permission to file an amicus curiae ("friend of the court") brief on Mapp's behalf. The OCLU, a chapter of the American Civil Liberties Union (ACLU), was interested in the case because it believed the case provided an excellent opportunity to challenge the constitutionality of the Ohio obscenity statute. The ACLU allows its affiliates to handle more than 80 percent of the ACLU's legal cases. Most affiliates, like the one in Ohio, have a small paid staff and a number of volunteer "cooperating attorneys." These attorneys dedicate their time for the cause. Participating on the OCLU brief was Livingstone, along with attorneys Bernard A. Berkman and Julian C. Renswick. Justice Carl V. Weygandt granted the OCLU's motion to participate in the case, and in December the attorneys filed their brief.

Three major arguments were presented in the legal brief: the Ohio statute violated the due process clause of the Fourteenth Amendment, it interfered with an individual's privacy rights under the Fourth and

Fourteenth Amendments, and it violated the equal protection clause of the Fourteenth Amendment.

To illustrate the due process violation, the OCLU attorneys argued that the statute was not a valid exercise of Ohio's general "police powers." After noting that states did have the right to advance public health, safety, welfare, and morals, the attorneys remarked that these laws must meet general constitutional standards. The standard traditionally used is that the legislation serve a public purpose and that it be reasonably related to a legitimate government purpose that is reasonably adapted to the accomplishment of that purpose. The legislation must also not be arbitrary or excessive. The legislative purpose behind the Ohio statute, the lawyers claimed, was "to prevent abnormal or depraved sexual attitudes and overt anti-social behavior," and, they argued, the state had not proved that the law was related to this purpose because there was no "relationship, direct or remote, between the possession of obscene literature and depravity or overt anti-social conduct." The brief listed a summary of several sociological and psychological studies in support of this contention and concluded that there was "no positive finding by anyone that possession and/or reading of obscene literature by adults leads to depravity and/or overt anti-social conduct."

The second major line of argument was that the legislation interfered with individual "private rights" under the Fourth, Fifth, and Fourteenth Amendments "to a greater degree than the necessities of the situation require," and that, in particular, it interfered unnecessarily with the constitutional "right to read," which can be fulfilled only if one has the "right to possess literature." These privacy rights are threatened, the civil liberties lawyers argued, where "police authorities are able to arrest and detain persons for private possession of obscene material." The brief quoted several law review articles that described the common-law basis for this general right to privacy. Returning to the Ohio antiobscenity statute, the OCLU attorneys conceded that while there might be instances where outlawing private possession of obscene material may "in some few instances" eliminate potentially destructive practices, "the danger to society arising out of sanctioning police interference in the private lives of our citizens far outweighs any good that might be derived from uncovering and destroying allegedly obscene material."

To support the third argument, that the Ohio antiobscenity statute violated the equal protection clause of the Fourteenth Amendment, the attorneys noted that the statute included several exceptions and that, "when a statute grants a privilege or immunity to one and denies it to another in the same class it denies equal protection of the laws."

———

The Ohio Supreme Court handed down its decision on March 23, 1960, almost two years after Mapp was arrested at her Milverton Road home. What initially appeared as a win turned out to be a loss. Four of the seven judges on the state's highest court voted to reverse the court of appeals decision, concluding that the Ohio obscenity law was unconstitutional. However, Mapp lost her appeal due to a quirk in the state constitution, which required a supermajority to declare a law unconstitutional. Under article IV, section 2, of the Ohio state constitution, "No law shall be held unconstitutional and void by the supreme court without the concurrence of at least all but one of the judges, except in the affirmance of a judgment of the court of appeals declaring a law unconstitutional and void." This meant that six of the seven Ohio Supreme Court justices would have to agree that a law was unconstitutional for it to be struck down. With only four justices voting to invalidate the state law on constitutional grounds, it was upheld.

Justice Kingsley A. Taft wrote the decision for the four-justice majority. A fifth justice agreed with the judgment but chose not to write a separate concurring opinion. Writing for the majority, Taft began the decision by stating that the lower courts correctly ruled that Mapp had obscene material in her "possession" or "control." He explained that "the evidence clearly discloses that defendant not only took possession and control of the room which she had rented but also of the belongings of her former tenant, including the books and pictures which the undisputed evidence shows that she knew to be lewd and lascivious." Thus, the state obscenity law applied to Mapp's case. But this did not settle the issue. Taft then considered whether the constitutional questions raised by the defense required a reversal of the judgment.

In regard to the Fourteenth Amendment due process challenge, Taft first addressed the police's claim that they searched Mapp's home with a valid warrant. He noted that he did not believe the police or prosecutor's testimony that there was a search warrant.

> There is, in the record, considerable doubt as to whether there ever was any warrant for the search of defendant's home. No warrant was offered in evidence, there was no testimony as to who issued any warrant or as to what any warrant contained, and the absence from evidence of any such warrant is not explained or otherwise accounted for in the record. There is nothing in the record tending to prove or from which an inference may be drawn, and no one has even suggested that any warrant that we may assume that there may have been described anything other than policy paraphernalia as things to be searched for.

The majority agreed with Kearns's conclusion that the police either never obtained a warrant or that, if they did, they failed to follow the state statutory and constitutional requirement that a warrant particularly describe the place searched and the things seized.

Justice Taft then declared that the absence of a warrant did not affect the outcome of the case because, according to the precedent, *State v. Lindway* (1936), Ohio courts could admit unlawfully seized evidence in criminal prosecutions. The right of states to do so, he added, was appropriate according to the U.S. Supreme Court decision *Wolf v. Colorado*, where it held "that the Constitution of the United States does not usually prevent a state court from so holding." Nor did Taft believe the "methods" used by the police "offend[ed] 'a sense of justice' requiring exclusion of evidence" under *Rochin v. California*. Because he did not believe the police search met the "shock the conscience" test, Justice Taft concluded that there was no due process violation, despite the fact that the conviction was based on unlawfully seized evidence.

The second constitutional question regarding the statute criminalizing possession of obscene literature was more troubling for two justices in the majority. After noting that the statute was of recent vintage and had yet to be reviewed for its constitutionality, Justice Taft interpreted the meaning of the statute strictly: "Under our statute as now worded, mere possession is forbidden even where the possessor does not have a purpose of again looking at the books or pictures; and, in the instant case, the jury could have found the defendant guilty and she could have been (as she was) sentenced as a felon, even though it believed her evidence that she had innocently acquired possession of these articles, had no intention of ever looking at them again and was merely keeping them pending instructions for their disposition from the owner." Taft hypothesized that using this interpretation, a person could come across such material innocently and then, after learning of "their lewd and lascivious character," they would "at that instant" have such material in their possession or under their control as prohibited by the statute. Such a statute, he explained, was constitutionally suspect.

The justice likened the Ohio statute to one struck down by the U.S. Supreme Court in *Smith v. California* (1959). The California statute made it "unlawful for any person to have in his possession any obscene or indecent writing, or book in any place of business where books are sold or kept for sale," and the Supreme Court concluded that such a strict statute would restrict the public's access to reading material in violation of the First Amendment. Taft believed the Ohio statute would have a similar effect on individual behavior. He explained that "if anyone looks at a book and finds it lewd, he is forthwith, under this legislation, guilty of a serious crime, which may involve a sentence to the penitentiary similar to the one given to this defendant. As a result, some who might otherwise read books that are not obscene may well be discouraged from doing so and their free circulation and use will be impeded." Based on this possible "chilling effect" on First Amendment rights, Justice Taft concluded that it was the opinion of four members of the court (two in the majority and two in the dissent) that the state's antiobscenity statute was "constitutionally invalid, and, for that reason, the judgment of the Court of Appeals should be reversed." However, he continued, the court was unable to declare the law unconstitutional because section 2 of article IV of the state constitution required that six of seven justices reach that conclusion to do so. As a result, despite the fact that four of the seven justices believed the state antiobscenity statute violated the freedom of speech and press clauses of the First and Fourteenth Amendments to the U.S. Constitution, the Ohio Supreme Court was bound under the state constitution to affirm the court of appeals decision.

Two justices, although agreeing with two justices in the majority that the Ohio statute violated the First Amendment, wrote a separate dissent calling attention to the *Lindway* precedent. They argued that the majority erred in its application of *Lindway* to Mapp's case, thereby allowing the admission of unlawfully seized evidence in her criminal trial. The dissent suggested that the court use this opportunity to abandon *Lindway*, which they believed undermined Ohioans' right to be secure from unlawful police intrusions: "It seems to me to be far too comprehensive and susceptible to abuse by police and prosecution authorities. As a rule, abuses by such officials rarely occur but when they do the constitutional rights of the private citizen should be fully protected." *Lindway*, the dissenters argued, led them "to the inescapable conclusion that in too many instances it virtually sterilizes" article I, section 14, of the Ohio state constitution, which provides, "The right of the people to be secure in their persons, houses, papers, and possession, against unreasonable searches and seizures shall not be violated; and no warrant shall issue, but upon probable cause, supported by oath or affirmation, particularly describing the place to be searched, and the person and things to be seized."

The dissent reasoned that this issue was of paramount importance in this case because of the state constitution's requirement of near unanimity to invalidate a state law on constitutional grounds: "Since under another provision of the Constitution a bare majority of this court is powerless to invalidate the portion of that section under which the defendant was convicted, we certainly should scan carefully the method by which the evidence was acquired for such conviction." The dissenting justices also explained that a reevaluation of *Lindway* was appropriate because the states were "about evenly divided" between the federal rule on search and seizure, that evidence illegally obtained must be excluded in federal criminal trials, and states that allowed admission of such evidence. Suggesting that this was evidence of a national trend "away from the *Lindway* rule since the time of its decision," the dissent concluded that *Lindway* "should be modified and clarified so that there will no longer be a judicial stamp of approval on the use of unlawful means to justify an end result."

The Ohio Supreme Court decision in *Mapp v. Ohio* must have been baffling to Mapp and her attorneys. All seven members of the court believed the police search of Mapp's home was illegal, and four justices believed the law criminalizing possession of obscene material was unconstitutional. A majority on the court, therefore, was in favor of reversing Mapp's conviction on constitutional grounds. However, an unusual requirement in the state constitution allowed the conviction to stand. And, two justices in the dissent called for abandonment of the *Lindway* rule, which allowed admission of the fruit of an illegal search. Mapp had lost once again.

Several days after learning of the Ohio Supreme Court decision, Kearns asked the court to rehear the case, which was denied a week later. The court did, however, grant his motion for a "stay of execution," which allowed Mapp to remain free on bail while the attorney pondered his next move.

Over the next few days Kearns and Greene deliberated the advantages and disadvantages of appealing the case to the U.S. Supreme Court. Although they had lost in the Ohio Supreme Court, they were encouraged that a majority of the justices found the state obscenity law constitutionally suspect. They felt they might have better luck before the U.S. Supreme Court, which was not restricted by a requirement of near unanimity to invalidate a state statute that contravened the Constitution. Kearns and Greene also believed that the Cleveland police's illegal search and seizure of evidence used against Mapp might provide an avenue for a reversal. Although the issue had not garnered a majority on the Ohio Supreme Court, which ruled that such evidence was admissible under *State v. Lindway*, there was the possibility that they could persuade the U.S. Supreme Court to consider the issue.

Exclusion of unlawfully seized evidence from federal criminal trials dated back to the beginning of the twentieth century, but exclusion from state criminal trials varied from jurisdiction to jurisdiction. To learn more about this remedy for police misconduct, it is instructive to review the history of the Fourth Amendment and the origins of the exclusionary rule.

The History of the Fourth Amendment and the Federal Exclusionary Rule

A. L. Kearns's insistence that the Ohio state courts suppress the illegally seized evidence from Dollree Mapp's home was based on his belief that exclusion was required under the U.S. Constitution. Although there was such an "exclusionary rule" for evidence unlawfully seized by federal officers, the U.S. Supreme Court had applied the rule only against state officers acting in the most extreme circumstances — where the police misconduct "shocked the conscience." As a result, state laws or state constitutions governed the issue of whether illegally seized evidence should be excluded from state criminal trials. This chapter details the historical background of the Fourth Amendment and the origins of the federal exclusionary rule. It includes a discussion of the "warrant preference" and "generalized reasonableness" construction of the Fourth Amendment and a review of Supreme Court decisions that illustrate the evolution of the exclusionary rule prior to the Court's decision in *Mapp v. Ohio*.

Introduction and passage of the Fourth Amendment to the U.S. Constitution was strongly influenced by the early American experience with the English and American governments. Historians Jacob Landynski, in his book *Search and Seizure and the Supreme Court*, and Nelson Lasson, in his monograph *The History and Development of the Fourth Amendment to the United States Constitution*, provide valuable insight into the Fourth Amendment and the origins of the exclusionary rule.

The colonies experienced problems with England because of Parliament's effort to protect English businesses by imposing import duties on goods from non-English territories. Smuggling was common in the colonies, and several British statutes enacted in the late seventeenth century gave British authorities extensive power to use writs of assistance to enforce regulations that governed navigation and trade. A writ of assistance is generally described as an unparticularized general warrant that allowed customs officers to search for goods imported in violation of British tax laws. The writs significantly empowered customs officials, who were granted almost complete discretionary authority to enter and search homes, businesses, or other areas where they suspected smuggled goods, and if they found any, to seize those goods acting under the color of law. Because customs officials were not required to specify the products being searched or the location of the search, they could enter one's property "at will." To secure a writ, the official need only make a request; justification did not have to be supported by sworn information presented to a magistrate or judge. The writs were also open-ended — valid during the sovereign's lifetime in which they were granted.

Writs of assistance were most widely used in colonies that engaged heavily in trade, especially Massachusetts and New Hampshire, and soon "caused profound resentment." Dissatisfaction with the writs extended beyond the body politic. In many states colonial judges questioned their legality, contending that they gave government officials too much discretionary power that violated individual privacy and property rights.

By the close of 1760, the level of public outcry against the writs had grown significantly. The controversy escalated with the death of King George II in 1761 when the legitimacy of writs of assistance came under scrutiny because, according to custom, the writs would expire six months after the death of the sovereign, and officials were required to request their reissue. Later that year, sixty-three Boston merchants launched a legal challenge against the writs of assistance in the Massachusetts Superior Court. The merchants were represented by James Otis Jr., who would later earn prominence in the Revolutionary War, and Oxenbridge Thatcher, a Boston attorney. In addition to challenging the writs as not applicable in the colonies, not justified under common law, and in conflict with the Magna Carta, Otis called for greater restrictions on the writs: that they be limited to a "single occasion" and be "based upon particularized information under oath." The attorney general for the Massachusetts Bay Colony, Jeremiah Gridley, offered a contrary view, arguing that the writs were

{ *Chapter 2* }

allowable under English law and necessary to crack down on smuggling and to enforce the customs laws that protected the collection of revenue to support the colonial governments.

In his arguments before the court Otis stated, "I will to my dying day oppose with all the powers and faculties God has given me all such instruments of slavery on the one hand, and villainy, on the other, as this writ of assistance is. It appears to me the worst instrument of arbitrary power, the most destructive of English liberty and the fundamental principles of law, that was ever found in an English law book." He called attention to the breadth of power granted to customs officers and the writs' impact on one's privacy:

> This was a power that placed the liberty of every man in the hands of every petty officer. Anyone with this general warrant could be a tyrant and reign secure in his petty tyranny. That a man's house was his castle was one of the most essential branches of English liberty, a privilege totally annihilated by such a general warrant. This writ, if it should be declared legal, would totally annihilate this privilege. Custom house officers may enter our houses when they please — we are commanded to permit their entry — their menial servants may enter — may break locks, bars and everything in their way — and whether they break through malice or revenge, no man, no court can inquire — bare suspicion without oath is sufficient. . . . Every man prompted by revenge, ill humor, or wantonness to inspect the inside of his neighbor's house may get a writ of assistance.

Despite Otis's passion, the superior court upheld the writ as legal. However, the legal challenge did have an impact on those present to watch the proceedings. A young John Adams, one of many in the courtroom, wrote in a letter to William Tudor, "I do say in the most solemn manner, that Mr. Otis's oration against the Writs of Assistance breathed into this nation the breath of life." He continued, "He was a flame of fire! Every man of a crowded audience appeared to me to go away, as I did, ready to take up arms against Writs of Assistance. Then and there was the first scene of opposition to the arbitrary claims of Great Britain. Then and there the child Independence was born." The revolutionary fires were fueled when Parliament passed other laws, including the Sugar Act (1764) and the Stamp Act (1765), to protect Britain's revenue stream and the Townshend Act (1767), which reiterated customs officials' authority to use general writs of assistance to search for and seize smuggled goods.

After declaring independence, several of the newly created states limited government's power to search in their state constitutions. Between 1776 and 1787 seven states adopted provisions in their declarations of rights protecting their citizens against unreasonable searches and seizures. Most condemned the use of general warrants, but several also implied that citizens were granted a substantive right against arbitrary searches and seizures. The first state to act was Virginia, which amended its declaration of rights in 1776 to condemn general warrants, calling them "grievous and oppressive" which "ought not be granted." Later, North Carolina adopted similar language in its declaration. The states of Pennsylvania and Maryland went a step further, both declarations noting that warrants made without oath or affirmation would not be granted. The Pennsylvania declaration also affirmed the people's substantive right "to hold themselves, their houses, papers, and possessions free from search and seizure," and Maryland's declaration also condemned warrants that did not specify the area to be searched or items seized. Vermont, while not one of the original colonies, would eventually duplicate Pennsylvania's provision in its own declaration of rights. To some observers, this language describing people's general right to be free from illegal searches and seizures implied that searches made without a warrant were unreasonable.

Massachusetts followed form, amending its declaration of rights in 1780 to state, "Every subject has a right to be secure from all unreasonable searches and seizures of his person, his house, his papers and all his possessions. All warrants, therefore, are contrary to this right, if the cause or foundation of them be not previously supported by oath or affirmation." Also included was a "particularity" clause prohibiting warrants that did not specify the place, person, or object to be searched. New Hampshire later copied the Massachusetts declaration verbatim. These early state declarations would later influence the writing of the Fourth Amendment to the U.S. Constitution.

The federal Constitution produced by the Constitutional Convention of 1787 did not include a bill of rights, much to the consternation of Anti-Federalists, who feared an overreaching federal government. However, this shortcoming was rectified during the ratification debates when the issue was revisited. Among the arguments made in the states was that the Constitution include a provision that forbade indiscriminate searches and seizures. In 1789 James Madison put forth a proposal forbidding general warrants: "The rights of the people to be secure in their persons, their houses, their papers and their property, from all unreasonable searches and seizures shall not be violated by warrants issued without probable cause, supported by oath or affirmation, or not particularly describing the places to be searched, or the persons or things to be seized." The draft was referred to the House Select Committee of Eleven, which consisted of representatives from each state. Apparently the phrase "by warrants issued" was objected to by Egert Benson of New York, the committee chair, who wanted it altered to "no warrant shall issue," but the change was defeated. When put forth before the House, however, Benson's revision was included nonetheless, and the draft that passed both the House and the Senate, and was later ratified by the states, included his change. Despite substantial debate, the amendment that was ratified was very similar to that introduced by Madison.

The Fourth Amendment to the Constitution contains two clauses; the first establishes "the right of the people to be secure in their persons, houses, papers, and effects, against unreasonable searches and seizures," and the second outlines what is required for a warrant — that "no Warrants shall issue, but upon probable cause, supported by Oath or affirmation, and particularly describing the place to be searched, and the persons or things to be seized." The provision has, as Landynski observed, "both the virtue of brevity and the vice of ambiguity." Fourth Amendment scholar Thomas Davies explained in his article "Recovering the Original Fourth Amendment," that "there is a difficulty embedded in the apparently obvious meanings of the two clauses, however — the text does not indicate how they fit together. It does not say whether a valid warrant should be the usual criterion for a 'reasonable' police intrusion, or whether 'Fourth Amendment reasonableness' should be assessed independently of use of a warrant. Put more concretely, it does not indicate whether or in what circumstances arrests or searches must be made pursuant to a warrant."

The interaction between the two clauses has been the subject of considerable controversy among constitutional scholars, who fall into one of two camps. One camp argues that the two clauses should be read together and that, in particular, the "warrant" clause informs the judiciary that searches conducted with a warrant are per se reasonable. Landynski, who endorses this perspective, suggests that interpreting the two clauses together makes rational sense: "It would be strange, to say the least, for the amendment to specify stringent warrant requirements, after having in effect negated these by authorizing judicially unsupervised 'reasonable' searches without warrant. To detach the first clause from the second is to run the risk of making the second virtually useless." Called the "warrant preference" construction of the Fourth Amendment, this interpretation believes a warrant is a precondition of a reasonable search or seizure, and that searches or seizures without a warrant are unreasonable "subject only to few specifically established and well-delineated exceptions." Those endorsing this perspective argue that the two clauses must be read together to allow the courts to effectively check against abuses of government authority. This warrant preference construction is regarded as the "traditional" approach to the Fourth Amendment because it dominated the Supreme Court's interpretation of the provision up until the late 1960s.

In the other camp are scholars who believe the two clauses should be interpreted independently of one another. Those who subscribe to this "generalized reasonableness" construction believe the reasonableness clause articulates only a general reasonableness standard to guide government searches and seizures without a warrant, and that the warrant clause refers only to what is necessary if a warrant is actually issued. Those falling into this camp also argue that warrantless arrests and searches, which were allowable in English common law, were anticipated by the Framers. Historian Telford Taylor embraced this view in his book *Two Studies in Constitutional Interpretation* (1969). He argues that the Framers were primarily concerned with judicial abuse of authority because judges authorized general writs of assistance. "Our constitutional fathers were not concerned about warrantless searches, but overreaching warrants," he states. Instead, they wanted to "prohibit the oppressive use of warrants, and they were not at all concerned about searches without warrants. They took for granted that arrested persons could be searched without a search warrant, and nothing gave them cause for worry about warrantless searches."

Those who favor the primacy of the reasonableness clause of the Fourth Amendment argue that the presence of warrantless searches and seizures during the colonial era and the first few years after ratification of the Constitution illustrates how the Fourth Amendment required only that searches be governed by the reasonableness, rather than the warrant, clause of the Fourth Amendment. This approach to the Fourth Amendment is of relatively recent vintage; it has emerged only recently in the literature, which previously focused on the "warrant preference" construction of the amendment. However, it has now found an audience with a majority of the justices on the Supreme Court, who have embraced the generalized reasonableness construction since the mid-1970s.

To find support for their positions, scholars in both camps look to the Framers' intent, an exercise rife with problems. First, the historical record is slim. As Fourth Amendment scholar Wayne LaFave noted, "Framers' intent is of limited utility in shedding light on the meaning of the Fourth Amendment, and second, and perhaps more problematic, it is an inherently subjective exercise." Law professor Yale Kamisar, who has written dozens of articles on the Fourth Amendment quipped, "It is a remarkable if familiar fact that law professors, like Supreme Court Justices, almost always find that the Framers' view mirrors their own." Perhaps the most honest assessment of intent of the Framers in writing the Fourth Amendment is provided by Davies, who observed that "[a] number of historical commentaries on the Fourth Amendment have either favored or rejected a warrant requirement. However, none have supported their answer with persuasive historical evidence. If one turns to the historical sources themselves, the mystery initially deepens: the participants in the historical controversies that stimulated the framing of the Fourth Amendment simply did not discuss when a warrant was required. Odd as it may seem, the Framers simply were not troubled by the most salient issue of the modern debate." However, after independently researching the issue, Davies concluded that the "warrant-preference construction is more faithful to the Framers' concerns than the generalized-reasonableness construction" because "ultimately the purpose of the Fourth Amendment was to curb the exercise of discretionary authority by officers."

Like all the Bill of Rights guarantees, the Fourth Amendment is silent regarding what should happen if one is the victim of an illegal search or seizure. While some argue that an exclusionary remedy is implied in the Fourth Amendment, others suggest that it is merely a judicially created remedy. There is scant historical evidence that the exclusionary rule was intended by the Framers; in fact, opponents to the rule argue that because illegally seized evidence was admitted in England, the Framers would have endorsed this view as well.

―――――

Despite the Fourth Amendment being called "one of the most litigated provisions of the National Bill of Rights," there were few search and seizure cases decided by the U.S. Supreme Court in its first hundred years. As one commentator observed, the Fourth Amendment was "a sleeping giant." The paucity of cases was not unusual during this period, as the Court paid little attention to those rights protected by the first ten amendments to the Constitution. There were also few cases involving illegal searches and seizures because it was not until the latter part of the nineteenth century that Congress enacted federal legislation addressing illegal drugs and liquor, weapons possession, and gambling. These new laws led to a greater number of federal prosecutions and, as a result, more searches and seizures. Also, a constitutional challenge was not the preferred solution for victims of illegal searches, who chose instead to sue the government for trespass in civil court. As a result, there was little occasion to interpret the meaning of the Fourth Amendment.

The first significant search and seizure case decided by the Supreme Court was *Boyd v. United States* (1886). Boyd and his brother were arrested for fraudulently importing glass without paying a duty in violation of a federal statute. The federal district court judge directed the merchants to produce private papers and records of their business transactions, which they did under protest. They were found guilty, and the glass in question was confiscated by the government. The issue before the Court was whether compulsory production of a person's private papers, to be used as evidence against him, constituted an unreasonable search and seizure in violation of the Fourth and Fifth Amendments.

Writing for a seven-person majority, Justice Joseph P. Bradley first stated that by trying to "extort from the party his private books and papers to make him liable for penalty or to forfeit his property," the government action amounted to an unreasonable search and seizure because the defendant had no choice under the law but to produce the papers. This was in violation of the Fourth Amendment, he explained, because the forfeiture proceeding was of a "quasi-criminal nature." Bradley next addressed whether the unlawfully seized evidence could be used in the trial. He noted the "intimate relation" between the Fourth and Fifth Amendments, which "run almost into each other," and reasoned that the Fifth Amendment, which protects one from incriminating oneself, "throws light on the question as to what is an 'unreasonable search and seizure' within the meaning of the fourth amendment." He concluded that the law forcing compulsion of the papers and the admission of the illegally seized evidence was therefore "erroneous and unconstitutional" in violation of the Fourth and Fifth Amendments.

While the Court did not directly address whether exclusion of the illegally obtained evidence was constitutionally required by the Fourth Amendment alone, its decision in *Boyd* that evidence unlawfully seized in violation of the Fourth Amendment, when used to incriminate an individual in violation of the Fifth Amendment, was significant because it was the Court's first announcement that illegally obtained evidence would not be admissible in federal criminal trials.

The Supreme Court would not decide another Fourth Amendment case for eighteen years, and once it did, the ruling put the *Boyd* decision in some doubt. The case, *Adams v. New York* (1904), concerned an individual convicted of knowingly possessing gambling paraphernalia. State police seized the policy paraphernalia under a valid warrant and, at the same time seized some of Adams's private papers. The papers, which were not included in the warrant, were later used as evidence against Adams under his protest, and he was found guilty.

The bulk of the majority decision, written by Justice William Day, was dedicated to a review of the common-law rule that trial courts should "not stop to inquire as to the means by which the evidence was obtained," which he characterized was a "collateral issue." The Court's primary focus, he explained, must be the guilt or innocence of the accused. Moreover, he added, the seizure of the private papers in this case was not unconstitutional because they had been discovered during a lawful search for illegal gambling paraphernalia. Day differentiated the case from *Boyd*, noting that in *Boyd* the appellants had been "virtually compelled" to testify against themselves, which was not an issue in the present case. He announced that evidence obtained as a result of such an illegal search could be admitted.

The decision appeared to contradict the Court's earlier finding regarding the exclusion of illegally obtained evidence announced in *Boyd*. Also significant was the fact that *Adams* involved an illegal search by state, and not federal, officers, and the Court could have easily dismissed the case, reasoning that the Fourth Amendment applied only to searches by federal authorities.

The confusion over the state of the exclusionary rule deepened a decade later when the Court once again addressed whether evidence seized by law enforcement in violation of the Fourth Amendment should be excluded from trial. The case, *Weeks v. United States* (1914), involved an individual suspected of using the mail for gambling purposes in violation of federal law. Weeks was arrested by a state police officer at his workplace; at the same time, other state officers entered his home without a warrant and seized personal papers and material, which they turned over to a U.S. marshal. The marshal then went to the home with the state officers and conducted his own warrantless search and seizure of items. Although some items were returned, Weeks had to petition for the return of the remaining unlawfully seized items, which included private correspondence. The petition, filed prior to the trial, was denied because the judge ruled that the materials constituted evidence. Weeks was convicted in federal court and appealed to the Supreme Court, arguing that the trial court's failure to exclude the evidence was in error.

In a unanimous decision, the Supreme Court reversed, ruling that the illegally seized evidence should have been excluded from trial. The majority opinion, written by Justice Day, concluded that the search violated the Fourth Amendment because *federal* officers could enter a home only "when armed with a warrant issued as required by the Constitution, upon sworn information and describing with reasonable particularity the thing for which the search was to be made." Weeks's right to his personal property was protected against such unwarranted seizures by the federal government. However, Day added, the evidence seized by the *state* officers was admissible because the Fourth Amendment was "not directed to individual misconduct of such officials. Its limitations reach the Federal Government and its agencies."

Justification for the exclusion of evidence seized by federal officers, Day reasoned, was required to enforce the Fourth Amendment. "If letters and private documents can thus be seized and held and used in evidence against a citizen accused of an offense, the protection of the Fourth Amendment declaring his right to be secure against such searches and seizures is of no value, and, so far as those thus placed are concerned, might as well be stricken from the Constitution." Also important to the Court was the fact that admission of the illegally seized evidence would undermine the integrity of the judicial process. Law enforcement officials who "obtain criminal convictions by means of unlawful seizures," Day observed, "should find no sanction in the judgment of the courts which are charged at all times with the support of the Constitution." He suggested that judicial approval of such actions "would be to affirm by judicial decision a manifest neglect, if not an open defiance of the prohibitions of the Constitution, intended for the protection of the people against such unauthorized action."

Despite acknowledging that the ruling would negatively affect federal law enforcement efforts, Day concluded that a more important principle was at stake. "The efforts of the courts and their officials to bring the guilty to punishment, praiseworthy as they are, are not to be aided by the sacrifice of those great principles established by years of endeavor and suffering which have resulted in their embodiment as the fundamental law of the land." The sticky issue of the *Adams* precedent, which Day also authored, was addressed with his analysis that *Weeks* should be differentiated because in *Adams* the request for the return of the seized items was made prior to the trial, and because when admitting the evidence, the district court "conceded" the illegal seizure. Day's attention in the earlier case to the common-law approach, which allowed the admission of excluded evidence, was explicitly rejected in *Weeks*. In retrospect, it appears that *Adams*, which was largely inconsistent with the general principles expressed in *Boyd* and *Weeks*, may have been an anomaly.

Weeks was a landmark decision, and the unanimity of the Court in regard to the exclusionary rule helped clear up some of the ambiguity inherent in *Boyd* and *Adams*. The Supreme Court ruled decisively, and for the first time, that evidence seized in violation of the Fourth Amendment was inadmissible in a federal criminal proceeding. In its reasoning, the Court focused on the rationale that the exclusionary rule was an essential part of the Fourth Amendment and that one had a "right to exclusion" of illegally seized evidence. The Court also emphasized that introduction of such evidence would undermine judicial integrity. There was no mention that the exclusionary rule was a "remedy" to repair the Fourth Amendment violation or that its purpose was to deter police misconduct.

The next major case involving the exclusionary rule was handed down several years later. In *Silverthorne Lumber Co. v. United States* (1920), the Court expanded the exclusionary rule's reach to include situations where illegally seized evidence leads police to the discovery of legally seized evidence, later known as the "fruit of the poisonous tree doctrine." The case involved a U.S. marshal unlawfully entering a business and seizing books and documents, which were later returned to the owners but were photographed prior to their return. The photographed evidence was then used to secure a new indictment against the defendants. The district court judge ruled that the originals be returned and the copies retained by the court as evidence. He then authorized federal authorities to issue subpoenas requesting the original documents. The subpoenas were refused by the defendants, who were subsequently imprisoned for contempt.

Justice Oliver W. Holmes, writing for seven members of the Court, reversed the conviction, reasoning that "the essence of a provision forbidding the acquisition of evidence in a certain way is that not merely evidence so acquired shall not be used before the Court, but that it shall not be used at all." Otherwise, he added, the Fourth Amendment would be reduced "to a form of words." He argued that suppression was required "when its discovery is causally traceable to an initial Fourth Amendment wrong." The wrong in this case was the unlawful search and seizure, which yielded the photographed evidence leading to the second indictment. Two decades later this would be known as the "fruit of the poisonous tree" doctrine. Holmes also used this opportunity to articulate the "independent source" exception to the doctrine, reasoning that "where knowledge of the illegally seized evidence is derived independently of the initial taint, the chain of illegality is broken and the evidence is admissible." The "fruit of the poisonous tree" doctrine was later made more explicit in *Nardone v. United States* (1939) in a decision by Justice Felix Frankfurter, which also included another exception, known as "attenuation," which allows the admission of the evidence, even if it was not the result of an "independent source," so long as the connection between the illegal and legal search "may have become so attenuated as to dissipate the taint."

In 1921 the Court handed down two decisions expanding the reach of the exclusionary rule. In *Gouled v. United States*, a unanimous Court excluded evidence obtained by the federal government using subterfuge, reasoning that it constituted an unlawful search and seizure. The Court was unpersuaded by the government's contention that the search was legal because it did not involve force or coercion. In this decision, the Court also practically reversed *Adams*, where it concluded that illegally obtained evidence could only be challenged prior to trial in order to be considered for exclusion. The majority noted, "A rule of practice must not be allowed for any technical reason to prevail over a constitutional right." The Court arrived at a similar result in *Amos v. United States* (1921). Later, in *Agnello v. United States* (1925), the Court, relying on the Fourth and Fifth Amendments, excluded drugs found during a warrantless search, thus extending the exclusionary rule beyond private papers to also include contraband.

In two 1927 cases the Supreme Court announced what would later be known as the "silver platter doctrine," where federal courts allowed federal law enforcement officers to introduce evidence seized illegally by state officers. The Court's rationale behind this exception to the exclusionary rule was that federal officials had not participated in an illegal search. Rather, the majority held, the evidence discovered by state law enforcement was "turned over to the federal authorities on a silver platter." In *Byars v. United States*, the Court acknowledged "the right of the federal government to avail itself of evidence improperly seized by state officers operating entirely upon their own accounts." However, the Court also placed certain parameters on the doctrine, noting that if there was collusion between state and federal officials, and the search was essentially "a joint operation of the local and federal officers," that the evidence must be excluded. Because this is what occurred in *Byars*, the defendant's conviction was reversed. Similarly, in *Gambino v. United States*, the Court threw out the defendant's conviction for violating the National Prohibition Act because although the state officers who unlawfully seized the liquor were acting independently, the Court reasoned that there was no reason for them to believe Gambino was violating a state law, which did not prohibit liquor possession. Thus, the arrest was "made solely on behalf of the United States."

Perhaps the strongest statement that the *Weeks* exclusionary rule was a constitutional imperative was announced in *Olmstead v. United States* (1928), a case involving federal wiretaps, which were lawful at the time. Although the Court was closely divided on whether wiretaps were unconstitutional — it split five to four on this question — all the justices agreed that the exclusionary rule was required under the Fourth Amendment. Most of the majority decision was dedicated to the holding that wiretapping did not constitute a search under the Fourth Amendment because authorities gathered the incriminating evidence by "the use of the sense of hearing and that only," and that no seizure had taken place because the amendment was limited to "tangible items."

The majority also declined to consider whether the evidence should be excluded because it was seized in violation of a state antiwiretapping law. Rather, it observed that the exclusionary rule should be limited to only those instances where evidence was seized in violation of the Constitution. "The striking outcome of the *Weeks* case and those which followed it was the sweeping declaration that the Fourth Amendment, although not referring to or limiting the use of evidence in courts, really forbade its introduction if obtained by government officers through a violation of the Constitution."

Olmstead is most famous for the dissenting opinions by Justice Louis Brandeis and Justice Holmes, which are often invoked by exclusionary rule proponents. Both called for applying the exclusionary rule in *Olmstead* because the government violated a state law. The dissents characterized the rule as a device for holding government accountable. Brandeis stated:

> Decency, security, and liberty alike demand that government officials shall be subjected to the same rules of conduct that are commands to the citizen. In a government of laws, existence of the government will be imperiled if it fails to observe the law scrupulously. Our government is the potent, the omnipresent teacher. For good or for ill, it teaches the whole people by its example. Crime is contagious. If the government becomes a lawbreaker, it breeds contempt for law; it invites every man to become a law unto him-

self; it invites anarchy. To declare that in the administration of the criminal law the ends justifies the means — to declare that the government may commit crimes in order to secure the conviction of a private criminal — would bring terrible retribution. Against that pernicious doctrine this court should resolutely set its face.

Separately Holmes added:

> The government ought not to use evidence obtained and only obtainable by a criminal act. . . . It is desirable that criminals should be detected, and to that end that all available evidence should be used. It also is desirable that the government should not itself foster and pay for other crimes, when they are the means by which the evidence is to be obtained. If it pays its officers for having got evidence by crime I do not see why it may not as well pay them for getting it in the same way, and I can attach no importance to protestations of disapproval if it knowingly accepts and pays and announces that in the future it will pay for the fruits. We have to choose, and for my part I think it a less evil that some criminals should escape than that the government should play an ignoble part.

———

The relative agreement of the Court in its approach to the exclusionary rule (many of these early cases were decided by a strong majority, or a unanimous Court) ended in 1949 when the Court handed down several decisions that revealed a division in its exclusionary rule jurisprudence. It was at this point in the Court's history that several justices cast the exclusionary rule in a new light, characterizing it as a judicially created remedy intended to deter police misconduct, rather than a constitutional necessity to protect Fourth Amendment rights. This change was significant because it would later be used as controlling precedent by future Courts to limit the application of the exclusionary rule.

The most significant ruling came in *Wolf v. Colorado* (1949) when the Court directly considered whether the Fourth Amendment and the exclusionary rule should be extended to the states. The case involved an obstetrician who was being investigated by state authorities suspecting that he might be performing abortions in violation of state law. A deputy sheriff raided the doctor's office and found an appointment book implicating him. After interrogating some of the doctor's patients, the state charged him with conspiracy to commit abortions, and he was later convicted.

A unanimous Supreme Court agreed that the search of the doctor's office and the seizure of evidence were unconstitutional. For the first time the Court ruled that the Fourth Amendment prohibition against unreasonable searches and seizures was applicable to the states through the due process clause of the Fourteenth Amendment. Prior to this date, the Court used its "selective incorporation approach" to "incorporate" other Bill of Rights guarantees to the states. This approach, described in *Palko v. Connecticut* (1937) as applicable to those rights "rooted in the traditions and conscience of our people as to be ranked fundamental," had been used to incorporate the First Amendment right to freedom of speech, press, and assembly, as well as the right to free exercise of religion and the right against the establishment of religion. However, the Court also declined to incorporate other guarantees, including the right to indictment by grand jury, the privilege against self-incrimination and double jeopardy, and the right to a jury trial.

In *Wolf*, a unanimous Court used the selective incorporation approach to apply the Fourth Amendment, the first Bill of Rights guarantee outside of the First Amendment, to the states. Justice Felix Frankfurter, writing for the majority, reasoned,

> The security of one's privacy against arbitrary intrusion by the police — which is at the core of the Fourth Amendment — is basic to a free society. It is therefore implicit in "the concept of ordered liberty" and as such enforceable against the states through the Due Process Clause. The knock at the door, whether by day or by night, as a prelude to a search, without authority of law but solely on the authority of the police, did not need the commentary of recent history to be condemned as inconsistent with the conception of human rights enshrined in the history and the basic constitutional documents of English-speaking peoples.

However, the Court was sharply divided on the question of whether the exclusionary rule, which the *Weeks* Court concluded was a necessary part of the Fourth Amendment, should be extended to the states. Writing for six members of the Court, Frankfurter refused to do so. He noted that the Court "must hesitate to treat this remedy as an essential ingredient of the right." He argued that the exclusionary rule was "not derived from the explicit requirements of the Fourth Amendment" but was rather "a matter of judicial implication." It was the first time the Supreme Court had ever described the exclusionary rule as a "remedy" to correct a Fourth Amendment wrong rather than a constitutional imperative. Frankfurter also, and for the very first time, characterized the purpose of the rule as deterrence of police misconduct.

Frankfurter, who strongly endorsed a philosophy of judicial restraint, based his decision not to extend the exclusionary rule to the states on the principle of federalism. He reasoned that it was up to each individual state to address the admissibility of illegally seized evidence, and that the exclusionary rule was only one of several approaches to addressing Fourth Amendment wrongs. He noted that at the time, of the forty-seven states that have passed the *Weeks* doctrine, only sixteen states had adopted the exclusionary rule, while thirty-one states and the United Kingdom rejected it. Frankfurter explained that "it is not for this Court to condemn as falling below the minimal standards assured by the Due Process Clause a State's reliance upon other methods, which, if consistently enforced, would be equally effective." He also used this opportunity to suggest alternatives to the exclusionary rule, including use of internal police disciplinary procedures, civil torts against government, and public opinion. However, Frankfurter did not foreclose the exclusionary rule as an option, noting that Congress might be able to impose the rule on the states through section 5 of the Fourteenth Amendment, its enforcement clause.

Justice Hugo Black wrote a brief concurring opinion, noting, "I agree with what appears to be a plain implication of the Court's opinion that the federal exclusionary rule is not a command of the Fourth Amendment but is a judicially created rule of evidence which Congress may negate." Justice William O. Douglas wrote a one-paragraph dissent, arguing that the exclusionary rule was the only effective sanction to Fourth Amendment violations. And Justice Frank Murphy, joined by Justice Wiley B. Rutledge in a separate dissent, stated, "It is disheartening to find so much that is right in an opinion which seems to me so fundamentally wrong." He reasoned that the Fourth Amendment required the suppression of the illegally seized evidence because the alternatives suggested by Frankfurter were ineffective: "There is but one alternative to the rule of exclusion. That is no sanction at all."

Murphy also provided the first empirical assessment of the exclusionary rule. He sent questionnaires to thirty-eight police chiefs asking about the exclusionary rule and law enforcement practices. Those residing in states with the exclusionary rule indicated that they were well instructed in the law of search and seizure. Murphy interpreted these results as evidence that the rule served to educate law enforcement about how to conduct constitutional searches and seizures. While the results were hardly scientific, his curiosity about the effectiveness of the exclusionary rule would later come to dominate the Supreme Court's analysis of the subject.

Wolf was a landmark decision. By declaring the Fourth Amendment applicable to the states, the Supreme Court expanded Americans' right to be free from illegal searches and seizures by both federal and state government authorities. However, the decision also reflected the Court's disagreement about the consequences of such a Fourth Amendment violation. By choosing not to include the exclusionary rule as part of the Fourth Amendment, the Court cast doubt on whether it was a constitutional necessity. According to one commentator, "The Court dealt the rule a blow from which it has never recovered." Also important was Frankfurter's characterization regarding the purpose of the federal exclusionary rule. With the Court's suggestion that the purpose of the rule was deterrence of police misconduct — reasoning that had not been used by the Court previously — the earlier rationales for the rule (that it was a constitutional necessity, and that exclusion was necessary to preserve judicial integrity) moved to the background. In two exclusionary rule cases decided in 1949, *Wolf*'s rationale for the exclusionary rule, and not *Weeks*'s, would be cited as authoritative. For instance, in *United States v. Wallace and Tiernan Co.* and *Lustig v. United States*, also decided that year, the Court mentioned the deterrence rationale as the reason for the exclusionary rule. Finally, *Wolf* presented a practical problem. While the exclusionary rule was available for federal law enforcement violations, it was not available in states that had yet to adopt the exclusionary rule, thus creating a two-tiered system.

Also relevant to the discussion of the history of the exclusionary rule is a trio of decisions that indirectly addressed who had "standing" to raise a Fourth Amendment challenge to illegally seized evidence. A relaxed view of standing allows a broader range of victims of illegal searches to raise an exclusionary rule challenge, while a more restrictive reading of this jurisdictional issue limits the range of victims who can make this claim. In these early years, the Supreme Court offered a very broad reading of who has standing, declaring in *McDonald v. United States* (1948), *United States v. Jeffers* (1950), and *Jones v. United States* (1960) that third parties with a private property interest in evidence illegally seized were protected under the Fourth Amendment.

Justice Frankfurter would return to the due process clause of the Fourteenth Amendment several years later in another illegal search and seizure case. The case, *Rochin v. California* (1952), concerned a particularly outrageous illegal search and seizure by state authorities. Three Los Angeles deputy sheriffs, believing Rochin was selling narcotics, entered his home without a warrant, forced open his bedroom door, and found him, partially dressed, in bed with his wife. Upon seeing the police, Rochin grabbed two capsules from the table and swallowed them. The officers tried to retrieve the capsules by squeezing his throat but were unsuccessful, so they brought him to the hospital and directed the physicians to force a tube of solution into his stomach to make him vomit. After the procedure the capsules were recovered, tested, and found to be morphine. They were admitted into evidence, and Rochin was convicted of illegal drug possession.

Writing for six members of the Court, Justice Frankfurter announced that in cases where evidence was obtained by egregious police conduct, the evidence should be suppressed from trial under the due process clause of the Fourteenth Amendment. Although he recognized that the due process clause offered "the least specific and most comprehensive protection of liberties," which "as a historic and generative principle precludes defining," he believed it protected criminal defendants from convictions "brought about by methods that offend a 'sense of justice.'"

Frankfurter explained that the police conduct in *Rochin* "shocks the conscience." It was, he observed, "bound to offend even hardened sensibilities. They are methods too close to the rack and screw." He concluded that evidence so obtained should be excluded from state criminal trials. Frankfurter added that exclusion was also necessary to protect judicial integrity, reasoning that "to sanction the brutal conduct . . . would be to afford brutality the cloak of law. Nothing would be more calculated to discredit law and thereby to brutalize the temper of society."

Although Frankfurter found a way to exclude *some* illegally seized evidence by state authorities after rejecting a broad rule disallowing all illegally seized evidence in *Wolf*, other members of the Court questioned this approach. In a concurring opinion, Justices Black and Douglas expressed concern about the indeterminate nature of the "shock the conscience" test. They suggested instead that Rochin's conviction be reversed on grounds that the police conduct violated the Fifth Amendment prohibition against self-incrimination, which they argued should be applicable to the states.

The subjectivity of the "shock the conscience" test was revealed two years later in *Irvine v. California* (1954), where the Court refused to extend the exclusionary rule to situations that did not involve "coercion," "violence," or "brutality." In *Irvine*, police repeatedly entered the defendant's home over a three-week period in an effort to uncover evidence of illegal bookmaking. Several holes were bored into the walls of his house, including his bedroom, and a tap was placed on his phone. Police eventually obtained enough evidence to convict the defendant for illegal gambling. The Court sustained the conviction by a five-to-four vote in five separate opinions. Justice Robert H. Jackson, writing for four members in the plurality, observed that "few police measures have come to our attention that more flagrantly, deliberately, and persistently violated the fundamental principle declared by the Fourth Amendment." However, he concluded, the actions fell short of the "shock the conscience" test established in *Rochin*. Jackson also used the opportunity to reaffirm *Wolf v. Colorado* and to offer his belief that the federal exclusionary rule did little to deter police misconduct. Other sanctions fared as poorly; he dismissed them as "of no practical avail."

Justice Tom C. Clark's concurring opinion revealed his unhappiness with the Court's approach to the exclusionary rule. Noting that had he been on the Court when it decided *Wolf*, he would have voted to apply the exclusionary rule to the states, he concurred with the majority's opinion in the present case "with great reluctance" based on the precedent, stating, "Thus *Wolf* remains the law and, as such, is entitled to the respect of this Court's membership." Clark also expressed his displeasure with the Court's "shock the conscience" approach, stating that it made for "uncertainty" and "unpredictability." "In truth, the practical result of this ad hoc approach is simply that when five Justices are sufficiently revolted by local police action, a conviction is overturned and a guilty man may go free." Moreover, the former attorney general doubted the Court's case-by-case approach to due process would have an effect on police conduct. "[Although] we may thus vindicate the abstract principle of due process," he observed, "we do not shape the conduct of local police one whit; unpredictable reversals on dissimilar fact situations are not likely to curb the zeal of those police and prosecutors who may be intent on racking up a high percentage of successful prosecutions."

Clark's distaste for *Wolf* was also evident in a draft *Irvine* opinion that called for overturning the decision and extending the exclusionary rule to the states. The draft was not circulated among the conference but was sent only to Justice Jackson. In it Clark argued that "the fundamental error in *Wolf* was its failure to recognize the constitutional imperative in the language of *Weeks v. United States.*" He cited language from *Weeks* indicating "that the exclusionary rule [was] an essential part of the constitutional safeguards against unreasonable searches and seizures," as well as language from *Silverthorne Lumber Co., Gouled, Byars,* and *Olmstead,* to illustrate the Court's rather consistent declarations that the exclusionary rule was part and parcel of the Fourth Amendment. Clark reasoned, "If the Fourth Amendment ban against unreasonable searches and seizures by federal officers necessitates exclusion of unlawfully seized evidence from federal trials, *a fortiori*, the Fourteenth Amendment's ban against such seizures by state officers requires exclusion of tainted evidence from state trials." Overturning *Wolf* and applying the rule to the states, he reasoned, "would make the long line of federal cases since *Weeks* the rule of decision in this field and would dissipate the confusion now existing in our cases as to the protection the states must afford this important constitutional right of each of our citizens." Although the full Court never saw this draft, the opinion illustrates Clark's musings on extending the exclusionary rule to the states as a constitutional necessity almost a decade before *Mapp v. Ohio.*

In 1959 all nine justices voted to review *Elkins v. United States,* a case involving the "silver platter doctrine." Several of the Court's earlier decisions cast doubts on the legitimacy of the doctrine, especially *Wolf,* where the Court declared that illegal searches by state authorities violated the Fourth and Fourteenth Amendments. In *Elkins,* Oregon authorities failed to successfully prosecute the defendant for evidence seized through wiretapping in state court, which suppressed the evidence due to an invalid warrant, so state authorities turned the evidence over to federal officers for federal prosecution.

The Supreme Court used *Elkins* to discard the silver platter doctrine and make evidence seized illegally by state officers inadmissible in federal criminal trials as well. The Court was sharply divided in its decision, handed down in 1960. Writing for a five-justice majority, Justice Potter Stewart concluded that since the Court decided in *Wolf* that the Fourth Amendment was applicable against both state and federal law enforcement actions, it was appropriate that the evidence illegally seized by state authorities also be excluded from federal trials. He based the decision on the principle of healthy federalism, which, he observed, "depends on the avoidance of needless conflict between state and federal courts" and "the imperative of judicial integrity." The federal courts should not, he remarked, act as "accomplices in the willful disobedience of a Constitution they are sworn to uphold."

Stewart also used *Elkins* to evaluate the exclusionary rule. He noted the "ardent controversy" about the rule and emphasized that the reason for the rule was deterrence of police misconduct, as articulated in *Wolf*. Its purpose, he explained, "is to deter — to compel respect for the constitutional guaranty in the only effectively available way — by removing the incentive to disregard it." While Stewart conceded that there was no empirical evidence on the rule's efficacy, he acknowledged that since *Wolf*, a number of states had adopted a partial or complete exclusionary rule by legislation or court action, which was an indication that more states were embracing the exclusionary remedy.

Justice Frankfurter, joined by Justices Clark, Harlan, and Whittaker, wrote the dissent. He questioned Stewart's use of *Wolf* as a rationale for excluding evidence illegally seized by state authorities in silver platter cases, especially when he explicitly used the decision to declare that the exclusionary rule did not apply to the states. Like Stewart, he based his decision on the principle of federalism, but for different reasons. He explained that *Elkins* would likely prompt federal courts to question the legality of searches and seizures more extensively, which he believed would unduly interfere with federal-state relations. But the debate was lost, and *Elkins* was reaffirmed later that term in *Rios v. United States* (1960), a case also involving evidence seized illegally by state officers. But *Wolf*'s days were numbered. Both *Elkins* and *Rios* ultimately paved the way for its reconsideration and overruling in *Mapp v. Ohio*, which came before the Court the following year.

———

Justice Stewart's *Elkins* comments regarding the fact that a number of states had embraced the exclusionary rule since *Wolf v. Colorado* raises questions about why states were selecting the exclusionary rule sanction to Fourth Amendment violations at the same time the Supreme Court was refusing to impose it on the states. Insight into this question is revealed in the conversion of one state supreme court justice, Roger Traynor, who served on the California high court for three decades. Traynor, a highly regarded jurist, was heralded for his judicious approach to balancing respect for individual rights with society's need for effective law enforcement.

In 1942 Traynor wrote the majority opinion in *People v. Gonzales*, which allowed the admission of illegally seized evidence in state trials. However, he changed his position thirteen years later in *People v. Cahan* (1955). In his majority opinion Traynor explained that his transformation was motivated, in large part, because of his concerns about rampant police misconduct: "Without fear of criminal punishment or other discipline, law enforcement officers, sworn to support the Constitution of the United States and the Constitution of California, frankly admit their deliberate flagrant acts in violation of both Constitutions and the laws enacted thereunder. It is clearly apparent from their testimony that they casually regard such acts as nothing more than the performance of their ordinary duties for which the city employs and pays them." He concluded that the only way to address this problem was to adopt the exclusionary rule, which "opens the door to the development of workable rules governing search and seizure and the issuance of warrants that will protect both the rights guaranteed by the constitutional provisions and the interest of society in the suppression of crime."

Traynor explained that the exclusionary rule was the only way to force law enforcement officers to obey the Constitution because other alternatives were ineffective. "Experience has demonstrated . . . that neither administrative, criminal nor civil remedies are effective in suppressing lawless searches and seizures." He was also motivated by the rationale of judicial integrity, noting that accepting the tainted evidence made judicial officers parties to the unconstitutional activity. Traynor observed that effectively, failure of alternatives to the exclusionary rule created a situation where the courts had been "constantly required to participate in, and in effect condone, the lawless activities of law enforcement officers."

Several years later in a law journal article, Traynor more fully explained his transformation from a critic to a supporter of the exclusionary rule:

> My misgivings . . . grew as I observed that time after time [illegally seized evidence] was being offered and admitted as a routine procedure. It became impossible to ignore the corollary that illegal searches and seizures were also a routine procedure subject to no effective deterrent; how else could illegally obtained evidence come into court with such regularity? It was one thing to condone an occasional constable's blunder, to accept his illegally obtained evidence so that the guilty would not go free. It was quite another to condone a steady course of illegal police procedures that deliberately and flagrantly violated the Constitution of the United States, as well as the state constitution.

———

On the eve of *Mapp v. Ohio*, the Supreme Court's exclusionary rule jurisprudence was less than clear. As one commentator noted, "From 1914 when the Court adopted the exclusionary rule for federal courts and began developing search and seizure standards, to 1961 when it imposed the exclusionary rule on the states, the Court created a body of doctrine regarded by judges and scholars as confusing, irrational, and incomplete." There were three major problems with the Court's exclusionary rule jurisprudence. First was the Court's early use of both the Fourth and Fifth Amendments to justify exclusion of illegally seized evidence. While this was most notable in *Boyd v. United States*, several other decisions in the first few decades after *Boyd* also discussed the Fifth Amendment in justifying the exclusionary rule. These decisions cast some doubt on whether the rule was based on the Fourth Amendment alone, or on the Fourth and Fifth Amendments combined.

Second was the Court's decision in *Wolf v. Colorado*, where it used the Fourteenth Amendment's due process clause to incorporate the Fourth Amendment to apply to the states while at the same time rejecting incorporation of the exclusionary rule. This decision put the Fourth Amendment in a vulnerable position because it acknowledged the states' capacity to commit a constitutional violation, but it did not authorize a remedy to address the violation.

Third was the evolution in the exclusionary rule's rationale between *Weeks v. United States* (1914) and *Wolf v. Colorado* (1949). Although for several decades following *Weeks* a unanimous Court, or a very strong majority, appeared fully behind the exclusionary rule as a constitutional imperative that was also necessary to preserve judicial integrity, in *Wolf* the Court characterized the rule as a remedial device created by judicial implication to deter police misconduct. This confusion regarding the constitutional basis for the exclusionary rule and the controversy over its applicability to the states would continue and would deepen even further.

———

Meanwhile, in Cleveland, Ohio, Ms. Dollree Mapp was still trying to decide what to do in the wake of her defeat in the Ohio Supreme Court. The Supreme Court's exclusionary rule jurisprudence was clearly in a state of flux. Now there was the remote possibility that the Court might use her case to revisit the question of whether illegally seized evidence should be excluded from state, as well as federal, criminal trials as a requirement of the Fourth Amendment.

One Final Appeal

Dollree Mapp had one final avenue for judicial consideration of her conviction under the Ohio state antiobscenity law: an appeal to the U.S. Supreme Court. This chapter reviews her appeal, including the strategies employed by counsel, the arguments made at bar, and the participation of the American Civil Liberties Union as amicus. It also details the oral arguments in *Mapp v. Ohio.*

———

When she learned of the Ohio Supreme Court's final decision, Mapp was enormously disappointed, but she did not allow the loss to deter her intention to clear her name. She consulted with her attorneys regarding the next step, and Kearns and Greene informed her that her final option was an appeal to the U.S. Supreme Court. Mapp wanted to continue her fight but did not have the finances to pursue the case. The estimated cost of the appeal was $8,000. Fortunately, the friend who had assisted her with her earlier legal bills offered to fund an appeal to the high court. But finding a way to pay the legal costs was not as great a challenge as the hurdle that lay ahead. Even though many believe they have the right to "take their case all the way to the Supreme Court," few realize the Court is not obligated to hear the appeal.

Despite the long odds of having their case selected by the U.S. Supreme Court — at this time in the Court's history only one in approximately two hundred cases were granted review — Kearns and Greene believed there was a good possibility *Mapp v. Ohio* would catch the Court's attention. They felt the breadth of the Ohio antiobscenity statute made it susceptible to a constitutional challenge. In addition, a majority of the Ohio Supreme Court had declared the law unconstitutional, and only a quirk in the state constitution allowed it to stand. Moreover, obscenity cases had proved eye-catching to the Warren Court, which handed down the landmark *Roth v. United States* decision in 1957. And, in 1959, the Supreme Court decided *Smith v. California*, where it ruled that a state law prohibiting mere possession of obscene books by booksellers was a violation of the First Amendment. *Roth* and *Smith* were evidence the Court might be willing to break additional ground in this subject area.

The task of writing the petition requesting review fell largely to Walter Greene. The young attorney introduced five broad questions "presented by this appeal." The petition was surprisingly short; eight pages, with only a single page and several sentences dedicated to presenting why the Supreme Court should elect to review the Ohio Supreme Court decision in *Mapp v. Ohio.*

The three major arguments presented were that the Ohio obscenity statute violated the Fourth, Fifth, and Fourteenth Amendments to the U.S. Constitution; that Mapp's sentence constituted cruel and unusual punishment in violation of the Eighth Amendment to the U.S. Constitution; and that the police conduct violated the Fourth, Fifth, and Fourteenth Amendments to the U.S. Constitution. The two minor arguments were that the Ohio Court of Appeals' decision not to review Mapp's sentence and the trial judge's incorrect jury instructions violated Mapp's right to a fair trial under the Sixth Amendment to the U.S. Constitution.

After a one-page summary of the five questions, the bulk of the petition was dedicated to a review of the facts of the case, including the contention that the police acted inappropriately when they searched Mapp's home without a warrant. The petition also described how the legal questions presented were unsatisfactorily addressed by the Ohio Supreme Court. It concluded with the statement that the federal questions were substantial because the Ohio statute "violates one's sacred right to own and hold property, which has been held inviolate by the Federal Constitution," and because "the right of the individual to read, to believe or disbelieve, and to think without governmental supervision is one of our basic liberties, but to dictate to the mature adult what books he may have in his own private library seems to be a clear infringement of the constitutional rights of the individual." The case also raised a substantial federal question, wrote Mapp's attorneys, because the Ohio obscenity statute was being enforced vigorously in the state and "many convictions have followed that of the defendant . . . based upon this very same statute." Unless the statute was struck down, they predicted there would be "many such appeals." The petition ended with a summary statement about how the police conduct and the harsh sentence deprived the appellant of "her right to liberty and pursuit of happiness . . . and is a cruel and unusual punishment."

The petition was sent to the prosecutor's office in Cuyahoga County, Ohio, the same day it was sent to the U.S. Supreme Court. Upon receiving it, the county's prosecuting attorney, John T. Corrigan, and the assistant prosecuting attorney, Gertrude Bauer Mahon, had thirty days to file their "motion to dismiss or affirm." Mahon, who had been doing the lion's share of the work, was assigned the responsibility of writing the motion to dismiss. Her objective was to discourage the Court from granting review.

The state's motion began with an assessment of the events that took place at Mapp's home. This account of the search was far less inflammatory than the appellant's version. The state insisted that the police conducted the search with a valid warrant despite the fact that the police sergeant in charge, Carl Delau, had privately admitted to the prosecuting attorney's office that there was no warrant, and the Ohio Supreme Court acknowledged the lack of a warrant in its majority opinion. The state also continued its strategy to cast Mapp in a negative light, noting her "tussle" with the police and implying that she was responsible for the officers' actions.

The motion to dismiss included responses to Kearns's and Greene's three major arguments presented in the petition for review. The state countered that the obscenity statute was constitutional and necessary to eradicate obscenity; that evidence unlawfully seized by Ohio police was still admissible in a state criminal trial under judicial precedent; and that the penalty section of the obscenity statute was constitutional because it was an indeterminate sentence.

The bulk of the brief was dedicated to the constitutionality of the obscenity statute. In order to eradicate obscenity, the state argued, "the police powers of a state should be broad enough to ban every step in the progress of 'obscenity,' not only prohibiting the manufacture, advertising, sale and distribution but the ultimate scienter retained possession by an individual." To highlight the importance of prohibiting possession, the state posed the question, "Why prohibit distribution and sale of obscene books and pictures if the end result, namely, possession by an individual for private consumption and further circulation is constitutionally protected?" The response brief also differentiated the case at hand from Supreme Court precedent, *Smith v. California*, which was favorably cited by the Ohio Supreme Court majority to support its conclusion that the Ohio statute was unconstitutional. The state explained that the California ordinance in *Smith* made it unlawful for a bookseller to possess obscene books, regardless of whether the possessor had scienter, or knowledge, that the books were obscene, whereas in *Mapp v. Ohio* the lower courts emphasized that not only possession but also scienter was necessary for conviction. The vagueness of the California statute would lead to a greater risk of inhibiting or "chilling" constitutionally protected expression, whereas the Ohio statute required that one know he or she was in possession of obscenity in order to be convicted.

In response to the appellant's concerns about the police search and the confiscated evidence, the state admitted that the evidence found in Mapp's home would not have been listed on the search warrant because the police were looking for a bombing suspect, not obscene material. The admission meant that the search and seizure of the obscene material was unlawful. However, the attorneys continued, the lawfulness of the search was irrelevant because according to the Ohio precedent, *State v. Lindway*, the evidence was admissible. Moreover, the state added, the Supreme Court's own precedent in *Wolf v. Colorado* (1949) allowed each state to set its own standards regarding the admission of unlawfully seized evidence. Because the appellant provided "no sound reason for departing from the *Lindway* decision, or modifying it in its application to this case," the lawyers reasoned, the decision should stand. The state also offered a more restrictive reading of an individual's Fourth Amendment rights, contending that while it is necessary to protect the lawful activities of individuals, "nothing is said in that provision guaranteeing security and immunity in the commission of crimes."

The final section addressed whether Mapp's sentence was unconstitutionally cruel and unusual. The state responded that this was not the case because the penalty for violating the statute was a "general one, and not fixed in duration," and that as an indeterminate sentence, the defendant could earn early release on parole "at any time after she started serving her sentence." The brief concluded with a recommendation that the Supreme Court exercise restraint and not grant review because the case had been decided on an "adequate not-federal basis," and a plea that the states be given enough latitude under their police powers to "eradicate obscenity."

The briefs were filed, and it was now up to the Warren Court to determine if the appeal was meritorious.

———

Mapp v. Ohio was one of almost 2,000 petitions for review sent to the U.S. Supreme Court in 1960. At this time, the Court was granting review to approximately 250 cases a year. A little less than half of these cases were disposed of summarily, which is to say the Court bypasses oral arguments and issues a judgment based on the written briefs. These per curiam (by the Court) opinions are generally uninformative and consist of only a short memorandum setting forth the issue, law, and decision. The remaining cases, approximately 140 at this period in the Court's history, received plenary review or "full dress treatment," which includes oral arguments and a written opinion.

An examination of the conference deliberations over whether *Mapp v. Ohio* should be accepted for review reveals that the case caught the eye of almost all the justices on the Court. However, they were paying attention to the case for reasons other than what was presented in the petition for review of *Ohio v. Mapp*. Several justices' conference notes reveal that they, like the Ohio Supreme Court, were interested in the case because they believed the Ohio obscenity statute potentially violated the First and Fourteenth Amendments to the Constitution. For example, Justice Tom C. Clark's law clerk wrote a three-page memorandum stating that the case presented a First Amendment question. It may, the clerk wrote, "discourage law abiding people from even looking at books and thus interfere with the freedom of speech and press. . . . I think it should fall under *Smith v. California*." The clerk noted that "this argument convinced 4 of the 7 justices of the st. ct. but the Ohio constitution prohibits a finding of unconstitutionality if more than one justice finds it constitutional."

The memorandum did acknowledge the appellant's due process challenge — that Mapp's conviction was on the basis of evidence obtained without a search warrant and should therefore be excluded —

but responded that Ohio "accepts such evidence and the facts here do not appear to bring this case under the ban of the *Rochin* due process standard." *Rochin* was the Court's 1952 decision where a majority, led by Justice Felix Frankfurter, suggested that situations where police actions "shock the conscience" may prompt suppression of illegally obtained evidence. The clerk ended the memo with the remark that the other issues presented by the appellant "have little merit." His assessment that *Mapp v. Ohio*'s major issue on appeal was the First Amendment challenge to the Ohio statute was shared by other law clerks. Justice John Marshall Harlan's clerk, for example, recommended review, writing, "This is an obscenity case."

Chief Justice Earl Warren opened the discussion of *Mapp v. Ohio* in the weekly judicial conference. He summarized the facts and legal questions and announced that he would vote to review. The other justices then voted in order of seniority. Justice Clark's docket book, which recorded the votes, indicates that all but one of the justices were in favor of review. The lone holdout was Frankfurter, who voted to dismiss the case because he believed possession of obscenity was clearly criminal under the state statute. There is also the possibility that Frankfurter was concerned that the appellant's focus on the legitimacy of the search would call attention to the issue of whether illegally seized evidence should be excluded in state criminal trials. He was well known for refusing to revisit his opinions, and he may have believed the case might be used to overturn *Wolf.* As is the tradition, the most junior member of the Court, on this occasion, Justice Potter Stewart, provided the results to the clerk of the Court, who then contacted the attorneys on both sides of the case.

———

Mapp was delighted when informed that the Supreme Court chose to hear the appeal. She had one final opportunity to prevail in court. Kearns and Greene were pleased as well. Encouraged that a majority on the Ohio Supreme Court believed the antiobscenity statute was unconstitutional, they predicted that the U.S. Supreme Court would invalidate the statute on similar grounds. They also knew that the odds of a reversal were in their favor; on average, the Supreme Court reverses two-thirds of the cases it chooses to review. For their part, the state's attorneys were confident as well. Corrigan and Mahon had won at every stage in the Ohio courts and had little reason to believe they would not prevail before the high court. Both sides began the task of preparing their formal legal briefs.

Walter Greene was given the assignment to prepare the "Brief of the Appellant on the Merits." Upon hearing the Court had granted review, he had forty-five days to file the brief with the Supreme Court. The brief duplicated the five questions presented in the petition for review and provided additional reasoning and citation of court precedent to support the arguments for reversal.

In support of the first argument, that the antiobscenity statute was unconstitutional, Mapp's attorneys favorably cited the Ohio Supreme Court majority ruling — and the dissent — where the justices declared that the law infringed upon one's right to freedom of speech and the press. Although there had not been a sufficient number of votes to strike down the law under the Ohio Constitution, Kearns and Greene believed the reasoning was sound because both opinions illustrated how the breadth of the statute might discourage law-abiding people from even looking at books and pictures, potentially "chilling" constitutionally protected speech. The attorneys also found support in the U.S. Supreme Court's opinion in *Smith v. California* (1959), a decision, they wrote, analogous to the case at bar in its effect. Curiously, although the Ohio Supreme Court in *Mapp* and the U.S. Supreme Court in *Smith* decided these cases on First Amendment grounds, Kearns and Greene insisted that the Ohio statute was unconstitutional under the Fourth, Fifth, and Fourteenth Amendments to the Constitution. Although it was not entirely clear from their legal brief, they were implicitly arguing that one had a right to possess this type of material as part of a general right to privacy under the Fourth and Fifth Amendments, extended to the states under the Fourteenth Amendment.

To support the second argument, that the sentence of seven years for violating the statute constituted cruel and unusual punishment, Kearns and Greene highlighted the extreme nature of the current Ohio antiobscenity statute by comparing it to other state laws that criminalized mere possession of obscene material, as well as the previous Ohio antiobscenity law. The earlier Ohio law, for example, classified violations as misdemeanors subject to minor fines between

$25 and $100 and sentences of 30 to 100 days if obscene material were delivered to a minor child, and fines between $50 and $500 and 30 days to six months in jail if one posted obscenity in a public place. That the current law criminalized mere possession as a felony subject to a fine of $2,000 and a sentence of one to seven years was characterized as "excessive" and "cruel and unusual."

For the third major argument, regarding the unlawful search, Mapp's attorneys returned to *Rochin v. California.* They repeated their earlier claim that the Cleveland police's conduct in Mapp's case portrayed "a shocking disregard of human rights" analogous to the situation in *Rochin.* The attorneys also did not give up on their effort to persuade the Court to reevaluate the state's *Lindway* decision, which allowed the admission of illegally seized evidence in Ohio. However, in case the Supreme Court chose not to do so, the attorneys argued that if *Lindway* were to stand, then Mapp's case was distinct and should not be evaluated under this standard. To support their argument, the brief favorably quoted the dissenting opinion from the Ohio Supreme Court in *Ohio v. Mapp* that the case should be distinguished from *Lindway,* and the illegally seized evidence should be excluded, because in the latter case the defendant was accused of the crime of manufacturing bombs in the basement of a home, an offense so grave that "neither the Constitution nor State law was intended to provide security for such dangerous enemies at our public peace," compared with Mapp's offense, where "mere private possession of such literature by an adult constitute[d] a crime."

The attorneys' justification for the remaining two arguments, that Mapp did not receive a fair trial because the appellate courts did not review the sentence handed down by the trial court, and that the trial court judge had given incorrect jury instructions, was only a few sentences long. The attorneys merely reminded the Supreme Court that the appellate courts should have given these matters greater attention to ensure the appellant received a fair trial.

The state of Ohio had thirty days to respond to the appellant's legal brief. It appears that the attorneys for the state spent even less time on their brief on the merits than they did on their motion to dismiss the case. The brief was only fourteen pages long and repeated most of what was included in the earlier motion. There were only two new additions, and both reflected the state's concern that the appellant's continued focus on the search warrant issue may have struck a chord with the Supreme Court. First, apparently weary of the focus on the Cleveland police conduct and whether or not there was ever a valid warrant to search Mapp's home, the state agreed that "the police officers who made the search and who were witnesses in this case, testified that they did not obtain the search warrant," but, not yet willing to give up on the issue, the state added that the officers believed the lieutenant arriving on the scene had a warrant and had waited for him before proceeding with the search. And, the attorneys argued, "no question was raised on the trial that no search warrant had been obtained and Lt. White was as available to the defense on subpoena as to the State. It was not incumbent upon the State to offer a search warrant into the evidence as an element of the offense to be proven in this trial." *However, the state finally conceded, almost as an afterthought, "it is admitted that such a search warrant was not secured."* Finally admitting in the official record that there was no search warrant must have been difficult for the state's attorneys, and may provide one reason why the state put such little time into its brief before the Court.

The second new argument was a response to the appellant's charge that the police conduct "shocked the conscience," thereby providing the Supreme Court with the opportunity to exclude the unlawfully seized evidence under *Rochin.* The state differentiated the circumstances in *Mapp* from this precedent, stating that in the present case, "no physical examination of the appellant was made to secure the evidence which was the basis for this prosecution," and that "there was no misconduct on the part of the police in securing the evidence." The attorneys also repeated their earlier claim that it was Mapp who was responsible for the "scuffle" that had ensued between her and the police. "By her conduct, the appellant provoked the situation which made it necessary for the police to handcuff her if a peaceable search was to be conducted."

Aside from these two additions, the state's legal brief was essentially the same as the motion to dismiss; the attorneys argued that extensive police powers were necessary to eradicate the problem of obscenity, that the indeterminate sentence imposed by the trial court did not constitute cruel and unusual punishment, that illegally obtained evidence could still be admitted in Ohio state criminal trials, and that the trial court judge acted appropriately and did not violate Mapp's right to a fair trial.

———

Once again, *Mapp v. Ohio* attracted the attention of the Ohio Civil Liberties Union, an affiliate of the American Civil Liberties Union. The Ohio chapter had been involved in the case since the time it went before the Ohio Supreme Court, when it filed an amicus curiae brief in favor of reversing the Ohio obscenity statute as a violation of the First Amendment to the U.S. Constitution. After hearing that the U.S. Supreme Court granted review in the case, the OCLU joined with the American Civil Liberties Union to request permission to prepare an amicus curiae brief to the Court to argue the constitutionality of the Ohio statute. In order to appear as amici, the OCLU and the ACLU first had to obtain permission from the attorneys and later from the Supreme Court. Participation of amicus before the Supreme Court is important because they often raise questions not considered by direct parties to a case and usually cast legal questions in terms of their broader effect on the development of constitutional law or public policy.

The Ohio chapter began working with the national organization on the amicus curiae brief before the U.S. Supreme Court. The ACLU has had an active national litigation campaign since its inception in 1917, usually providing funding or counsel to litigants or, alternatively, filing amicus briefs in major cases. It also frequently collaborated with other civil liberties groups on cases appealed to the Supreme Court. The ACLU has appeared before the Supreme Court more than any other organization except the federal government, including participation in a number of the Court's landmark decisions. While early litigation struggles focused on the rights of political dissidents, the ACLU's participation in *Mapp v. Ohio* and a number of other cases involving criminal procedure rights significantly shaped the Court's interpretation of the Fourth, Fifth, Sixth, and Eighth Amendments to the Constitution.

The board of directors for the OCLU assigned four volunteers to the amicus brief in *Mapp v. Ohio.* The committee consisted of the three young lawyers, Bernard A. Berkman, Fred J. Livingstone, and Julian C. Renswick, who wrote the amicus curiae brief before the Ohio Supreme Court, as well as Ralph Hertz, an experienced attorney who also had judicial experience, having served as a judge on the Court of Common Pleas of Cuyahoga County. In addition to these four, another attorney, Jack G. Day, who would later serve on the Ohio Court of Appeals for the Eighth District, served briefly on the committee but resigned. Day would later write a short article, "Words That Counted — A Vignette," for the fortieth anniversary of *Mapp v. Ohio*, where he explained that he "resigned because of stylistic objections to the brief. With that act I walked out of a significant piece of legal history into obscurity. *Sic simper* snob!"

Contrary to his ex post facto hand-wringing, however, Day did play an important role in the writing of the brief. He recalled that the three younger attorneys were "anxious to brief the constitutionality of the suppression issue." However, the committee's interest was initially stymied by the resistance of Judge Hertz, whom Day recounts "thought the issue was foreclosed by *Wolf v. Colorado* and would not budge." The attorneys approached Day to get the judge to change his mind. "We need a son-of-a-bitch and you are our first choice," they told him. "Will you try and soften the Judge on this issue?" Day agreed and approached Hertz, "emphasizing the history of the high court in modification of principle." The judge relented and supported the committee's effort to include the argument about search and seizure.

The amicus curiae brief filed on behalf of the Ohio Civil Liberties Union and American Civil Liberties Union was similar to the earlier brief to the Ohio Supreme Court. It focused on the constitutionality of the Ohio state antiobscenity law: that it violated the due process clause of the Fourteenth Amendment, interfered with an individual's privacy rights under the Fourth and Fourteenth Amendments, and violated the equal protection clause of the Fourteenth Amendment. However, there was one important addition. It also included a very short section asking the Supreme Court to reexamine its *Wolf v. Colorado* decision. Albeit brief, that section would later prove to be the most important argument before the Supreme Court. In a single paragraph at the end of the brief, the attorneys suggested Mapp's conviction should be overturned because she was convicted by the "use of evidence obtained in an illegal search and seizure," which, they argued, "violates the due process clause of the Fourteenth Amendment."

Their justification for the argument consisted of only eleven typewritten lines: "This case presents the issue of whether evidence obtained in an illegal search and seizure can constitutionally be used in a State criminal proceeding. We are aware of the view that this Court has taken on this issue in *Wolf v. Colorado*. It is our purpose by this paragraph to respectfully request that this Court re-examine this issue and conclude that the ordered liberty concept guaranteed to persons by the due process clause of the Fourteenth Amendment necessarily requires that evidence illegally obtained in violation thereof, not be admissible in state criminal proceedings."

With the briefs filed and later disseminated to each of the justices' chambers, it was now time for oral arguments, scheduled for March 29, 1961. Unbeknownst to the two sets of attorneys representing Mapp and the state of Ohio, their legal briefs to the Court may have done more harm than good. One of Chief Justice Earl Warren's law clerks noted in a bench memorandum, "The briefs of the parties in this case are among the worst I have seen all year. Happily, however, the amicus brief of the American Civil Liberties Union and Justice Taft's opinion in the court below tend to bring the major issues into focus." The arguments at bar would no doubt be interesting.

———

In the two months prior to oral arguments before the U.S. Supreme Court, Dollree Mapp would frequently phone Kearns, her primary attorney, for information about the case. "I was following the case closely," she recalled. "I demanded that I be told everything they did." Kearns told Mapp that he was encouraged about their chances and informed her that his office had presented several arguments on appeal that would likely persuade the Court to reverse her conviction. However, Kearns never mentioned the OCLU and ACLU's participation as amici curiae. Nor did he tell Mapp that several weeks prior to oral arguments, one of the OCLU's attorneys working on the case, Bernard Berkman, phoned him to ask if he could present his arguments directly before the Supreme Court during oral arguments. Because each side was limited to a single hour for oral arguments, Berkman was requesting that Kearns share his allotted time. Kearns told the young civil liberties lawyer he would honor his request as long as the Court agreed. Berkman then wrote a letter to the Supreme Court formally requesting to be allowed time during oral arguments to present his case. Several weeks later the Supreme Court granted the request. It was the first time the Court allowed oral arguments time to a chapter of the ACLU participating as amicus curiae. Unbeknownst to Ms. Mapp, several other attorneys, representing the premier civil liberties organization in the country, had joined her case. The ACLU and OCLU's reasons for participating were far broader than those of Mapp's attorneys. While Kearns and Greene were focused on reversing Mapp's conviction, the civil liberties organizations were primarily concerned with persuading the U.S. Supreme Court to overturn the Ohio antiobscenity law, which they believed threatened the privacy rights of all citizens in the state.

Several days before oral arguments in *Mapp v. Ohio*, Kearns and Greene arrived in Washington, D.C., where they continued with last-minute preparations. Kearns, the more experienced attorney, would be presenting oral arguments before the Court. It was Greene's responsibility to review strategy with the veteran Cleveland attorney, who, although this would be his first appearance before the Supreme Court, appeared nonplussed about presenting before the highest court in the land. Driving separately to Washington was Bernard Berkman. He arrived two days before the scheduled arguments with two goals in mind: first, to observe the Supreme Court in action to increase his comfort level before his first appearance before the Court, and, second, to meet with Kearns to coordinate their presentations. Although they both lived and worked in Cleveland, and Berkman had reached out to Kearns several times, the attorney was always too busy to meet with him. In the end, Berkman was able to observe the Court in session, but he was unable to track down Kearns. In fact, he would not set eyes on the Cleveland attorney until moments before oral arguments began.

On the morning of March 28, 1961, the day before the Supreme Court would hear *Mapp v. Ohio*, Dollree Mapp and a friend drove from Cleveland to Washington, D.C., to observe the proceedings. After checking into a motel, they went to the capital to see the sights. Included was a tour of the Supreme Court building, which was open to the public. During the tour, Mapp spoke with one of the bailiffs. She told him she was an appellant in a case the next day and asked him several questions about the Court. The young man warmed to her and spent several minutes describing how the Court functions.

Late the next morning Mapp and her friend came to the Marble Palace and waited for the case, which was scheduled to begin at noon. Although the surroundings were grand, she was not intimidated, just as she was not intimidated by the police search two years earlier. Four decades later, Mapp can still recall how important the day felt to her: "I got such good vibrations from being there. It made me feel good. Being raised in a modest family, it made me feel important to be at the Court and to think they would be talking about me." She was not surprised by the media attention, given the salaciousness of the material police allegedly found in her home. "They wrote up stories about the case all the time," Mapp recalls. "I'm sure people said, 'There goes that girl with the dirty books.'"

The Supreme Court hears oral arguments from the beginning of its term in October until the end of April. Traditionally, oral arguments are held on Mondays, Tuesdays, and Wednesdays and are scheduled several months after a case has been accepted for review. The Court first began to limit the amount of time allotted for oral arguments in 1848 to eight hours, or two hours for each of two attorneys representing their clients. In 1871, this time was cut to two hours for each side, then down to ninety minutes in 1911 and to one hour in 1925. In 1970 the Supreme Court set the current time limit, which is thirty minutes for each side. Most of the attorneys appearing before the Supreme Court are doing so for the first, and often only, time in their careers. For this reason they are considered "one-shotters." There are, however, some "repeat players," or members of the legal elite who specialize in Supreme Court litigation. These are usually members of the Office of the Solicitor General, which represents the U.S. government before the Court, or state attorneys general. Over the last several decades, there have also been a growing number of small law firms that specialize in appellate litigation before the Supreme Court.

Supreme Court justices exhibit different styles during oral arguments. Some, such as Frankfurter, a former law professor, are known for aggressively asking questions of the attorneys appearing at bar. Others use oral arguments as an opportunity to communicate with each other. Because oral arguments are one of only three times the Court is seated together to discuss a case (the other times being the weekly conference to consider requests for review and the conference to discuss the case after oral arguments), it is one of the few instances when justices communicate with one another directly.

Even Supreme Court justices disagree about whether oral arguments affect the outcome of a particular case. Chief Justice Earl Warren has stated that litigants' appearances were "not highly persuasive," while Justice William O. Douglas once remarked that "oral arguments win or lose a case." The one thing justices are in agreement about, however, is the poor quality of lawyering before the Court. Because most of the attorneys are presenting before the Court for the first time, this is not unexpected, but to the justices it must be highly irritating.

Appearing first on behalf of the appellant was A. L. Kearns, Mapp's lead attorney. An experienced criminal attorney back in Ohio, Kearns was confident about his abilities and chose to address the Court in the same folksy, casual manner he used before the local judges back home. He started his presentation with a vivid depiction of the police search of Mapp's home. Speaking in a loud voice, he spent more than sixteen minutes describing the facts of the case, slowly reciting details he thought would grab the Court's attention, such as the number of police cars and officers present at the home, the forceful retrieval of the piece of paper claimed to be a warrant from Mapp's bosom, and the fact that his client had been handcuffed and denied access to her attorney during the search. Kearns also emphasized how the police conducted the search without a warrant. It was a claim he had made from the beginning — and now he finally had the state's admission that the police never had a warrant. Raising his voice and pounding the podium, Kearns exclaimed, "Now, the evidence discloses that no search warrant existed although they claimed there was a search warrant. There is absolutely no evidence of any magistrate that had been asked for a search warrant; there was no record of a search warrant. We asked during the trial of the case that the search warrant be produced and it was not. The fact of the matter is that our own supreme court found that it was very questionable as to whether there was a search warrant in this case."

Kearns's detailed recital of the facts was too much for Justice Frankfurter, who, apparently weary of his presentation, interrupted the lawyer. "May I trouble you to tell us what do you deem to be the questions that are open before this Court?" he asked. Momentarily confused, Kearns stumbled before answering. He told the Court that he wanted it to review *State v. Lindway*, the 1936 case where the Ohio Supreme Court ruled that illegally seized evidence could still be admitted in a state criminal trial. Shuffling through the papers before him, Frankfurter informed Kearns that the Ohio Supreme Court had not focused on the search and seizure issue but rather ruled that the state antiobscenity statute violated the First Amendment. But, he added, "Is there anything open before us beyond what the court decided or perchance what it refused to decide that you pressed them and they didn't decide?"

Kearns stuck to his script. He wanted the Court to focus on the Fourth Amendment issue. He answered, "One thing that I say that I am asking this Court to decide is the question of the deprivation of eight and a half million citizens of the state of Ohio depriving them of their constitutional rights against unlawful search and seizure . . . and that's the *Lindway* case." The Cleveland attorney stated that *Lindway* was "advocating anarchy" because if police searched a person's home without a warrant, they would be considered trespassers, and homeowners could "use force to keep them out of your home."

Frankfurter then asked Kearns if he was actually requesting that the Court revisit *Wolf v. Colorado*, a decision he authored, which stated that while the Fourth Amendment applied to the states, the *Weeks* exclusionary rule did not. Because, he added, "I notice it isn't even cited in your brief." Kearns hesitated for a moment, apparently unfamiliar with *Wolf*. He then ignored Frankfurter's question and returned to his written notes, stating that there were two questions raised in the case, the constitutionality of the Ohio statute, and "the search and seizure proposition." Frankfurter prompted him again, "That means you're asking us to overrule *Wolf v. Colorado*?" Kearns replied, "No, I don't believe we are." The justice then tried to coax the attorney into realizing the connection between the two cases. He asked Kearns about the *Lindway* decision, stating, "And that holds that, although evidence is illegally procured, it is admissible?" When Kearns replied that that was correct, Frankfurter reminded him, "That's the familiar doctrine in so many states in this Union, and which we dealt with in the *Wolf* case. Which you don't even cite in your brief!"

Justice Frankfurter was clearly annoyed. Not only did he believe the Ohio Supreme Court had settled the search and seizure question when it authoritatively cited *Lindway*, but he quickly realized that the more Kearns spoke, the more evident it was that he had not even read *Wolf v. Colorado*, where the Supreme Court ruled that each state was free to decide how it would remedy Fourth Amendment violations. However, throughout the exchange, Kearns appeared surprisingly unruffled by Frankfurter's sharp questioning, and he soldiered on though his notes. He ended his presentation by repeating his argument that, presuming the Supreme Court found the Ohio statute constitutional, Mapp's sentence of seven years for possession of obscene material constituted cruel and unusual punishment in violation of the Eighth Amendment to the Constitution. His lengthy recital of the facts and his exchange with Frankfurter had taken more than thirty minutes, and he had yet to make a complete justification for why the state court decision should be reversed. Kearns then introduced Bernard Berkman, from the OCLU, whom he had met just moments before oral arguments, to the Court.

Berkman, sensing that the Court knew better than Kearns that he was implicitly arguing that the Supreme Court revisit *Wolf v. Colorado*, turned immediately to the eleven-year-old decision. "The American Civil Liberties Union and its Ohio affiliate . . . are asking this Court to reconsider *Wolf v. Colorado* and to find that evidence that is unlawfully and illegally obtained should not be permitted into a state proceeding and its production is in violation of the federal constitution's Fourth Amendment and the Fourteenth Amendment. We have no hesitancy in asking the Court to reconsider it because we think it is a necessary part of due process."

After Berkman's opening statement, one of the justices inquired whether the Court should instead consider excluding the evidence used to convict Mapp under *Rochin v. California* because of the police conduct during the search. While Berkman conceded that such an argument "could be made," he reiterated that the ACLU was not "raising that technical argument" and that "our principal reason for appearing on behalf of the American Civil Liberties Union and its Ohio affiliate is to urge the unconstitutionality of the Ohio obscenity law."

The civil liberties lawyer then turned to this major argument. He reminded the Court that the appellant had not been charged with criminal intent or with distributing the obscene material, but rather was guilty only of possession. While noting that "we deplore the appellant's

{ *Chapter 3* }

bad taste in the selection of her literature, and we are not now arguing in favor of pornographic literature for the population," Berkman remarked, "the central issue in considering the validity of this statute is this: Is this an area in which the individual has the right to be let alone, to be free of governmental restraint?" He cited Justice Brandeis's dissent in *Olmstead v. United States* (1928) that this was "the most comprehensive of rights and the right most valued by civilized men" and was protected by the Fourth and Fourteenth Amendments.

Berkman also characterized the Ohio statute as a violation of the due process clause of the Fourteenth Amendment: "We submit that interposing a policeman between a normal adult and his library is not a proper means of accomplishing what might otherwise be a valid legislative purpose. We contend that the statute is arbitrary and excessive." He told the Court that not only did the Ohio statute infringe "upon the concept of ordered liberty embodied in the Fourteenth Amendment," but that "the evil sought to be controlled here can be met by less drastic statutory means without limiting the liberties of the citizens of the State of Ohio." Berkman referenced the sociological and scientific studies cited in the ACLU's legal brief to demonstrate that the statute was not "reasonably related to, nor adapted to the accomplishment of any legislative purpose." At the end of his presentation, although acknowledging that the First Amendment did not protect obscenity, he suggested the statute might also be overbroad because of its "inhibiting effect upon freedom of expression." The young lawyer sat down, saving approximately ten minutes for Kearns's rebuttal to the state's presentation.

Gertrude Mahon, the state's lead attorney as *Mapp* moved through the Ohio courts, stood to represent the appellee, the state of Ohio. It was her first time before the Supreme Court, and either out of nervousness or because she believed that what she was about to say was significant, she began her presentation with an embarrassing admission:

At the outset I want to say this, that when this case was pending in the Supreme Court of Ohio, or just after its deposition, one of the State's exhibits disappeared, one of the obscene books. And when the exhibits were returned to the Clerk of the Court of Common Pleas, there was just the cover of this one obscene book that came back, and we don't know what happened to it. I'm only mentioning this because you may be wondering, if you examined the exhibits, why one of the books only has a cover and the rest of it is gone.

This provoked a brief exchange between Justice Potter Stewart and Mahon about the missing material. "Has the Clerk been indicted?" he quipped, to a rumble of laughter in the courtroom. Mahon paused for a few beats but then recovered quickly, replying, "Well that shows you the necessity for the provision in this statute against possession, knowing possession."

Her response prompted Justice William Brennan to question her about what constituted "possession" under the law. He reminded Mahon that "your supreme court in this very case has construed this as meaning that if you have possession, naked possession, with knowledge that it's obscene, you're guilty of a crime under the statute." Mahon agreed with Brennan's interpretation and added that "inherent in the element of possession is the opportunity for circulation."

Stewart and Brennan's focus on the breadth of the Ohio antiobscenity statute piqued the interest of Justice Frankfurter, who was also clearly relieved that the oral arguments were now focusing on the First Amendment question. He chimed in, asking Mahon if having any book in one's personal library constituted "possession" under the Ohio law? Mahon remarked that, yes, any "knowing possession of obscenity" was prohibited by the statute. Frankfurter pressed the issue. Ever the former law professor, he presented her with a hypothetical situation involving an individual who owned a personal library. "He's a bibliophile and he collects first editions, not for the content, but because they are first editions," stated the justice. "Any book on his shelf — on my shelves — which I know to be obscene in content, a matter of great indifference to me because I'm interested in the fact that it was published in 1527 — That makes me . . . a violator of this statute. Is that correct?" Mahon answered, "I would say so, your Honor. Any collection of obscenity would be." Frankfurter could not help himself. He interjected, "Well, Mark Twain had one of the biggest collections, and I could tell you now where it is, but it's outside your jurisdiction." For the second time, the courtroom erupted into laughter. Frankfurter pressed on, "But you said that the purpose of this — the aim of this statute is to prevent circulation, dissemination. Now, having it on a shelf isn't disseminating it, quite the opposite. There are no more miserly people in the world than bibliophiles." The laughter continued.

Mahon attempted to regain her footing by focusing on her legal argument, suggesting that anyone who possessed obscene material could always potentially disseminate it, but Frankfurter ended the discussion by reminding Mahon that there was no proof Mapp was trying to circulate the obscene books. Although at the end of her presentation Mahon would return to the issue of what constituted possession under state law, it was clear from the exchange that at least Stewart, Brennan, and Frankfurter were troubled by the Ohio statute's far-reaching implications.

After her shaky start, Mahon turned her attention to the three major issues before the Court: the constitutionality of the antiobscenity statute, the argument that the evidence used to convict the appellant had been unlawfully obtained and should be excluded, and the challenge that Mapp's sentence constituted cruel and unusual punishment. Mahon's response regarding the constitutionality of the Ohio statute was brief. Noting Justice Brennan's majority opinion in *Roth v. United States* (1957) that obscene material was "utterly without redeeming social importance" and "not within the area of constitutionally protected speech or press," Mahon stated that regulation of obscenity was a "proper exercise of the police powers of the State" and likened the state action to the state's interest in regulating narcotics or other contraband.

Next, the assistant prosecuting attorney addressed the police search and seizure of the obscene material. She reminded the Court of the Ohio rule established in *Lindway*, which allowed the admission of illegally obtained evidence. She also referenced *Wolf*, noting, "This Court has held that the state has a right to, and it is not in violation of the Fourteenth Amendment to so admit evidence, even though obtained without a search warrant." Mahon characterized the exclusionary rule, as had Frankfurter in *Wolf*, as "a judicial rule of evidence" and appeared repulsed at the idea that evidence of a crime be excluded from a trial, remarking that "the absence of a search warrant can be no defense to a crime." Moreover, she added, the Ohio constitution and state law provided many procedural rights to individuals accused of crimes, but "neither the laws of Ohio nor the Ohio courts are solicitous to a person accused of a crime in concealing the evidence of their guilt." Mahon explained that under state law "the fact that there was a search warrant would not make the evidence any more competent or the fact that there was no search warrant would not make it any less competent. It has no bearing whatsoever on the evidence itself proving the corpus delicti of the crime."

In the short time remaining, Mahon addressed the constitutionality of Mapp's sentence. She repeated the argument made in the legal brief: that the Ohio statute offered the option of a fine and/or prison time, and that the penalty could be in the range of one to seven years. Individuals convicted under such an indeterminate sentence, she explained, could potentially serve a short time, depending on the decision of the state Pardon and Parole Commission.

Mahon then summarized her major points as the time expired. In the middle of her concluding remarks, the question of the search warrant came up once again. Chief Justice Warren asked, "Is the search warrant in existence?" Mahon admitted, "Insofar as the record is concerned, it doesn't show any . . . there's no record that there was a search warrant." But, she quickly explained, the two officers at the scene who had "nothing to do with obtaining the warrant" believed before proceeding with the search that the lieutenant who arrived at the scene had a search warrant.

Kearns had approximately ten minutes remaining, and he summarized his main arguments. He also used his final minute to take a dig at the Cleveland police. Kearns told the Court that Mapp was in an awkward position after she found the obscene material: if she had destroyed the material after she found it, she would be in violation of another state statute that carried a prison sentence of one to seven years in prison if the value of the destroyed property was more than $100; if she stored it, as she had, she was guilty of the state's antiobscenity law. One of the justices then interjected, "I suppose she could have called the attention of the police to it, couldn't she?" To which Kearns replied, "Well, if she called it to the attention of the police, she would still be in possession under this statute. . . . And if the police were of the type that they were, and doing the things that they did and they usually do in Cuyahoga County, using their badges as supreme authority, they would have done the same thing, by prosecuting her."

———

It is always difficult to predict how the Court might rule based on oral arguments, and this case was no different. The justices, and especially Justice Frankfurter, were likely disappointed with Kearns's inadequate preparation on *Wolf*, particularly given its importance to his claim that *Lindway* be reconsidered and the illegally seized evidence used to convict his client excluded. Despite this, several members of the Court appeared concerned with the breadth of the Ohio antiobscenity law, and Kearns needed only five justices to declare the law unconstitutional and void. Counsel for both sides naturally predicted they would prevail when the Court handed down its decision. However, like the rest of the country, they would have to wait and see.

Walking out of the courtroom, Dollree Mapp encountered the Court bailiff she had befriended the previous day. She asked him, "How long before I can expect a decision?" He told her the Court announced its decisions every Monday until the end of the term, but that it was difficult to predict the actual date the Court would rule on a particular case. Mapp was anxious to hear the results, so she asked the bailiff, "Will you do me a favor? Phone collect every Monday? I won't be able to stand it not knowing. Call me anyhow, whether they decide the case or not — every Monday."

CHAPTER 4

The Supreme Court Deliberates

Although there is no official record of the immediate events that transpired after oral arguments in *Mapp v. Ohio*, information gleaned from judicial biographies, justices' private papers, and post hoc musings on the decision sheds light on the Supreme Court's deliberations in this landmark decision. This chapter pieces together these events, illustrating how a straightforward First Amendment obscenity case was transformed into one of the most important criminal procedure decisions in history.

———

Supreme Court conference deliberations, like the review of certiorari petitions, are conducted entirely in secret. While the insular nature of its decision-making process no doubt appears foreign to Americans living in a constitutional democracy, the Court famously protects its prerogative to do so, and many justices believe it enhances the institution's ability to effectively conduct its business. Justice Lewis F. Powell once stated, "The integrity of judicial decision making would be impaired seriously if we had to reach our judgments in the atmosphere of an ongoing town meeting. There must be candid discussion, a willingness to consider arguments advanced by other Justices, and a continuing examination and re-examination of one's own views. The confidentiality of this process assures that we will review carefully the soundness of our judgments. It also improves the quality of our written opinions." It also adds to the Court's mystique.

Because there is no official public record of the Court's conference deliberations, judicial scholars have few options but to re-create what may have transpired during these meetings. They could interview justices after they have left the bench in hopes they will shed light on their time on the Court, but few are fortunate enough to have such access, and because the Court decides so many cases, it would be difficult for a justice to recall all but the most prominent or contentious cases. Interviews with the justices' law clerks are more common, but they provide secondhand recollections of what happens after a conference and depends on how much information a justice provides his or her clerk.

Insight from the conference is best gleaned from a review of the private papers of retired or deceased justices. A justice's private papers often include copies of docket books that record votes on petitions for review and tentative votes from conference, drafts of opinions, memoranda between the justices, personal notes on cases under consideration, and miscellaneous material. While the quality of these private papers varies, they are the best resource for scholars trying to learn of the inner workings of the Court. Although most of the justices in the nineteenth and early twentieth century destroyed their papers, in recent years many have donated them to the Library of Congress or their law school alma mater, thus providing a firsthand account of Supreme Court deliberations. Access is governed by rules set up by the donor, such as making the papers available only after the justice has passed away or until all of his or her former brethren have left the bench.

Some of these private papers are of more use than others. Although one can only surmise so much from hastily written notes — some justices avoid writing notes at all, and if they do, the notes are rarely comprehensive because they are paraphrasing their brethren's comments — the drafts and memoranda to the conference provide valuable insight into the opinion-writing process. In particular, these papers illustrate how justices bargain and negotiate with one another, and often broker compromises to maintain or achieve a majority. Because the justices do not meet to discuss cases outside of conference, but rather, deliberate alone and communicate with each other through these opinions and memos, it is only through these papers that one gets a true picture of how this collegial institution arrives at a decision.

An inside look at the Supreme Court's deliberation in *Mapp v. Ohio* is best provided by an examination of the private papers of Justice Tom C. Clark, who wrote the majority opinion. Chief Justice Earl

Warren's papers provide additional material on the Court's deliberation in this case.

———

On March 31, 1961, the day after oral arguments in *Mapp v. Ohio*, the Court met in the conference room to discuss the case. As was the tradition during several of the Warren Court years, the conference was held on a Saturday. Chief Justice Warren's and Justice Clark's private papers reveal that the conference discussion focused primarily on the constitutionality of the Ohio obscenity statute. Warren started the discussion, noting the vagueness of the Ohio law, which, he stated, "cuts across First Amendment rights. It's too broad a statute to accomplish its purpose, and on that basis I'd reverse." Justice Stewart observed, "If this stuff isn't covered by the First and Fourteenth Amendments, it was hard to see what would be." And Justice John Harlan characterized the law as a "thought control statute." All the other justices agreed. Although Kearns and Greene, and separately the ACLU, argued the statute be reversed on Fourth and Fourteenth Amendment grounds because it infringed on one's privacy rights, the Court characterized the case as primarily presenting a First and Fourteenth Amendment issue because of its overbreadth.

The Fourth Amendment search and seizure issue and *Wolf v. Colorado* received only brief attention. Justice William O. Douglas was the first to suggest the case could be decided on these grounds. He announced that *Mapp* could be used to overrule *Wolf* and apply the exclusionary rule to the states. The idea was attractive to Warren and Brennan, who agreed they would go along with such an approach. In his docket book, Clark paraphrased Brennan's comments, "This is a candidate for overruling *Wolf* — officers have no warrant — they go through [the] cellar and find this stuff in box belonging to someone else — he will overrule *Wolf*." However, without the support of a majority, the idea stalled. Warren, Douglas, and Brennan then joined the rest of the Court in its decision to reverse Mapp's conviction by invalidating the constitutionality of the Ohio statute on First Amendment grounds. Several weeks later, in a memorandum to Clark, Justice John Marshall Harlan summarized the conference deliberation: "I would have supposed that the Court would have little difficulty in agreeing (as indeed I thought the whole Court had) that a state prohibition against mere knowing possession of obscene material without any requirement of showing that such possession was with a purpose to disseminate the offensive matter, contravenes the Fourteenth Amendment, in that such a statute impermissibly deters freedom of belief and expression, if indeed it is not tantamount to an effort at thought control."

At the end of the conference discussion Warren assigned the majority opinion to Clark. Each chief justice has his own style in the assignment of opinions. He may choose to keep the most important cases for himself, assign opinions based on an individual's area of expertise, or take into consideration the workload of each individual justice to ensure he or she is not overburdened. A chief justice might also strategically assign an opinion to a justice in the center rather than at the extreme end to ensure that justice maintains a majority. Warren, considered one of the greatest chief justices who possessed the "instinctive qualities of leadership," used an egalitarian approach in his opinion assignments, making sure each justice was assigned a similar number of "stars" and "dogs" each term. According to Brennan, Warren "bent over backwards in assigning opinions to assure that each Justice, including himself, wrote approximately the same number of Court opinions and received a fair share of the more desirable opinions."

Clark left the conference knowing the Court unanimously voted to invalidate the Ohio statute on First and Fourteenth Amendment grounds. Although votes taken at conference are tentative and members may change their minds during circulation of opinions, the unanimity of agreement meant that it would be an easy decision to write. However, something happened over the next few minutes to change Clark's mind. Justice Potter Stewart, who wrote about *Mapp v. Ohio* in a 1983 *Columbia Law Review* article, stated, "What transpired in the month following our conference on the case is really a matter of speculation on my part, but I have always suspected that the members of the soon-to-be *Mapp* majority had met in what I affectionately call a 'rump caucus' to discuss a different basis for their decision." The rump caucus was held in the elevator.

According to a judicial biography of Chief Justice Warren, there was an impromptu gathering of three justices in the elevator after the conference discussion. Clark, pondering Douglas's suggestion from the conference, turned to Justices Hugo Black and Brennan and asked,

"Wouldn't this be a good case to apply the exclusionary rule and do what *Wolf* didn't do?" "Are you serious?" Black and Brennan replied. Yes, said Clark; he had shifted to the Douglas position. Their response must have been positive enough for Clark to further consider the idea. A quick count indicated he might have majority support to overturn *Wolf* and require states to adopt the exclusionary rule. In conference, Douglas, Brennan, and Warren had already agreed to such a position. With himself on board, there were four justices in favor of reversing *Wolf*. The fact that Black had not adamantly opposed the idea in the elevator would raise the tally to five, a majority. But Black was not explicit in his support, and Clark would have to persuade him to sign on.

Clark knew Black would be a hard sell. In past decisions he had narrowly interpreted the reach of the Fourth Amendment. Even worse, Black wrote a concurring opinion in *Wolf* in which he declared that the exclusionary rule was a "judicially created rule of evidence" rather than a "command of the Fourth Amendment." He also wrote a unanimous decision in *United States v. Wallace and Tiernan Co.* (1949) where he noted that the rule was "one of judicial origin." What occurred over the next two months was a flurry of opinions between Clark and Black as the Texan worked to attract Black to his position. At the same time, Black maneuvered to use the case for his own ends.

Unbeknownst to Clark, Douglas was pursuing his own plan to use *Mapp* to overturn *Wolf*. After the conference he returned to his chambers and started preparing a draft concurring opinion, which he completed on April 3. In it he wrote, "I would apply the Fourth Amendment with full force to the States, making the exclusionary rule part and parcel of the constitutional guarantee. *Wolf v. Colorado* should be modified to that extent. As so modified, it would remove the entire underpinning of this case. The evidence seized and used in evidence having been unconstitutionally obtained, the judgment of conviction should be set aside." However, the opinion was only circulated to Justice Brennan. At this point it was unnecessary to persuade a majority to overturn *Wolf* because Justice Clark would endorse this position in his majority opinion.

Despite these initial musings over whether *Mapp* could be used to overrule *Wolf*, it is important to recognize the Court's unanimity in conference over the unconstitutionality of the Ohio obscenity statute on First Amendment grounds. This meant that Dollree Mapp's conviction was going to be reversed, and she would be free. What was not known at this point was whether this would be a straightforward First Amendment case or whether Clark would use this opportunity to do something he had considered for years — overturn *Wolf* and hand down a landmark decision applying the exclusionary rule to the states.

———

Justices differ in their approach to opinion writing; some delegate the task of writing the first draft to their law clerks, with the justice then revising this initial draft; others take a more active role in opinion writing, such as writing the opinion and having law clerks provide supplementary research such as footnotes. Regardless of each individual justice's approach, once the opinion writer is satisfied with the draft, it is circulated among the brethren. Justices then have the option of joining the majority opinion, writing a concurring opinion, where they agree with the result but for different reasons, or writing a dissenting opinion. Justices communicate to one another through a "memorandum to the conference," which is circulated to the entire Court, or a memorandum to an individual or select group of justices. Draft opinions are often circulated three or four times, and even more if the issue is a contentious one or if the Court is closely divided. It is through this circulation of opinions that real deliberation takes place. Justices will often negotiate and compromise at this stage as the author of the majority opinion tries to maintain his or her Court.

Justice Clark liked to handwrite preliminary draft opinions on a yellow legal pad and give them to his support staff to proofread and type. Although Clark's conversation in the elevator indicated that he might use *Mapp* to reverse *Wolf* and apply the exclusionary rule to the states, when he actually sat down with a pen and paper to write the initial draft, he was uncertain about the wisdom of overturning *Wolf*. According to his first, four-page handwritten draft, Clark was going to adhere to the decision. The draft begins with a quick recap of the lower court action and then states, "We have concluded that the conviction of the appellant is violative of the due process clause of the 14th Amendment to the Constitution of the United States which results in a reversal of the judgment." Written in the margin, however, is the note, "On the 4th Amendment question the Court adheres to its rule announced in *Wolf v. Colorado* . . . and hence this contention of the appellant is denied." The draft then recites the facts of the case in great detail, notes that the state of Ohio did not have an exclusionary rule, and then abruptly ends. A typewritten version of this handwritten draft continues for several more pages, with Clark examining *Wolf*'s rationale, and stating that four years after the decision, in *Irvine v. California* (1954), the Court had been urged to reconsider *Wolf*, as it was doing today. However, before Clark could begin a defense or a challenge to *Wolf*, this draft ended as well.

At no point in this early draft did Clark address the issue that dominated the Court's conference discussion — that the Ohio antiobscenity statute was overbroad and violated the First Amendment under the precedent provided in *Smith v. California*. Even at this early stage, Clark appeared intent on focusing on the Fourth Amendment issue.

One can only speculate at this point, but the lengths to which Clark went to describe the facts of the case and the fact that he opened the draft with the comment that Mapp's conviction violated the due process clause of the Fourteenth Amendment lead one to believe the justice may have been considering using *Rochin*'s "shock the conscience" test to conclude that the police conduct was so egregious that the illegally seized evidence should be excluded from the case. Whatever the reason, after attempting to write an opinion overturning Mapp's conviction without actually reversing *Wolf*, Clark realized this may not be the best course. The only thing clear from this initial draft is that Clark had chosen not to write an opinion in line with the unanimous agreement of the Court that the Ohio antiobscenity statute violated the First and Fourteenth Amendments.

Clark's indecision may have been due to the way he viewed his role on the Court. According to one judicial scholar, Clark was guided by a strict obedience to the law, which included the fact that justices "should never, therefore, show a contempt for or indifference to the law," which Clark believed occurred when a judge dissented from one of its doctrines. According to Clark, "Through such an action, a United States Supreme Court justice defied its precedents — thereby holding himself or herself above the law."

Clark exhibited some of this behavior in previous cases involving the exclusionary rule. For example, his distaste for *Wolf v. Colorado* but his allegiance to the Court's rule of law was outlined in his concurring opinion in *Irvine v. California*. He stated that had he been on the Court when *Wolf* was decided, he would have parted with the majority and applied the exclusionary rule to the states, but that he would nevertheless concur with the *Irvine* majority based on the *Wolf* precedent because it "remains the law and, as such, is entitled to the respect of this Court's membership." However, his disapproval of the precedent was so strong that he also wrote a ten-page draft concurring opinion in *Irvine*, circulated only to Justice Robert Jackson, where he directly called for its reversal and application of the exclusionary rule to the states. One can only assume that he abandoned the effort because he was unable to assemble majority support.

Clark had wanted to overturn *Wolf* for years, and now he decided that *Mapp* might be the right vehicle for doing so. However, merely arguing that a Supreme Court decision should be reversed — especially a decision only a decade old — is a risky move. Clark first had to find out if he had doctrinal support for the argument that the exclusionary rule was constitutionally required, and should therefore be applied to the states. Then he would have to find majority support for his position.

———

Justice Clark asked his law clerks to research cases decided since *Weeks v. United States*, the 1914 decision where the Supreme Court ruled that illegally seized evidence must be excluded from federal criminal trials. In particular, he instructed his clerks to look for decisions that described the exclusionary rule as required under the Fourth Amendment. The clerks went to work. Clark's private papers include a dozen pages with strips of yellow and white legal paper taped to them. On each strip is a single Supreme Court decision, or several decisions, and a summary of its holding in each case. Most of the strips of paper also contain the clerks' notes regarding whether the decision could be used to justify the argument that the exclusionary rule was constitutionally required. The results must have been disheartening for a justice wanting to find support for such a position. Although there were several cases that seemed to include language that would support this argument, there were almost three times as many that worked against it, and several dozen that were irrelevant.

The strongest language in support of the contention that the exclusionary rule was constitutionally required was found in *Weeks* and

Olmstead v. United States (1928). Working against these decisions, however, were almost a dozen cases where the Court, or justices writing separate opinions, suggested it was not. Included in this group of cases was Justice Black's unanimous opinion in *United States v. Wallace* (1949) and his concurring opinion in *United States v. Rabinowitz* (1950), where he discussed the exclusionary rule as a rule of evidence rather than a constitutional mandate. Also in this group was *United States v. Jeffers*, a 1951 decision written by Justice Clark. The clerks' notes on this decision exclaimed, "This language hurts us because it says the exclusionary rule is court made and implies congress can change it, and particularly, because Clark, j. said it!" One of Clark's own opinions was working against him.

Regardless of the disheartening outcome of the clerks' research assignment, Clark went about writing his draft opinion. He was intent on using *Mapp* as a vehicle to apply the exclusionary rule to the states. With little judicial precedent to support this position, he would have to rely on what was available and also offer sound judicial reasoning for overturning *Wolf*. He sat down and composed a new, seventeen-page draft in his tight cursive writing. Believing he already had support from three justices, he knew the swing vote would be Justice Black, so he focused his effort on earning support from the Alabaman. The first draft of Clark's *Mapp* opinion was sent only to Black on April 22, 1961. The cover letter noted, "At your convenience I would appreciate your criticisms. This is the first draft and will need some 'polishing.'"

The opinion began with Clark directly confronting *Wolf v. Colorado*. Clark stated that since the case was decided, "there has occurred a series of events which undercuts the continued vitality of the considerations which found expression in its basic reasoning," and "the scales are weighted in favor of the *Weeks* doctrine." Among these considerations was the fact that more states had adopted the exclusionary rule since *Wolf*, including California, which reached that conclusion "because other remedies completely failed to secure compliance with the constitutional provisions."

Clark characterized alternative remedies to Fourth Amendment violations as "worthless and futile" as evidenced by statistics from cities like Chicago, where police committed thousands of unlawful searches and seizures each year. He also directly confronted the remedies to Fourth Amendment violations Frankfurter suggested in *Wolf*, responding that private remedies to unlawful searches were rarely pursued and public opinion as a remedy was impractical because the likely targets of unlawful searches were criminal defendants, who were hardly sympathetic plaintiffs. Because these suggested alternative remedies had provided a basis for Justice Frankfurter's decision in *Wolf* not to extend the exclusionary rule to the states, Clark concluded, the decision must be reevaluated.

Clark next reviewed recent Supreme Court decisions that corrected some outstanding Fourth Amendment issues left open since *Wolf,* such as *Elkins,* where the Court ruled that federal courts could no longer use evidence illegally seized by state officers in a federal criminal trial. He remarked that in *Elkins* the majority had expressed reservations about *Wolf,* noting that it "operated to undermine the logical foundation of the *Weeks* admissibility rule." Clark then set up his argument, announcing that "the only remaining basic incongruity now facing us is the double standard that this Court permits in enforcement of the Amendment. A federal prosecutor may make no use of evidence unconstitutionally seized, but a state attorney operating under the enforceable prohibition of the same Amendment, may. Thus the state, by admitting evidence unlawfully seized, indirectly, but nonetheless actually, serves to encourage disobedience to the federal Constitution which it is bound to uphold."

Clark observed that such an approach created a double standard that might induce federal officers in nonexclusionary states to "step across the street to the state's attorney with their unconstitutionally seized evidence." He stated, "Prosecution on the basis of that evidence is then had in a state court in utter disregard of the enforceable Fourth Amendment. If the fruits of an unconstitutional search were inadmissible in both state and federal courts, this inducement to evasion would be eliminated." Clark then used this reasoning to provide the first of three rationales for applying the exclusionary rule to the states: the promotion of healthy federalism. He opined that if the exclusionary rule were applied to states in the same manner as to the federal government, "federal-state cooperation in the solution of crime under constitutional standards would be promoted."

A second rationale in support of the exclusionary rule, Clark explained, was the imperative of judicial integrity, which had been alluded to in *Elkins.* He revised Justice Benjamin Cardozo's famous aphorism, "The criminal is to go free because the constable has blundered," observing, "The criminal goes free, if he must, but it is under the law. Even Titus has rights. . . . What can destroy a government more quickly than its failure to observe its own laws, or worse, its disregard of the charter of its own existence?" Clark also cited Brandeis's dissent in *Olmstead* in support of this rationale: "Our government is the potent, the omnipresent teacher. For good or for ill, it teaches the whole people by example. . . . If the government becomes a lawbreaker, it breeds contempt for law; it invites every-man to become a law unto himself; it invites anarchy."

It was toward the end of the draft that Clark presented the third and, he believed, primary rationale for applying the exclusionary rule to the states: that it was constitutionally required. He cited *Boyd v. United States*, where the Court held that the Fourth Amendment applied "to all invasions, on the part of the government and its employees, of the sanctity of a man's home and the privacies of his life. It is not the breaking of the doors and the rummaging of his drawers that constitutes the essence of the offense; but it is the invasion of his indefensible right of personal security, personal liberty and private property." Clark asked, "If that be truly the case, does it adequately safeguard the 'indefensible right of personal security' to relegate the individual who suffers its invasion to a suit for damages for the "breaking of doors?" The answer, he observed, was provided several decades later in *Weeks v. United States* when the Court concluded that it was the exclusionary rule that protected one's rights under the Fourth Amendment, without which "the protection of the Fourth Amendment declaring his right to be secure against such searches and seizures, is of no value, and, so far as those thus placed are concerned, might as well be stricken from the Constitution."

The draft ended with Clark's observation that since *Wolf* established that Fourth Amendment protection against unreasonable searches and seizures was "implicit in the concept of ordered liberty," it must therefore be enforced. And, "Since no other methods of sanction have been at all successful, the remedy of exclusion must be available by 'judicial implication.' " Other fundamental rights were strictly enforced by a single standard by dual sovereigns, wrote Clark, and "the honest and real enjoyment of such rights is wholly determined by the aggregate strength of the available remedies and enforcement devices which an individual and his community are able to muster in their defense." He concluded, "Having once recognized as was done in *Wolf* that the right is nothing less than constitutional in origin, we can no longer abstain from drawing upon the same source for its safeguard. No longer can we permit it to be revocable at the whim of every policeman who, in the name of law enforcement itself, chooses to suspend its enjoyment."

Justice Black must have responded quickly because Clark sent him a second draft only three days later. The short cover page accompanying it stated, "Hugo, I hope this is better. I have re-arranged and inserted new material. Thanks for the suggestions." This draft placed a greater emphasis on the constitutional foundation for the exclusionary rule. Clark more clearly explained how *Boyd* and *Weeks* made the rule a constitutionally required safeguard of the Fourth Amendment and moved this section to the beginning of the opinion. The section on *Wolf* and Clark's critique of the "factual considerations" upon which the decision was based was moved to the middle. Clark also strengthened his criticism that *Wolf* applied the Fourth Amendment to the states without appropriate enforcement. "In short," he added, "the creation of the new constitutional right could not admit the denial of its most important constitutional privilege, namely, the exclusion of the evidence constitutionally protected from seizure. To hold otherwise is but to grant the right but withhold its privilege." Preserved in this second draft were the two other rationales for application of the exclusionary rule to the states: promotion of healthy federalism and the imperative of judicial integrity. Moreover, added Clark, it "made good sense."

The two justices corresponded once again, and Clark worked on the draft opinion to accommodate Black's concerns. In particular, Black reminded Clark that *Boyd* rested on both Fourth and Fifth Amendment grounds and implied that a similar approach could be used in *Mapp*. He then gave Clark his approval to circulate the opinion to the other justices; written in the top right-hand corner of his working draft was the note, "TCC draft after OK from HLB, 4/27/61." It would go to the full Court the next day.

This third draft, which was being circulated to the full conference for the first time, contained several important changes that reflected Black's influence. For instance, after introducing *Boyd v. United States*,

Clark, for the first time, included the *Boyd* Court's statement that the Fourth and Fifth Amendments run "almost into each other." He also added language about how the two amendments enjoyed "an 'intimate relation' in their perpetuation of 'principles of humanity and civil liberty'" and how "the philosophy of each [was] complementary to, although not dependent upon, that of the other." More explicitly citing the Fifth Amendment along with the Fourth to justify application of the exclusionary rule to the states, Clark hoped, would solidify Black's support.

Also included in this revision was Clark's response to those who suggest that the exclusionary rule was a rule of evidence rather than constitutionally required. While he conceded that the Court had made such "passing references" to such a position, he contended that "the plain and unequivocal words of *Weeks* — and its later paraphrase in *Wolf* — to the effect that the *Weeks* rule is of constitutional origin, remains entirely undisturbed." He cited *Olmstead* as before and added two additional precedents to support his position: *Byars v. United States* (1927), where the majority stated that admission of unlawfully seized evidence could not "be tolerated *under our constitutional system,*" and *McNabb v. United States* (1943), where it observed that "a conviction in the federal courts, the foundation of which is evidence obtained in disregard of liberties deemed fundamental by the Constitution, cannot stand." While these few cases only implied that the exclusionary rule was constitutionally required, it was all Clark could muster after his clerks' detailed review of Supreme Court precedent since *Weeks* in 1914.

In the next section Clark refined his critique of the Court's decision in *Wolf* not to extend the exclusionary rule to the states. He stated that the Court's reasons for doing so "were bottomed entirely on factual considerations" and responded that while these factual considerations were "not relevant to the constitutional consideration," his primary basis for *Mapp*, they "could not, in any analysis, now be deemed controlling."

At the end of the draft, Clark included new language about the need for the exclusionary rule to realize the promise embodied in the Fourth Amendment. "In short, the admission of the new constitutional right by *Wolf* could not consistently tolerate denial of its most important constitutional privilege, namely, the exclusion of the evidence which an accused had been forced to give by reason of the unlawful seizure. To hold otherwise is to grant the right but without its privilege and enjoyment." Clark also elaborated on his earlier assessment that the exclusionary rule makes good sense, noting "There is no war between the Constitution and common sense."

Justice Clark's third draft of *Mapp v. Ohio*, and the first to be circulated to the full Court, contained no mention of the constitutional issue that was central in the Ohio state courts and the Supreme Court's conference deliberations — that the Ohio antiobscenity statute violated the First and Fourteenth Amendments. Clark had produced a decision that reversed Mapp's conviction because the Cleveland police unlawfully searched her home and illegally seized evidence, which was used to convict her. If the opinion garnered another four votes, Mapp would be free, and the exclusionary rule applied to the states.

———

The Court reacted quickly to the Clark draft. The first response came from Justice Douglas the following day. He wrote, "Dear Tom: That is a mighty fine opinion you have written in No. 236— Mapp v. Ohio. Please join me in it." The response from Justice Brennan on May 1 was even more effusive: "Dear Tom: Of course you know I think this is just magnificent and wonderful. I have not joined anything since I came with greater pleasure." Chief Justice Warren's response the next day was short but favorable: "Dear Tom: Re: No. 236— Mapp v. Ohio I agree." Clark had the support of three members of the Court — not quite a majority.

The expected disapproval was not far behind. The first of May brought two critical responses. Potter Stewart, who indicated in an article years later "how amazed I was when the Justice Clark circulation in *Mapp v. Ohio* hit my desk," wrote Clark a memorandum, in which he commented, "As I am sure you anticipated, your proposed opinion in this case came as quite a surprise." His assessment was more practical than anything:

In all honesty, I seriously question the wisdom of using this case as a vehicle to overrule an important doctrine so recently established and so consistently adhered to. Without getting into the merits, I point out only that the idea of overruling *Wolf* was urged in the brief and oral argument only by amicus curiae and was not even discussed in the Conference, where we all agreed, as I recollect it, that the judgment should be reversed on First Amendment grounds. If *Wolf* is to be reconsidered, I myself would much prefer to do so only in a case that required it, and only after argument of the case by competent counsel and a full Conference discussion.

Justice Harlan was equally troubled. His frank, four-page memorandum began, "I hope you will not mind my writing you candidly as to my concern over your opinion in this case." He reminded Clark of the conference discussion over the First Amendment issue and questioned his decision to decide the case in a manner that was "highly debatable and divisive." Harlan then presented three reasons why overruling *Wolf* was "unnecessary and inadvisable": first, that it threatened a "jail delivery of uncertain, but obviously serious, proportions"; second, that it would "prompt much, and perhaps confusing, writing among the Brethren"; and, third, that the decision "derives no support from the rule of avoidance of constitutional issues. It simply substitutes one constitutional ground for another." Then, despite acknowledging that it was not the time for "a discussion on the merits of what you are holding," Harlan made two observations about Clark's opinion. He challenged his contention that the rule was constitutionally based and remarked that, even if it were, this did not mean the Fourteenth Amendment applied the exclusionary rule to the states: "*Wolf* itself, let alone the uniform course of the Court's decisions, has laid that ghost to rest."

On the final page, Harlan questioned Clark about what led him to this "juncture" to force the exclusionary rule on the states. He earnestly asked him to "reconsider the advisability of facing the Court, in a case which otherwise should find a ready and non-controversial solution with the controversial issues that your proposed opinion tenders." The memo ended with a conclusion that was already evident from the content of the correspondence: "Perhaps you will have gathered from the foregoing that I would not be able to join you in your present opinion!" Then, before sending it, Harlan added a postscript in his own hand, "If you don't mind my saying so, your opinion comes perilously close to accepting 'incorporation' for the Fourth A., and will doubtless encourage the 'incorporation' enthusiasts." He was referring to the fact that several members on the Court were intent on applying multiple criminal procedure guarantees from the Bill of Rights to the states.

Clark's response arrived at Harlan's desk three days later. He addressed his concerns in turn. First, he admitted that the case could be decided on First Amendment grounds, but, he reminded Harlan, the *Wolf* question had also been raised in conference, and "three gave the latter as an alternate ground for reversal." In response to Harlan's criticism that *Wolf* had been followed as precedent in recent cases, thereby making it difficult to reverse, he replied that the Court had done so only "grudgingly" and pointed out that in *Elkins*, for instance, the Court indicated the decision did more harm than good and "had muddied the waters." He was also unconcerned with the "jail delivery" where defendants would request a new trial, seeing this type of attack as a "collateral one which raises other problems for the claimants."

Clark then went on the offensive. He stated, "There is, of course, as in all controversial cases, ground for disagreement. I have a Court and therefore my theory at least has support." The trouble, he told Harlan, stemmed not from *Mapp* but rather from *Wolf*, which "enunciates a constitutional doctrine which has no escape clause mitigating against the present inexorable result, i.e., if the right to privacy is really so basic as to be constitutional in rank and if it is really to be enforceable against the states *(Wolf)*, then we cannot carve out of the bowels of that right the vital part, the stuff that gives it substance, the exclusion of evidence." Clark then reiterated his position that exclusion of evidence was, in his mind, constitutionally derived, noting that "even *Wolf* says it is a constitutional rule formulated by 'judicial implication.'" And, while he conceded that the decision rested on the "fundamentals of federal-state relations," he countered that "I believe that the present result achieves a necessary measure of symmetry in our constitutional doctrine on both federal and state exercise of those powers incident to their enforcement of criminal law which deal most directly with individual freedom and pose perhaps its greatest threat." Clark replied that the reasons for not extending the exclusionary rule no longer existed and that since *Wolf* made privacy enforceable against the states, they were "obliged to enforce it as we do other basic rights."

At the end of his memo he responded to Harlan's penned comment about the decision being a "windfall to incorporation enthusiasts."

Clark wrote that he did not believe that to be the case, but that "if it is, then *Wolf* brought it on." Then, to soften the remark, he added, "However, I adhere to all that is said in *Palko* and will be glad to say so if I am understood presently to be saying otherwise." Clark was referring to the Court's decision in *Palko v. Connecticut* (1937), where it announced its "selective incorporation" doctrine regarding the due process clause of the Fourteenth Amendment. Under this doctrine, the Court indicated that some of the guarantees in the Bill of Rights were in a "preferred position" and "so rooted in the traditions and conscience of our people as to be ranked fundamental," and should thus be absorbed into the Fourteenth Amendment and applied against the states.

After receiving correspondence from all justices except Felix Frankfurter and Charles Evans Whittaker, Clark sent a revised draft to the full Court on May 4. There were three significant changes. First, at the beginning of the opinion, Clark added two pages detailing the facts of the case. He established how the police forcibly entered Mapp's home, physically subdued her, and illegally confiscated the obscene material. He also noted the Ohio Supreme Court's conclusion that there was "considerable doubt" regarding the existence of a warrant, but that this was not determinative because Ohio did not have a rule excluding unlawfully obtained evidence, which was the state's prerogative.

Second, no doubt in response to Harlan's criticism that his opinion would "encourage the 'incorporation' enthusiasts," Clark replaced the language that explicitly said the Fourth Amendment was fully incorporated to apply to the states with language about how the "security of one's privacy against arbitrary intrusions by the police" was "implicit in 'the concept of ordered liberty' and as such enforceable against the States through the Due Process Clause." And, in several other passages where Clark discussed the Fourth Amendment's application to the states, he used the more nebulous phrases the "right to privacy" or the "Fourth Amendment's right of privacy." The term "incorporation" was replaced with "enforceable against the States through the Due Process Clause."

Third, in the paragraph where he introduced *Boyd* and the language about the Fourth and Fifth Amendments "running together," Clark elaborated on his selected quotation from the decision to illustrate the interplay between the two amendments and also to highlight the similarity between *Boyd* and *Mapp*. "Breaking into a house and opening boxes and drawers are circumstances of aggravation, but any forcible and compulsory extortion of a man's own testimony or of his private papers to be used as evidence to convict him or to forfeit his goods is within the condemnation . . . [of those Amendments]." However, he clarified that his use of *Boyd* and the decision's statements about the Fourth and Fifth Amendments running together did not suggest that the decision also implied that the Fifth Amendment was enforceable against the states. Clark stated that instead, they enjoyed an "intimate relation" in their perpetuation of "principles of humanity and civil liberty" and that they "express 'supplementing phrases of the same constitutional purpose — to maintain inviolate large areas of personal privacy.'" In order to clarify that his holding was not dependent on both the Fourth and Fifth Amendments, he remarked, "The philosophy of each Amendment and of freedom is complementary to, although not dependent upon, that of the other in its sphere of influence — the very least that together they assure in either sphere is that no man is to be convicted on unconstitutional evidence."

Meanwhile, as Clark refined his opinion, Justice Harlan was hard at work on his dissent, the first draft of which was circulated at the end of May. It began with a statement that is familiar to those who know Harlan's judicial philosophy. He criticized the Court for overreaching and forgetting its "sense of judicial restraint which, with due regard for stare decisis, is one element that should enter into deciding whether a past decision of this Court should be overruled." Harlan remarked that the case could have been easily decided by invalidating the Ohio statute on First and Fourteenth Amendment grounds, "a simpler and less far-reaching" question. He lamented the fact that Clark's majority decision ignored the issue that dominated the Court's conference deliberations and noted that had he done so, the outcome as far as Ms. Mapp's criminal conviction would have been the same: "Justice might well have been done in this case without overturning a decision on which the administration of criminal law in many of the States has long justifiably relied." Harlan also remarked that using the present case to overrule *Wolf* was inappropriate because the issue "was briefed not at all and argued only extremely tangentially," and that the Court's "obligation to the States, on whom we impose this new rule, as well as the obligation of orderly adherence to our own processes would demand that we seek that aid which adequate briefing and argument lends to the determination of an important issue." He observed, "To all intents and purposes the Court's present action amounts to a summary reversal of *Wolf,* without argument."

Harlan addressed the merits of Clark's majority opinion in the second section of his dissent. He included the argument from his earlier memo to the justice about how he doubted the *Weeks* exclusionary rule was of "constitutional origin," and that even if it were, this did not necessarily mean that enforcing the rule against the states was constitutionally required. Rather, Harlan characterized the rule as a remedy "which, by penalizing past official misconduct, is aimed at deterring such conduct in the future," and stated that it was inappropriate to impose such a remedy on the states, in part because "problems of criminal law enforcement vary widely from State to State." He warned, "this Court should continue to forebear from fettering the States with an adamant rule which may embarrass them in coping with their own peculiar problems in criminal law enforcement." Harlan also challenged Clark's contention that applying the exclusionary rule to the states made "good sense" and promoted "mutual obligation to respect the same fundamental criteria" in federal and state governments' approach to law enforcement. Rather, he argued, the Court was overstepping its bounds, and such a position "disfigures the boundaries of this Court's functions in relation to the state and federal courts." The Fourth Amendment, he exclaimed, did not empower the Court to "mould state remedies effectuating the right to freedom from 'arbitrary intrusion by the police' to suit its own notions of how things should be done."

Finally, Harlan took Clark to task for implying that the application of the exclusionary rule to the states could be justified, in part, by the Fifth Amendment protection against self-incrimination. He stated that the Court not only had refused to reverse state convictions resting on coerced confessions but that this is a *"procedural right,* and that its violation occurs at the time this improperly obtained statement is admitted at trial. . . . This, and not the disciplining of the police, as with illegally seized evidence, is surely the true basis for excluding a statement of the accused which was unconstitutionally obtained. In sum, I think the coerced confession analogy works strongly *against* what the Court does today."

Harlan ended the dissent with an aside about how Clark's good intentions undermined the Court's legitimacy: "I regret that I find so unwise in principle and so inexpedient in policy a decision motivated by the high purpose of increasing respect for Constitutional rights. But in the last analysis I think this Court can increase respect for the Constitution only if it rigidly respects the limitations which the Constitution places upon it, and respects as well the principles inherent in its own processes. In the present case I think we exceed both, and that our voice becomes only a voice of power, not of reason."

The dissent immediately attracted the support of Justices Frankfurter and Whittaker. Frankfurter also sent a memo informing the Court that he would be filing his own separate opinion "in due course" but, in the end, must have concluded that Harlan satisfactorily expressed his own concerns about the error of overturning *Wolf* because one was never circulated. Justice Stewart also joined part of Harlan's dissent. Separately, he wrote a "Memorandum" opinion stating that he agreed fully with the first part of Harlan's dissent where he criticized the Court for "reaching out" to overturn *Wolf*. Stewart had privately expressed this view to Clark several days after the first draft was circulated, and he now put it to paper. However, unlike Harlan, Stewart wrote that he "express[ed] no view as to the merits of the issue which the Court today decides." Instead, he contended, he would reverse on grounds that the Ohio obscenity statute violated the constitutional guarantees of free thought and expression, the argument the Court unanimously agreed upon in its conference deliberation.

Justice Douglas circulated a concurring opinion the next day. He used a large portion of the uncirculated draft he originally penned after the Court's conference deliberations. It is clear from this opinion that the circumstances surrounding the unlawful search of Mapp's home made quite an impression on the civil libertarian. More than half of it was dedicated to a review of the Cleveland police's "lawless" behavior. The remainder was critical of *Wolf*, a decision that he stated undermined the Fourth Amendment. He remarked that while the majority's decision not to extend the exclusionary rule to the states had "the necessary votes to carry the day," that "with all respect it was not the voice of reason or principle." *Wolf* was wrong, Douglas argued, because "when we allowed States to give constitutional sanction to the 'shabby business' of unlawful entry into a home . . . we did indeed rob the Fourth Amendment of all meaningful force."

Douglas ended his concurring opinion by calling attention to the inadequacies of two other possible remedies for Fourth Amendment violations. Disciplinary action within a police department was a "lofty ideal," he stated, and its "exaltation reaches new heights if we expect a District Attorney to prosecute himself or his associates for well-meaning violations . . . during a raid [they have] ordered." Further, an action of trespass by the homeowner is "onerous and difficult" and the relief "meager" if the victim prevails.

It was the first week of June, and every member of the Court had joined either the majority opinion or the dissent except Justice Black, the swing vote in the case. Although he had initially corresponded with Clark on his preliminary drafts, Black had yet to formally air his views to the full Court. Then, on June 8, he circulated a concurring opinion. Several days previous, he sent a typed draft to Justice Clark for feedback. Only one part of the opinion troubled Clark, who was doubtless relieved that he finally had a fifth vote to reverse *Wolf*, but it was an important issue, and it prompted a dialogue between the two. It was Black's paraphrasing of Clark's majority opinion. Near the end of his draft concurring opinion, Black had written, "As I understand the Court's opinion in this case, we . . . now definitely hold that the Fifth Amendment's protections against unreasonable searches and seizures have both been extended to the states through the Fourteenth Amendment."

Justice Black was suggesting that *Mapp v. Ohio*, in addition to overruling *Wolf*, would also overrule *Adamson v. California*, a 1947 case that reaffirmed its earlier holding in *Twining v. New Jersey* (1908) that the Fifth Amendment protection against self-incrimination did not apply to the states! In retrospect, Justice Black's move was to be expected. He was regarded as an "incorporation enthusiast" who strongly believed that all of the Bill of Rights guarantees should also be binding on the states, and he was particularly keen on incorporation of the Fifth Amendment. In a well-researched and lengthy dissent in *Adamson*, he argued that the Fifth Amendment privilege against self-incrimination should be fully incorporated into the Fourteenth Amendment due process clause, and included a thirty-page appendix that provided historical and doctrinal support for this position. Nevertheless, Black's maneuver must have stunned Clark, who had explicitly remarked that *Mapp* did not incorporate the Fifth Amendment to apply against the states. The Texan realized Black had mischaracterized his constitutional basis for applying the exclusionary rule to the states in order to achieve his own objective of extending the right against self-incrimination to the states.

Clark had to handle the situation delicately because he needed Black's vote to reverse *Wolf*. He wrote him a brief memo. It gently began, "As you know, I certainly would not wish you to change any statement of *your* understanding of the Court's opinion." However, he continued, it was not his intention to use the case as a vehicle for applying the prohibition against self-incrimination to the states. "It was not necessary to do so," said Clark, because he was "personally satisfied that the Fourth Amendment, standing alone, is sufficient authority for a constitutional rule of exclusion." He explained that he had only drawn on the Fifth Amendment for "analogous support for that conclusion." He also reminded Black that "testimonial compulsion at trial is, of course, not involved in this case." Justice Clark's memo must have made an impression on Black, because he softened this initial statement in his revised draft to the full Court. Rather than suggest that Clark had relied on both the Fourth and Fifth Amendments to overturn *Wolf*, Black made it very clear that this was the basis for his concurring opinion.

Justice Black's opinion to the full Court began with him confronting the fact that he had written a concurring opinion in *Wolf*, stating that "the federal exclusionary rule is not a command of the Fourth Amendment but is a judicially created rule of evidence which Congress might negate." He explained that while he was still not persuaded that the Fourth Amendment, standing alone, barred the introduction of illegally seized evidence in trial, "reflection on the problem, however, in the light of cases coming before the Court since *Wolf*, has led me to conclude that when the Fourth Amendment's ban against unreasonable searches and seizures is considered together with the Fifth Amendment's ban against compelled self-incrimination, a constitutional basis emerges which not only justifies but actually requires the exclusionary rule. The close interrelationship between the Fourth and Fifth Amendments, as they apply to this problem, has long been recognized and, indeed, was expressly made the ground for this Court's holding in *Boyd v. United States.*" Black explained that this had been Justice Rutledge's rationale in his *Wolf* dissent, remarking that, "although I rejected the argument at that time, its force has, for me at least, become compelling with the more thorough study of the problem brought on by recent cases." He then cited *Rochin v. California* as "an almost perfect example of the interrelationship between the Fourth and Fifth Amendments" and stated that he had concurred in *Rochin* on those very grounds.

Black ended the opinion by restating the comment that led to Clark's memo several days previously. He replaced his explicit statement that the majority opinion extended the Fifth and Fourth Amendments to the states with the remark that he understood the majority opinion as setting aside Mapp's conviction "in reliance upon the *Boyd* constitutional doctrine." He also added a quotation from Justice Bradley's decision in that case about how the two amendments "upon which the *Boyd* doctrine rests are of vital importance in our constitutional scheme of liberty and are both entitled to a liberal . . . interpretation."

Justice Black circulated a second draft of his concurring opinion, which included minor stylistic changes, on June 12. He then turned his attention to Clark's majority opinion and found himself troubled by one of Clark's recent changes. He sent a one-page memo to the justice several days later. It began with his admission that *Mapp* would not be a good vehicle for overturning *Twining v. New Jersey* and *Adamson v. California* and applying the Fifth Amendment protection against self-incrimination to the states because the facts of the cases were "so different that the two cases can be distinguished on that basis." Black also removed his contention that *Mapp* overturned *Twining* in his concurring opinion. That battle would have to wait for a more opportune time.

It was another part of the majority opinion that troubled Black. He believed that in this most recent draft, which was a response, in part, to Justice Harlan's criticisms, Clark had taken a more narrow approach to incorporation than he had been led to believe. Black wrote that he was disturbed that Clark had written that "since the Fourth Amendment's *right of privacy* has been declared enforceable against the States through the Due Process Clause of the Fourteenth, it is enforceable against them by the same sanction of exclusion as is used against the Federal Government." He remarked that the statement "makes it necessary for me to say that my agreement to your opinion depends upon my understanding that you read *Wolf* as having held, as we are holding here, that the Fourth Amendment *as a whole* is applicable to the States and not some imaginary and unknown fragment designated as the 'right to privacy.' This was why, Black explained, he had been willing to use this case to address the scope of the Fourth Amendment. Then he stated, "If I am wrong in this and your opinion means that the Fourth Amendment does not apply to the States *as a whole*, I am unwilling to agree to decide this crucial question in this case and prefer to wait for a case that directly and immediately involves application of the Fourth Amendment to the Federal Government." He wanted Clark to clarify that the Fourth Amendment had been fully incorporated. "If this is not correct," he concluded ominously, "I think the case should be set down for reargument as the dissenters suggest."

Clark's short response arrived on Black's desk later that day. He tried to put him at ease. "The gist of the opinion is that *Wolf* held the entire Fourth Amendment to be carried over against the states through the Fourteenth," he wrote, "and therefore the exclusionary rule which *Weeks* applied to federal cases must likewise be made applicable to state prosecutions." Although Clark would not modify the language of the sentence that troubled Black, the brief exchange must have satisfied him. Clark finally had a majority agreeing to overturn *Wolf* and apply the exclusionary rule to the states.

The next decision to circulate to the full Court was a second draft of Harlan's dissenting opinion. This final version took Black's concurring opinion into account, with Harlan noting that only four members of the majority supported the argument that the Fourteenth Amendment due process clause enforced the exclusionary rule against the states. He emphasized that Justice Black did not subscribe to the view that the Fourth Amendment, standing alone, was enough to impose the exclusionary rule on the states: "It should be noted that the majority opinion in this case is in fact an opinion only for the judgment overruling *Wolf*, and not for the basic rationale by which four members of the majority have reached that result." But it was a halfhearted attempt. Harlan had lost the battle to retain *Wolf*.

In the final week before the decision was finalized and sent to the printer, Justice Clark's majority opinion went through two additional drafts. The changes were minor, and in many ways the final version was very similar to what he initially proposed to Justice Black: that the exclusionary rule was a constitutional one and was therefore enforceable against the states under the due process clause of the Fourteenth Amendment, thus requiring the reversal of *Wolf*; that the factual grounds upon which *Wolf* was based were no longer accurate; and that the exclusionary rule was necessary in order to realize the promise of the Fourth Amendment. Also, in addition to justifying the exclusionary rule as constitutionally required were the rationales that it was necessary for healthy federalism and the imperative of judicial integrity.

Years later Justice Clark offered insight into why he ultimately decided that the Court's decision in *Wolf v. Colorado* had to be reversed and the exclusionary rule applied to the states. "I couldn't understand why *Wolf v. Colorado* said that the fourth amendment applied to the states, but it just didn't seem to go all the way," he observed. "In fact it was just an empty gesture, sort of like what Chief Justice Hughes used to say: No use to have a Constitution — it's pretty, got all sorts of nice fringes around it, but it doesn't mean anything, just a piece of paper — unless you really live by it and enforce it. And so that's true with *Mapp* and the fourth amendment."

————

The Supreme Court ruling in *Mapp v. Ohio* tells only the beginning of the story about the exclusionary rule and the states. The consequences of the decision were yet to be realized. Its breadth was sure to provoke a spirited public debate over the exclusionary rule. And, because the decision would significantly alter police practices, it was possible that compliance with the Court's mandate would be unpredictable. An examination of the debate over *Mapp*, its implementation in nonexclusionary rule states, and the decision's effect on police behavior provide the next chapter in this story.

CHAPTER 5

Mapp Goes Public

Dollree Mapp was one of the first to hear of the Supreme Court ruling in *Mapp v. Ohio*. However, she was not the only one affected by the decision. *Mapp*'s reach extended far beyond her individual circumstances. The decision would affect every state in the union. Although almost half of the states called for exclusion of illegally seized evidence as a matter of state law, *Mapp* declared that all states were required to do so under the Fourth Amendment to the U.S. Constitution. The exclusionary rule, intended to ensure the promise of the Fourth Amendment, required police to significantly alter their practices regarding searches and seizures. If they failed to do so, exclusion of evidence could potentially alter the outcome of state criminal trials. The decision was about to become public, and the controversy over the Supreme Court ruling, and its implementation and impact, was not far behind.

After oral arguments in *Mapp v. Ohio*, Dollree Mapp returned to Cleveland and waited for news of the Court's decision. Over the next several months the young bailiff she befriended in Washington, D.C., would call her home weekly and give her the same message, "No decision today!" Then, on June 19, 1961, on the last "Decision Monday" of the 1960 Supreme Court term, Dollree Mapp received the call she had been waiting for. As Mapp recalls, "That thirteenth Monday, he called and he said, 'Dollree, you don't have to go to jail. It's all over.' That's the way he said it to me. That's all I heard." For Mapp, the result was anticlimactic. "Of course I was relieved that I didn't have to go to jail. But I felt empty. I didn't feel anything special."

If anything, Mapp was still resentful about her treatment by Cleveland's Bureau of Special Investigation, which she believed targeted her because of her race and the people she associated with rather than any evidence of wrongdoing on her part. She was angry. Over the last two years, with inadequate resources and a young teen to raise, she had faced many obstacles, including her court battle. However, thanks to a friend's financial support and motivated by her belief that she was unjustly treated by the state, she persevered and ultimately won her case. "I didn't buckle under," she states. "They thought I would be a pushover. I had experienced that before." Mapp had gone into battle with two plans in mind: what to do if her conviction was upheld, and what to do if it wasn't. When asked about what she would have done if her conviction was upheld, she replies, "I can only say that I wouldn't have gone to prison. . . . I don't think I would have allowed myself. I wasn't going willingly. It was a great relief that I didn't have to flee, that I didn't have to lose my daughter."

Mapp also believed throughout the arrest and lengthy court battle that she was fighting for more than her own rights. She was motivated by a higher purpose: "I was unhappy that I had to fight for my freedom. But I did so on the premise that all should be concerned with what happened to me." Later, when she learned of the significance of the ruling — that illegally seized evidence would be excluded from state criminal trials throughout the country — she says that she "was happy it resulted in something that would help others." Decades later, she is satisfied she saw the case through. "I would do it over again if I had to. I wouldn't change anything." Mapp would stay in Cleveland for several years after the Court decision. However, her story was far from over.

————

As pleased as Mapp was with the outcome of her case, there were others who were equally displeased upon hearing the Supreme Court decision. Carl Delau characterized it as "devastating." He also offered what would become one of the main criticisms of the Court's decision: that it would have an adverse effect on law enforcement activities. "If the Court threw the case out on the basis of illegal search and seizure, if they're going to be that technical," he exclaimed, "that ties our hands in law enforcement." Years later, in a letter to a professor researching *Mapp v. Ohio* for inclusion in a textbook, Delau elaborated upon the comment he made shortly after hearing of the decision.

"Has the *Mapp* decision harmed police enforcement?" he wrote, "[A] very definite Yes! Some law enforcement officers say it did not, and I have heard high-ranking officers say it has not, but I can only say that they have not performed police duties out in the street and prepared gambling cases for court."

Delau's assessment was based on his experience with Cleveland's Bureau of Special Investigation and years of work cracking down on the numbers racket. He also rationalized the police activity because their investigations always uncovered illegal activity. "Before *Mapp* and without search warrants, we at times forced doors but we always found violations that we knew were at that location." Delau described how the process of applying for a search warrant adversely affected the bureau's ability to do its job.

> After *Mapp*, after much surveillance on a location, obtaining the needed information for a search warrant, then going back to the prosecutor's office for the affidavit, to the clerk's office for the warrant, then to a judge for his signature, we then went back out into the street, hoping that the clearing office was still at the location where it had been previously observed. There is so much room for leaks to the violators in the numbers racket. Prior to *Mapp*, we forced a few doors, but never did we fail to find a good-sized gambling operation. After *Mapp* and armed with a search warrant, we often failed to find the operation that had been at the address in question.

Delau conceded that there was police error in the *Mapp* case, and that he and his officers did not have a warrant to search Mapp's home, an admission he first made in 1983 when he revealed they only had an affidavit for a warrant. "When the lieutenant went to get the search warrant . . . he went to the prosecutors and got a proper affidavit. He went to the clerk's office and had it signed, went to a judge, got a judge's signature. . . . He walked out with the affidavit. . . . He only got an affidavit! He never got a warrant. And as a result, when I finally looked at it outside the scene, and I seen it was just an affidavit . . . I wasn't going to make an issue over it. . . . So, were we going to say we only had the affidavit?" Delau provides an explanation for why this occurred: "The search warrant was faulty probably due to the lack of knowledge of the lieutenant who obtained same and delivered it to me on the scene. I have admitted that when I received the document at the scene, I did not study it in its entirety. It was after we arrived at police headquarters, I checked out the document and found the mistake." Delau said he did not make an issue of this at the time because he was reassured by the prosecutor that a warrant was not needed in order to proceed with the case because illegally seized evidence was allowable in criminal prosecutions in Ohio. However, he has yet to explain why he and the other officers testified at Mapp's trial that they were in possession of a warrant to search her home. Given Delau's observation that he and his unit "forced doors" but always found illegal activity, it is likely that the Cleveland police believed such actions were justified as part of the cost of fighting crime.

The *Mapp* decision certainly changed the way Carl Delau and the Bureau of Special Investigation did its job. It could no longer unlawfully search and seize property without risking the exclusion of evidence. And, because these searches most often occurred in communities of color, this meant that *Mapp*'s most immediate influence would be to protect populations traditionally targeted by police. As one observer noted, "The impact of *Mapp* was naturally greatest in the African-American community where Fourth Amendment violations were the most common. Whatever limited effect *Mapp* would have, it would be felt most where police conduct was the least restrained."

When *Mapp v. Ohio* was decided, twenty-four states, including Ohio, still admitted unlawfully seized evidence in state criminal trials. And, of the twenty-six states with the exclusionary rule, four states, Alabama, Maryland, Michigan, and South Dakota, had only partial exclusionary rules. These nonexclusionary and partial exclusionary states now had to conform to the requirement that illegally seized evidence be excluded from state criminal trials. In an instant, the Supreme Court imposed the exclusionary rule on half the states in the union. The breadth of the decision was extraordinary. Because practically all criminal cases are handled at the state and local level, the decision meant that the exclusionary rule could potentially be applied to thousands of cases involving illegal police searches every year. *Mapp* would significantly transform police investigatory activities and the conduct of state criminal prosecutions from that time forward. And, as would be seen later, the decision sparked the Warren Court's criminal due process revolution. It was the first in a number of decisions where the Supreme Court nationalized guarantees in the Bill of Rights to regulate police conduct and protect the rights of the criminally accused.

The significance of this landmark decision was clear. The *New York Times* called *Mapp* "historic" and "the most far-reaching constitutional step of the term." Even years after the ruling it has been characterized as "one of the most significant opinions rendered by the Court in the area of criminal procedure." Justice Abe Fortas referred to *Mapp* as "the most radical decision in recent times." And Justice Potter Stewart, who chose not to join the majority, opting instead to reverse Mapp's conviction on First Amendment grounds, would later describe *Mapp v. Ohio* as "perhaps the most important search-and-seizure decision in history."

Reaction to Supreme Court decisions varies according to the issue at stake, the population affected by the ruling, and its public policy implications. The exclusionary rule, no doubt unfamiliar to those outside of the law enforcement community, was introduced to many Americans for the first time. The rule is deceptively straightforward and carries potentially grave consequences, especially if suppression of illegally seized evidence results in a lost criminal conviction. As law professor John Kaplan explained, "From a public relations point of view, it is the worst possible kind of rule because it only works at the behest of a person, usually someone who is clearly guilty, who is attempting to prevent the use against himself of evidence of his own crimes." The decision's public policy implications were far-reaching; *Mapp* required significant changes in police searches and seizures, and its application would affect the prosecution and disposition of criminal cases. Everything was in place for a contentious debate over *Mapp v. Ohio* and the exclusionary rule.

The decision polarized the country. Many in the law enforcement community and members of conservative interest groups criticized *Mapp* because it was viewed as a hindrance to police and a threat to public safety. Those who favored the outcome, such as civil libertarians and liberal interest groups, did so on the basis that *Mapp* helped protect individual rights from an overreaching state. Politicians and the public, who focused on the practical implications of the decision, split according to their political ideology, with significant majorities questioning the rule. Members of the legal academy were also divided in their response, which was directed primarily at the Court's reasoning. There was heated rhetoric on both sides as *Mapp*'s proponents and opponents grappled with the actual and possible ramifications of the decision. This rhetoric captures the debate that took place over the exclusionary rule immediately after *Mapp v. Ohio* was handed down, and which continues today.

———

Criticism of *Mapp v. Ohio* was directed at the Warren Court's judicial activism, the possible "costs" of the rule to effective law enforcement and public safety, and the indirect effect of the exclusionary rule on the criminal justice system. Many also questioned whether the decision would have an effect on illegal police behavior. Other concerns include the unintended consequences of the exclusionary rule on police, prosecutorial and judicial behavior, and the fact that alternative remedies were available to encourage compliance with the Fourth Amendment.

Legal scholars critical of the decision denounced *Mapp* as the product of an activist, result-oriented Supreme Court. The Warren Court, already under criticism for its expansive interpretation of other individual rights and liberties under the Constitution, was portrayed as intentionally acting as a "super legislature." Harvard professor of government Robert G. McCloskey, echoing Justice Harlan's dissent that the Court unnecessarily overreached and boldly overturned *Wolf v. Colorado*, stated that "an important change in constitutional law should be preceded by full-dress argument, insuring the most sober kind of judicial consideration, especially when the prevailing rule has been laid down comparatively recently and when the issue is one of some intricacy." He explained that the Court's ruling also violated the principle of judicial restraint because the case could have easily been settled on the constitutionality of the Ohio state antiobscenity statute, which was argued in the lower state courts and discussed in the Court's conference. "*Wolf* may have deserved to be buried," he quipped, "but it merited a more persuasive funeral oration." The scholar also had harsh words for Justice Tom C. Clark's majority reasoning. "*Mapp* must surely rank as one of the untidiest decisions in which the modern Court has announced a salient constitutional doctrine, which is saying a good deal."

Criticism also focused on the majority's argument that the exclusionary rule was of constitutional origin. *Mapp*'s detractors argued that the exclusionary remedy lacked support in the "original intent or meaning" of the Framers and was not expressed or implied in the Constitution, which is silent on the issue of consequences that might result from Fourth Amendment violations. Rather, the rule was characterized as a "judicial creation" of recent origin, having not been recognized until the beginning of the twenty-first century by the federal judiciary and several state courts. The exclusionary rule was described as contrary to common law because under early common law, search warrants were not required, and victims of unlawful intrusions had to sue for trespass to remedy the wrong. As a practical matter, *Mapp* was denounced for intruding on the constitutional principle of federalism, because of the Court's effort to compose its view of "due process" upon the states.

Other critics focused on *Mapp*'s negative effect on law enforcement behavior. The decision directly impacted one of state and local government's primary functions — public safety. The law enforcement community's reaction was swift and hostile. Michael Murphy, the former police commissioner of New York City, which has the largest police force in the country, described *Mapp*'s impact as "dramatic and traumatic." He stated that "the decisions arrived at in the peace and tranquility of chambers in Washington, or elsewhere, create tidal waves and earthquakes which require rebuilding of our institutions sometimes from their very foundations upward." More generally, law enforcement opposed the Court's effort to "police the police." There were suggestions that the decision would "handcuff" them and negatively affect their ability to perform their duties. "What the Supreme Court is doing," Murphy stated, "is akin to requiring one boxer to fight by Marquis of Queensbury rules while permitting the other to butt, gouge and bite." Some police officers suggested that these legal restrictions would lead to an increase in crime. The decision was also criticized for giving criminal defendants an advantage in the courtroom, thus making convictions more difficult, and people sympathetic to the police — a considerable group because it is problematic to argue against law enforcement and in the narrowest sense argue in favor of the direct beneficiaries of the rule, criminal defendants — were displeased with the Court's attempt to judicially control police conduct.

The most persuasive rhetorical criticism against *Mapp* focused on the direct consequence of the exclusionary rule — the exclusion of reliable, often probative evidence, which potentially allows "obviously guilty criminals to go free." Because enforcement of the rule results in suppression of evidence, critics characterized it as a "technical loophole," which frees those who would otherwise be convicted at trial rather than punish those who violated the Fourth Amendment. As noted by evidence scholar Dean Wigmore, "Our way of upholding the Constitution is not to strike at the man who breaks it, but to let off somebody else who broke something else." The exclusionary rule, Wigmore suggested, therefore posed a danger to the community because it allowed criminals to return to the streets. Others predicted that thousands of criminals would go free because of imposition of the rule.

Closely related is the criticism that the exclusionary rule would alter the "truth-seeking" function of the criminal justice system by taking the focus away from the guilt or innocence of the criminal defendant to "a search for police error." Moreover, because the rule works to exclude "the truth from the fact-finding process," it was criticized for thwarting justice and turning the criminal justice system on its head. This, said critics, would inevitably lead to a loss of public confidence in the system as people learned of guilty criminals being freed on "technicalities." Moreover, the rule would impact the informal administration of justice — the disposition of cases through plea bargaining — because defense attorneys would focus on suppression motions, which are relatively costless, as a strategy to gain an advantage in their negotiations with prosecutors.

There was also speculation about possible unintended consequences of the rule, such as whether it would undermine the integrity of police, prosecutors, and judges. For example, some argued that police might now have an incentive to lie or misrepresent their investigative activities when faced with the consequences of exclusion. Or they may feel compelled to engage in tactics not intended to lead to arrest and prosecution, such as engaging in warrantless searches to get contraband off the streets, or tactics such as intimidation and harassment. Since their actions are not directed at the aequisition of physical evidence for criminal prosecution, the unlawful police action would not come to the attention of the courts. Prosecutors, on the other hand, may resort to accepting perjured testimony in order to avoid losing the case, and judges may face similar pressure when faced with a particularly heinous crime. Judges may also feel compelled to "stretch the law" to save a case, such as expanding the exceptions to warrantless searches or expanding the meaning of a legal search to avoid exclusion of evidence.

There was also the concern that the Supreme Court's conclusion that the exclusionary rule was the best way to halt unlawful police conduct precluded states from experimenting with other remedies. A number of other possible remedies were available to address unlawful police conduct, including civil lawsuits, which could provide injunctive and monetary relief; criminal suits where officials exceeding their authority would be subject to criminal penalties; and nonjudicial remedies such as internal police procedures, civilian disciplinary commissions, and the formation of an administrative agency to assess Fourth Amendment claims. Such remedies, exclusionary rule opponents claimed, would address the Fourth Amendment violation without negatively affecting the law enforcement community's ability to successfully convict criminals.

There were equally strong arguments presented in favor of the Court's ruling in *Mapp v. Ohio*. Its defenders praised the Court for extending the exclusionary rule to the states, noting that the decision was not activist as much as it was a response to recalcitrance on the part of the states for not enforcing the Fourth Amendment. It was also described as constitutionally and morally necessary to realize the promise of the Fourth Amendment. Regarding the potential "costs" of the rule, *Mapp*'s supporters suggested that it would actually help professionalize police, and that the costs were better characterized as the price of the Fourth Amendment rather than the exclusionary rule. In terms of possible unintended consequences, they noted the irony that the exclusionary rule, which was intended to deter the police from illegal behavior, was now being used as an excuse for future illegal behavior.

While conceding that *Mapp*'s reversal of *Wolf v. Colorado* was abrupt, proponents argued that states' unresponsiveness to the Court's suggestion in *Wolf* to do something to stop the prevalence of illegal police actions inevitably led to *Mapp v. Ohio*. As noted by one commentator, the twenty-four states without the exclusionary remedy had not established an alternative method for controlling police misconduct in the twelve-year period between *Wolf* and *Mapp*. *Mapp* was therefore characterized as making the Fourth Amendment guarantee against unreasonable search and seizure more than a "dead letter" by instituting a remedy with "teeth," which would actually ensure that the right was protected. Without such a remedy, police lawlessness would continue. As noted by law professor Stanley Ingber, "For constitutionally guaranteed rights to represent something beyond simple platitudes, the remedy provided for their violation must have some measurable consequence that vindicates the right in a manner which 'invokes and magnifies the moral and educative force of the law.'"

Supporters reiterated the Supreme Court's three rationales for the rule that were frequently overlooked by *Mapp*'s critics: that it was constitutionally required, promoted healthy federalism, and ensured judicial integrity. To counter critics who suggested the exclusionary rule was a judicial creation, rather than inherent in the Fourth Amendment, University of Michigan law school professor Yale Kamisar responded, "Most constitutional doctrine is made by judges." He asked critics to "cite even one Supreme Court case interpreting the Constitution which is not 'a matter of judicial implication.'" And, he added, the Constitution is usually silent on what occurs when a violation takes place, so it was entirely appropriate for the Court to fashion a remedy. Others heralded the decision for promoting healthy federalism by ensuring due process and equal treatment in every state in the country. Some were persuaded by the Court's rationale that the decision preserved the integrity of the judicial process by ensuring that it was not contaminated by partnership in police misconduct. As stated by Ingber, "The legitimate purpose of exclusion is not to place sanctions upon the specific officer, but to impose them upon the legal system in whose name he is functioning. Exclusion not only vindicates the right violated, but also eliminates the appearance of a system that encourages practically what it condemns rhetorically."

Proponents answered critics' concerns about the "costs" of the exclusionary rule by arguing that these costs are more accurately described as the costs of the Fourth Amendment, which had always prohibited unlawful searches and seizures. Kamisar, in an article responding to police complaints about court-imposed restrictions on their investigatory authority, answered, "but more often than not, what they are really bristling about is tighter *enforcement* of longstanding restrictions. Thus, many in law enforcement reacted to the adoption of the exclusionary rule as if the guarantees against unreasonable search and seizure *had just been written!* They talked as if and acted as if the exclusionary rule were the guaranty against unreasonable search and seizure. What disturbed them so much was that the courts were now operating on the same premise."

And, while some conceded that application of the exclusionary rule would result in the suppression of evidence of a crime, their response was that it was the unlawful police activity, not the exclusionary rule, that led to the suppression. More often than not, the evidence would not have been discovered were it not for the illegal search in the first place. As Ingber concluded, "This is not a political outcome impressed upon an unwilling citizenry by unbeknighted judges. It is the price the framers anticipated and were willing to pay to ensure the sanctity of the person, the home, and property against unrestrained governmental power."

Rather than harm law enforcement, *Mapp* was characterized as an incentive for local precincts to increase their professionalism by curbing police discretion and instituting formal rules to govern searches and seizures. Even law professor Dallin Oakes, a critic of the exclusionary rule, stated that police should restrain from saying they need to conduct illegal searches to do their job:

The whole argument about the exclusionary rule "handcuffing" the police should be abandoned. If this is a negative effect, then it is an effect of the constitutional rules, not an effect of the exclusionary rule as the means chosen for their enforcement. Police officials and prosecutors should stop claiming that the exclusionary rule prevents effective law enforcement. In doing so they attribute far greater effect to the exclusionary rule than the evidence warrants, and they are also in the untenable position of urging that the sanction be abolished so that they can continue to violate the rules with impunity.

In regard to the "unintended consequences" of the exclusionary rule — that it would lead to greater police illegality as police tried to circumvent it — *Mapp*'s defenders replied that not only had police used tactics such as intimidation and harassment prior to the decision, but that it was illogical to suggest that allowing police searches and seizures in violation of the Fourth Amendment would stop police from engaging in further illegal behavior. Nor could *Mapp* be blamed for an increase in crime. Ramsey Clark, Justice Tom Clark's son and former attorney general under Lyndon Baines Johnson, replied, "Court rules do not cause crime. People do not commit crime because they know they cannot be questioned by police before presentment, or even because they feel they will not be convicted. In the long run, only the elimination of the causes of crime can make a significant and lasting difference in the incidence of crime."

Mapp's supporters also bristled at the suggestion that criminals were the only beneficiaries of the exclusionary rule. They argued that the best way to look at the exclusionary rule was as a mechanism to protect all potential victims of police misconduct. As such, all Americans would profit from a society that respects and adheres to constitutional principles.

In response to the suggestion that there were other available alternatives to remedy Fourth Amendment violations, *Mapp*'s advocates responded that they had not worked to deter police misconduct in the past, and they were unlikely to do so in the future. Civil remedies were costly and rarely successful given deference to police and unsympathetic victims. Criminal remedies were even more elusive because district attorneys were reluctant to prosecute police offenders. Similarly, internal police procedures were ineffective because of the "blue wall of silence" and the strong police culture committed to the "crime-fighting" rather than the "due process" model of justice. And, remedies such as external civilian boards and administrative agencies suffered from a strong disposition in favor of law enforcement over the individual rights of criminal defendants. To support their contention that alternatives were ineffective, exclusionary rule supporters noted that many were available and underutilized prior to *Mapp*, and were therefore ineffective in deterring police misconduct and offering a remedy for Fourth Amendment wrongs.

Opponents of *Mapp v. Ohio* worked quickly to respond to the Supreme Court ruling. In October 1961, the National District Attorneys Association filed a petition to the Supreme Court requesting that it rehear the decision. It was a long shot. The Supreme Court rarely grants such petitions because a Court majority must agree to rehear the case. However, the association was hopeful because the dissenting justices had made a strong argument that the Court should have allowed a full briefing and argument on the issue of extending the exclusionary rule to the states. However, the effort was in vain. The Supreme Court issued a brief ruling denying the petition for rehearing several weeks later, and the debate over the exclusionary rule moved to the decision's impact on the administration of criminal justice.

———

For many political scientists, the study of events following the announcement of a Supreme Court decision is often more interesting than the decision itself. To explain and assess the response to a Supreme Court decision, it is useful to study compliance, implementation, and impact. As explained by one scholar, compliance research investigates whether lower courts or implementers of a decision abide by the "letter of the decision." Implementation research addresses the "spirit of the decision," or the degree to which those directly affected by it take steps to meet the decision's real goals. Impact research delves into a range of consequences stemming from a Supreme Court ruling, including the more obvious direct effects, such as whether it achieved its intended goal and changed public policy or behavior; and indirect effects, such as the social and political reaction to a judicial policy and the intended and unintended consequences of a decision. Impact research also examines the broader and longer-term effects of a judicial decision on society.

———

Compliance with Supreme Court decisions can range from active acceptance to overt resistance. A number of variables affect compliance, including the level of the Court's prestige, whether the Court clearly has jurisdiction over the subject matter, and the nature of the decision itself, including its level of specificity and whether it commands action from individuals who have the power to perform that act. Another important variable is the level of public support for the decision. If the decision is uncontroversial and in line with public opinion, or at least the opinion of those directly affected, compliance is likely. However, if it is controversial, especially in the minds of those immediately affected, noncompliance can drag on for years. And with the power of neither "the purse nor the sword," the Supreme Court does not institutionally have the resources to ensure compliance.

Successful implementation of a Supreme Court decision depends on the attitudes and actions of a range of individuals, including external political actors, such as elected and appointed officials in the executive branch, elected members of Congress and state legislatures, as well as members of special interest groups and the media. These actors may aid implementation by providing resources or hinder it by directly attacking the decision or the Court.

Other factors influencing implementation include how well the decision is communicated to those directly involved, the degree of behavioral change required, and whether there are adequate resources to fulfill the Court's mandate. Moreover, implementation of Supreme Court decisions often varies across the country, and even within an individual state, as regional and cultural differences come into play. The size of the jurisdiction affected is another important variable.

The impact of a Supreme Court decision can vary widely. Clearly, the decision most immediately affects the individual litigants in the case. However, because Supreme Court decisions frequently have wide-ranging public policy ramifications, it may take years before the consequences of a decision are fully realized. There are many different ways of measuring impact. While judicial impact most broadly refers to the general reactions and responses following a Supreme Court decision, it may also include whether a decision generates meaningful social and political change. However, measuring impact is difficult because it is not easy to separate the effect of a judicial decision from other influences on society.

One way to systematically study what occurs after the Court's decision is rendered is to focus on how affected populations respond to the Court's mandate. Political scientists Bradley C. Canon and Charles A. Johnson describe how four different populations of actors respond to a judicial policy: the interpreting population, consisting of judges in lower courts and other non-judges who play an official role in interpreting the law; the implementing population, which consists of the authorities whose behavior is directly affected by the judicial policy; the consumer population, consisting of those who would benefit from, or are disadvantaged as a result of, the decision; and the secondary, or residual, population, consisting of everyone else, such as government officials, interest groups, the media, and the public at large. They characterize these categories as primarily functional, so individuals can be members of different populations under different circumstances, and, depending on circumstances, there may also be linkages between the populations.

Responses to judicial opinions fall within two general categories: the "acceptance decision," which is the psychological reaction to a judicial policy, and the "behavioral response," which involves action that can be identified, and which illustrates the extent to which a judicial policy is realized. In the former, the intensity of a person's attitude toward the policy, his or her regard for the Supreme Court and perception of the consequences of a decision, and an individual's own role in society affect one's psychological reaction. A person's behavioral response is strongly influenced by the degree to which one has accepted a judicial decision.

For *Mapp v. Ohio*, the interpreting population consists of lower court judges, and the implementing population generally consists of police, prosecutors, and defense attorneys, each of whom may fall into the interpreting population as well. The consumer population consists of criminal defendants, although an argument can be made that all Americans fall into this category because the exclusionary rule, by enforcing the Fourth Amendment, serves a public interest beyond those formally accused of a crime. Politicians, special interest groups, academics, and the media fall into the secondary population.

State court judges were among the first to interpret *Mapp v. Ohio*. While it would be the trial court judges who would rule on motions to suppress illegally seized evidence in state criminal trials, the appellate court judges would interpret the Supreme Court's exclusionary rule jurisprudence and refine it in the process of deciding cases. Although the Supreme Court's directive was straightforward — evidence unlawfully seized by police had to be excluded from trial — other aspects of the decision were less clear. For example, the Court did not directly address whether, in addition to imposing the exclusionary rule on the states, it also intended to impose the federal standard of what was considered a "reasonable" search and seizure. As a result, state court judges did not know whether they should abide by federal search and seizure precedents or those of their own local jurisdiction. The U.S. Supreme Court would not address this dichotomy until 1963 in *Ker v. California*, when it ruled that federal standards should govern what is considered a reasonable search and seizure. The fact that this was not definitively settled for three years following *Mapp* helps explain some of the early challenges faced by the interpreting population.

Despite awareness of the decision, acceptance of *Mapp v. Ohio* by state court judges was not widespread, especially in the previously nonexclusionary states. Part of the reason for this lack of acceptance was because state judges, especially trial court judges far removed from the Supreme Court, have a tendency to be sympathetic to law enforcement. Also important was the fact that many state judges believed the Supreme Court was interfering with the administration of criminal justice, one of the primary functions of local government. There were even anecdotal cases of judges choosing to avoid *Mapp's* mandate. U.S. Senator Arlen Specter, then an assistant district attorney for Philadelphia County, wrote in 1962 that "the initial reaction in the Pennsylvania courts was one of dismay." He provided several examples of judges who questioned *Mapp's* wisdom, and at least one who refused to apply the exclusionary rule, noting that it was a split decision, and he "agreed with the dissenters."

However, notwithstanding their initial lack of enthusiasm for *Mapp*, most state court judges complied with the decision. An early study of state legal policies by David Manwaring three years after *Mapp v. Ohio* concluded that "in its most rudimentary purpose — to impose the exclusionary rule on those states not yet applying it — *Mapp v. Ohio* was wholly successful. This command was obvious, unambiguous and unavoidable." However, he also found that some state judges found creative ways to defy *Mapp*. For example, some judges would use state court precedents regarding what constituted a reasonable search, thereby controlling the situations where *Mapp's* exclusionary rule would apply. Based on these results, Manwaring concluded that compliance with federal search and seizure precedents "met with only partial and very spotty success." The study also revealed that previously nonexclusionary states were more likely than exclusionary states to follow federal search and seizure precedents because their state search and seizure law was undeveloped. Later, in 1964, after the Supreme Court clarified that states must abide by federal search and seizure precedents, compliance increased significantly.

There were two main implementing populations in *Mapp v. Ohio:* lower court judges and members of the law enforcement community. Examining the degree to which state judges applied the exclusionary rule both before and after *Mapp* is fraught with methodological challenges. First, as noted earlier, state court judges displeased with the decision could find ways to evade *Mapp's* mandate by expanding what was considered a "reasonable" search, thus eliminating the opportunity for application of the exclusionary remedy. This could be accomplished under both state and federal search and seizure precedents. Second, there are record-keeping challenges. Not only did half the states not have an exclusionary rule policy prior to *Mapp;* those that did were not systematic in their collection of data. For example, state trial court judge rulings on suppression motions in preliminary hearings are rarely recorded. Third, because a vast majority of criminal cases are disposed of informally through plea-bargaining, a judge often does not have the opportunity to formally rule on a suppression motion.

Overall, there was great diversity in how *Mapp v. Ohio* was formally implemented at the trial court level. David Horowitz, who also studied *Mapp's* implementation, concluded, "The uniform rule turns out to be enforced quite differently by the courts of various localities — a fact that may help to explain the finding that *Mapp's* effects on the police have also been uneven from city to city. Diverse local conditions of several kinds have profoundly affected the implementation of the supposedly uniform national rule."

In spite of limitations to empirical studies regarding implementation of the exclusionary rule, research on the number of suppression motions filed and granted in cities such as Philadelphia, Chicago, and New York illustrates that state court judges were in fact implementing the decision by applying the exclusionary rule in cases involving illegally seized evidence. Judicial granting of motions to suppress also increased in these early studies, although there was tremendous variation across jurisdictions. Clearly, lower court judges' behavioral response to *Mapp* was evident.

The other implementing population was the law enforcement community. Police complained bitterly about *Mapp*. There were several impediments to acceptance of the decision, including the fact that it was imposed by judges, that it required significant behavioral change, and that the police culture, which emphasizes "fighting crime," runs counter to the "due process" model, which emphasizes a more formal, legalistic approach to the rubber-meets-the-road police work.

Police argued that the justices who imposed the exclusionary rule were outsiders who did not fully understand the constraints under which law enforcement operates. As explained by sociologist Jerome Skolnick, police view the Court "with hostility for having interfered with their capacities to practice their craft." He described police as finding themselves in the awkward position of needing to do their job with this external pressure to abide by constitutional rules. "Their political superiors insist on 'production' while their judicial superiors impede their capacity to 'produce.' Under such frustrating conditions, the appellate judiciary inevitably comes to be seen as 'traitor' to its responsibility to keep the community free from criminality."

Skolnick observed that because "fighting crime" is more important than criminal convictions, police are more likely to do what their superiors want because they come from the same police culture as opposed to outsiders far removed from a police officer's job. Judges fall into this latter category and their decisions are not welcomed by police: "When an appellate court rules that police may not in the future engage in certain enforcement activities, since these constitute a violation of the rule of law, the inclination of the police is typically not to feel *shame* but *indignation*."

Another impediment to police acceptance of *Mapp v. Ohio* is that police culture dramatically affects police behavior more than court decisions. In his study of the effect of Supreme Court decisions on police organizations, Neal A. Milner described police as part of an isolated community, with strong internal cohesion and suspicion of outsiders that "fosters distrust for due-process-oriented change and a defensiveness toward its advocates." This distrust not only makes it less likely for police to implement court decisions, he explained, but it also makes them "less likely to appreciate the uncertainties and subtleties of legal constraints and more likely to attribute the difficulties in police work in general to the leniency of court decisions." The end result, Milner concluded, is that "the occupational ideology reinforces this distrust of legal change and exacerbates it." Even worse, it encourages circumvention of legal rules. "In short, the police occupational milieu fosters at best a view that the law is unrealistic and at worst a view that encourages police to evade the rules related to interrogation and search."

Because *Mapp* required significant behavioral changes, there were clearly challenges to law enforcement's implementation of the decision. Search and seizure requirements are potentially very difficult to understand and confusing in practice. To comply with *Mapp*, police need to know if their behavior is constitutional, including when they have to secure a warrant, what constitutes probable cause for a warrant, and when they can proceed with a search without a warrant. Moreover, search and seizure law was relatively undeveloped in previously nonexclusionary states, and, as noted previously, the Supreme Court did not declare conclusively that states were required to follow federal search and seizure law until 1964.

Despite complaining bitterly about *Mapp v. Ohio*, police, whether they liked it or not, had to change their way of conducting searches. Publicly, police reassured their constituencies that despite disagreeing with the decision, they would abide by it. New York's reaction to the decision provides an illustration of how the law enforcement community responded to the Court's mandate. Police Commissioner Murphy explained, "I state unequivocally that every effort was directed and is still being directed at compliance with and implementation of *Mapp*. While there was, and perhaps should have been, some grumbling and bitter realization that the criminal element had again gained an advantage, although not so intended by the Court, there was also and more importantly a good faith effort to conform to this new interpretation of the Constitution."

Other jurisdictions observed how *Mapp* prompted the law enforcement community to professionalize its officers. Stephen Sachs, a former Maryland state attorney general, noted, "In my state *Mapp* has been responsible for a virtual explosion in the amount and quantity of police training in the last twenty years." This executive director of the State Police Training Commission observed that "the increase in quality and quantity of training and education [can be attributed] directly to the need to adjust to the exclusionary rule."

Mapp's successful implementation was dependent on whether police received relevant information about search and seizure law, whether jurisdictions had resources for police retraining, and whether there was adequate communication between prosecutors' offices and police. New York City's implementation provides a model of how effective communication and adequate resources promoted implementation. Shortly after the decision was handed down, information on federal search and seizure precedents was published by the New York district attorney's office for use by police and judges, lecturers were sent to the police academy, and the district attorneys made themselves available to advise police on specific questions, including how to properly apply for a search warrant. In addition, the legal bureau of the city police counseled police officers about search and seizure law and assigned officers who were legally trained to city courts to aid their colleagues in applications for search warrants. Search and seizure law was emphasized at the police academy, and there was postacademy training for officers. As explained by Murphy, "Retraining sessions had to be held from the very top administrators down to each of the thousands of foot patrolmen and detectives engaged in the daily basic enforcement function. Hundreds of thousands of man-hours had to be devoted to retraining 27,000 men." Such retraining, he added, was not without its costs. "Every hour in the classroom was an hour lost from the basic function of the police department: the protection of life and property on the street."

Although New York City's implementation of *Mapp* was not typical of other jurisdictions — especially smaller police departments, which may not have the resources or expertise to appropriately train their officers — it was clear that the decision revolutionized the administration of criminal justice. There were dramatic changes in some jurisdictions, and minor changes in others. Many precincts imposed new policies and procedures to comply with the decision, such as more restrictive policies regarding searches and seizures. Supervision of officers was tightened, and internal sanctions for illegal search and seizure activity were imposed. Also, many departments instituted or expanded programs dealing with Fourth Amendment law and coordinated their efforts with local prosecutors to increase officer knowledge of constitutional restraints on police behavior. Some jurisdictions imposed internal sanctions for illegal searches.

In addition to police, prosecutors and defense attorneys reacted attitudinally and behaviorally in expected ways. Many prosecutors greeted the rule with some hostility, particularly if they were unfortunate enough to have a judge rule to suppress evidence because of an illegal police search. In some cases it created tension between police and prosecutors because, as one prosecutor noted, the problem with the exclusionary rule is that it most directly punishes prosecutors in terms of lost convictions, rather than the police who acted unlawfully in the first place. Defense attorneys, on the other hand, were happy to have another tool at their disposal to help clients. Behaviorally, both prosecutors and defense attorneys found themselves spending more time handling and arguing motions to suppress illegally seized evidence. The exclusionary rule also influenced the manner in which both parties informally disposed of cases, such as through the plea-bargaining process. It is difficult to make an empirical assessment of how much the plea-bargaining relationship was altered by *Mapp*, but logic dictates that the rule favors the defense. Motions to suppress require little time and few resources, and that small investment could lead to a potential windfall for a criminal defendant.

Criminal defendants, the most direct consumer population, were the obvious beneficiaries of the exclusionary rule. Increases in the number of motions to suppress illustrate that defense attorneys had incorporated this strategy into their repertoire. However, it is doubtful that criminal defendants were very familiar with the concept of the exclusionary rule, especially in the first several years after *Mapp v. Ohio*. It is even less likely that they altered their criminal behavior because of the possibility that illegally seized evidence would be excluded from trial.

Exclusionary rule advocates would argue that the consumer population extends well beyond these immediate beneficiaries to include all Americans who would benefit from the peace of mind that comes with knowing that police authorities cannot legally break into their homes or property without probable cause. Its critics would suggest that decreased police efficiency in combating crime actually works in the opposite manner and puts everyone at risk. However, it is difficult to measure this debate in any quantitative fashion.

Finally, the secondary population, consisting of politicians, interest groups, academics, and the public, reacted as one would expect. In general, individuals in these groups split along party lines, with conservatives blaming the courts for "coddling criminals" and "handcuffing the police," and liberals praising the Court for respecting individual liberty, which they felt could coexist with effective law enforcement.

It would take some time before the full impact of *Mapp v. Ohio* was realized. An early measure of the consequences of the decision was an evaluation of whether *Mapp* led to an increase in the use of search warrants by police as they tried to avoid situations where illegally obtained evidence might be suppressed. Although it is difficult to find comprehensive records on search warrant use both before and immediately after the decision, there is anecdotal evidence that applications for search warrants increased after 1961. Most of the evidence also reveals that search warrants were practically nonexistent prior to *Mapp*. For example, the American Bar Foundation conducted a survey of the Administration of Criminal Justice in 1957–1958 and found limited use of search warrants in three major cities. Only twenty-nine were issued in Detroit, thirty in Milwaukee, and seventeen in Wichita. In New York, Leonard Reisman, the deputy police commissioner in charge of legal matters, stated that before *Mapp* "nobody bothered to take out search warrants. Although the U.S. Constitution requires warrants in most cases, the U.S. Supreme Court had ruled that evidence obtained without a warrant — illegally if you will — was admissible in state courts. So the feeling was, why bother?" But, by 1966 more than 5,000 warrants were issued in the city. One of the most thorough before-and-after studies of warrant use was conducted by Michael Ban, who found that search warrant issuance in Boston increased from 100 per year prior to *Mapp* to 1,000 in 1963. He also found a similar increase, although fewer in terms of absolute numbers, in Cincinnati, which went from zero search warrants in the year prior to *Mapp* to 100 in 1963.

Other studies evaluated *Mapp*'s impact by evaluating if police search and seizure procedures changed following the decision. One of the earliest studies was conducted by Stuart Nagel in 1963. Nagel evaluated impact by comparing the behavior of the twenty-four states forced to initiate the exclusionary rule in response to *Mapp* ("initiating states") and the twenty-six states that already had an exclusionary rule or partial exclusionary rule ("non-initiating states"). He surveyed police chiefs, prosecuting attorneys, judges, defense attorneys, and representatives of the American Civil Liberties Union in each state and found that 75 percent of the respondents from the initiating states reported an increase in adherence to requirements for legal searches and seizures, compared with 57 percent from the non-initiating states. Nagel also discovered that across the country there was an increase in police education regarding parameters for legal searches, especially in the initiating states, where 51 percent of respondents noted that such education "increased substantially." However, his study provided little insight into whether there was friction between prosecution and police concerning police tactics in making searches.

In addition to finding an increase in post-*Mapp* legal searches and seizures and an increase in police education on the issue, Nagel's study also revealed that *Mapp* led to some "undesirable effects on police behavior" in the short run. Specifically, he found that 43 percent of respondents from the initiating states said police effectiveness in obtaining evidence by searches had decreased, compared with 9 percent in the non-initiating states. Respondents from the initiating states were also more likely to state that police morale and enthusiasm "with respect to making searches" appeared to decrease.

Nagel also discovered that *Mapp* led to behavioral changes in the courtroom. Both categories of states reported an increase in attorneys raising search and seizure issues in court, with 85 percent of respondents from initiating states reporting an increase, compared with 65 percent in the non-initiating states. However, the effect on judicial behavior was less dramatic. Respondents indicated little change in searches being declared illegal, and little change in judicial broadening of the definition of what constituted a legal search or "reasonable" police action that would avoid application of the exclusionary rule. In regard to the decision's effect on nonconvictions, Nagel found little change in the number of guilty persons released because of the exclusionary rule, although newly initiating states reported a slight increase over states that already had the exclusionary rule.

Nagel's study was duplicated by Michael Katz in 1966 for the state of North Carolina, which adopted the exclusionary rule in 1951. He was investigating whether *Mapp* "prompted" those states with the exclusionary rule to apply the rule more methodically after *Mapp*. Katz concluded that *Mapp* was generally well known and adhered to during the time studied (1961–1966) and that the decision had rapidly "passed into the collective consciousness of the participants concerned. The *Mapp* ruling seems to have captured the imagination of the legal profession and law enforcement officers throughout the U.S. to a marked degree." He also discovered that a significant minority of those returning the survey did not know that North Carolina had an exclusionary rule prior to *Mapp*. It was an interesting finding because it illustrated that even states with an exclusionary rule benefited from the heightened attention *Mapp v. Ohio* brought to the issue of illegal searches and seizures and the introduction of evidence in violation of the Fourth Amendment.

Katz also found that a significant majority of judges, prosecutors, and defense attorneys in the state believed the rule led to a decrease in the number of illegal searches. And, he revealed an unintended effect of the decision: almost 80 percent of those surveyed suspected that the exclusionary rule limited police morale and hindered law enforcement efforts. These early studies on the impact of *Mapp v. Ohio* would be revisited and elaborated upon in the years to come.

The debate over the impact of *Mapp*'s exclusionary rule, which began shortly after the decision was handed down, has yet to subside. Over the last forty years researchers have explored how the sanction of exclusion has influenced police search and seizure techniques, the nonprosecution and nonconviction of those accused of a crime, and police knowledge of search and seizure rules and willingness to obey these rules. These exclusionary rule studies shed light on the intended and unintended consequences of the rule and help shape the public and political debate over its legitimacy.

CHAPTER 6

"Is the Criminal to Go Free Because the Constable Has Blundered?"

In 1926, when deciding a case before the New York Court of Appeals, *People v. Defore*, which included the issue of whether illegally seized evidence should be excluded from trial, Judge Benjamin Cardozo stated, "There has been no blinking the consequences. The criminal is to go free because the constable has blundered." The phrase captures the sentiments of exclusionary rule opponents who argue that it thwarts justice by excluding what they deem to be valid, often probative evidence from trial, thus allowing the guilty to elude punishment. But what are the actual "costs" and "benefits" of the exclusionary rule? Because the debate surrounding the rule has moved away, as one scholar noted, from a "principled basis" that discusses it as a constitutional necessity to a "pragmatic discussion," even among Supreme Court justices, of "bloody knives" and violent criminals "getting off on technicalities," it is important to review empirical studies that shed light on the consequences of the exclusionary rule.

Exclusionary rule research falls into three main categories: early studies that examine whether it deters police misconduct; studies that investigate whether imposition of the rule results in "lost" convictions, including cases prosecutors decline to pursue; and studies that examine *Mapp*'s effect on police behavior, including whether it deters police misconduct, whether it contributes to increased knowledge of search and seizure law, and its possible unintended effects, including police perjury. This chapter reviews these studies in order to capture the exclusionary rule's impact on police behavior and the administration of criminal justice.

Initial study of *Mapp v. Ohio* focused on whether the exclusionary rule accomplished its intended goal and deterred illegal police searches.

The premise of these studies was that if *Mapp* was effective, then police misconduct — illegal searches and seizures — would decline. If the remedy to Fourth Amendment violations is the exclusion of evidence to compel constitutional police conduct, these researchers theorized, its effectiveness could be gauged by whether police engaged in constitutional searches and seizures.

One of the first major studies on the exclusionary rule's deterrent effect was conducted by Dallin Oakes in 1970. First, he surveyed existing research on the rule and found "no convincing evidence" that it deterred police misconduct. Then, his own study of arrest and conviction data for gambling, narcotics, and weapons crimes in Cincinnati, Ohio, for the five-year period before and the six-year period following *Mapp* revealed that the exclusionary rule did not have an appreciable effect on arrests or convictions for weapons or narcotics crimes. However, he did discover an effect on gambling arrests and convictions, which dropped by more than half in the six years following the decision. At the end of the article, while conceding that the results were "insufficient," Oakes called the exclusionary rule a "failure" that should be discarded once an effective alternative remedy was found.

Several years later James E. Spiotto investigated motions to suppress evidence in gambling, narcotics, and weapons cases involving searches and seizures in the Chicago municipal courts between 1950 and 1969. He found that motions to suppress evidence had "increased significantly," mostly in narcotics and weapons crimes, leading him to conclude that the number of illegal searches had actually increased following *Mapp*, "the opposite result of what would be expected if the rule had been efficacious in deterring police misconduct." Spiotto also contended that the exclusionary rule failed to deter police misconduct because his study revealed that a small number of officers repeatedly engaged in illegal searches.

To evaluate the exclusionary rule's "cost" to society, Spiotto took a detailed look at a sample of suppression motions in the city's narcotics, felony, and gun courts during the month of June 1971. He found that motions to suppress evidence were most frequently made by defendants with prior records; that these defendants were also more likely to have their motions granted; and that successful suppression motions disproportionately favored defendants charged with more serious drug crimes. Based on these results, Spiotto called for replacing the exclusionary rule with a tort remedy where victims of an illegal search could sue the government for damages.

Oakes's and Spiotto's research was sharply criticized by Thomas Davies, who challenged the results because the researchers neglected to control for external trends in population, changes in the crime rate and court caseloads, and the uneven time period studied. He also questioned whether examining the number of motions to suppress evidence could effectively account for the number of illegal searches by police, calling it a "crude measure." In regard to Spiotto's conclusion that the rule disproportionately benefited the most dangerous criminals in society, Davies noted that the study focused on only a limited number of offenses and suffered from an extremely small sample size. He also faulted the researcher's discussion of the results, which essentially equated drug offenders with "robbers" and "murderers" as the primary beneficiaries of the exclusionary rule. Davies interpreted the results differently: "In the end, Spiotto does tell us something about the 'countless guilty criminals' that escape through the exclusionary rule. They are not 'robbers' or 'murderers.' Instead the 'guilty victims' who escape are offenders caught in the everyday world of police initiated vice and narcotics enforcement. Their offenses are usually true victimless crimes in the sense that there is no civilian complainant."

Bradley Canon, who also characterized Oakes's and Spiotto's studies as "badly flawed," conducted two multicity studies to see if their results could be generalized to the broader population. Canon's 1974 study scrutinized motions to suppress evidence in narcotics, gambling, and weapons cases, as well as cases involving the possession and receipt of stolen property, in fourteen cities over a ten-year period (1956–1966). All fourteen cities were located in states that did not have the exclusionary rule prior to *Mapp*. Canon found wide variation in *Mapp*'s impact, leading him to conclude that the Oakes and Spiotto studies were not representative of how cities responded in *Mapp*'s wake. In four cities, he found *Mapp* had a minimal effect on the police's ability to make arrests; in four others it had a "significant impact," and in the remaining five, the results were "differentiated" depending on the crime.

Several years later Canon expanded the study to nineteen cities. He found that there was "a statistically significant decrease in arrests in all or most search and seizure crimes" in nine of the cities and a "minimal or absent" effect in the other ten cities. Noting the wide variation among the cities, Canon concluded that the exclusionary rule's impact "depended much on such factors as degree of professional training prevailing in a department, policies of chiefs of police and squad commanders, the attitudes of mayors, city councils and other officials, etc."

Over time, the Oakes and Spiotto studies were criticized for their inability to fully measure *Mapp v. Ohio*'s impact. It is problematic to measure the rule's effectiveness by looking only at the number of arrests and/or motions to suppress evidence. This approach does not take into account illegal searches that do not produce evidence to be suppressed, and it does not consider whether there may have been even more illegal searches were it not for the exclusionary rule. Moreover, it cannot examine the many variables that affect whether a motion to suppress is filed, including quality of defense counsel, the ability to prove an illegal search, and the individual circumstances presented by each victim of police misconduct.

––––––

Criticism of these early studies led researchers to investigate the exclusionary rule from a different perspective. These studies take a more pragmatic approach and empirically measure the rule's effect on the disposition of felony arrests. This research examines whether imposition of the exclusionary rule led to situations where "the criminal [has gone free] because the constable has blundered." In particular, the inquiry focused on the "cost" of the exclusionary rule measured in terms of cases that are not pursued by prosecutors on account of an illegal search and seizure (nonprosecution) and those cases where the defendant is acquitted because evidence was excluded from trial (nonconviction).

The first of these studies, a 1979 report by the General Accounting Office (GAO), analyzed 2,804 federal cases in thirty-nine U.S. attorney's offices over a two-month period. It revealed that 10 percent of all defendants whose cases were prosecuted filed a motion to suppress evidence, and of that percentage, in a fraction of cases (1.3 percent) evidence was excluded because of an illegal search and seizure. In more than half of those cases where evidence was excluded, the defendants were still convicted. The report also revealed that less than half a percent (0.4) of these cases were dropped voluntarily or declined by the prosecution because of an illegal search problem. While the

GAO study concerned federal rather than state cases, it provided general evidence of the rule's effect.

The next major study was the National Institute of Justice (NIJ) examination of the exclusionary rule's impact on felony arrests in California between 1976 and 1979. The results were quite different from the GAO study. NIJ researchers found that of the 86,033 felony arrests declined by prosecutors in California, 4,130, almost 5 percent, were rejected due to illegal search and seizure problems. Based on these findings, the researchers concluded that the exclusionary rule exerted a "major impact" on the state's prosecutions. They also determined that the rule's impact was most significant in drug cases. This latter finding was based on an analysis of drug cases from two prosecutors' offices, which revealed that approximately 30 percent of felony drug cases were rejected due to illegal police searches. Most disquieting was the researchers' conclusion that those released because their case presented a search and seizure problem had "serious criminal records," "continu[ed] to be involved in crime after their release," and posed a "risk to the community." According to the study, half of those whose cases were not pursued due to an illegal search or seizure were rearrested within a two-year period.

However, this study was sharply criticized for overstating its results. Thomas Davies argued that the NIJ researchers presented a "slanted interpretation of the data." The conclusion that the exclusionary rule had a "major impact" on disposition of felony arrests, Davies stated, was "misleading and exaggerated." He remarked that the NIJ researchers' conclusion that 5 percent of cases were declined because of the exclusionary rule was inaccurate because they cited the percentage of all cases declined for prosecution because of an illegal search and seizure problem out of all cases declined for prosecution. A more accurate way of measuring nonprosecution, Davies explained, was to calculate the percentage of cases rejected because of an illegal search as a percentage of the total number of arrests reported. According to Davies's reanalysis of the raw data, less than 1 percent (0.8 percent) of all felony arrests were rejected by prosecutors because of the exclusionary rule.

Davies also questioned the study's conclusion that those released because prosecutors declined to pursue the case were the most serious offenders. Rather, he found that they "tend not to have had especially serious records and not to have been charged with especially serious offenses; most would not have been sentenced to prison if convicted." Examining these cases further, he discovered that "illegal search problems were given as the reason for prosecutors' rejections of only 8 of 11,836 homicide arrests (0.06%), 13 of 14,328 forcible rape arrests (0.09%), 117 of 68,632 robbery arrests (0.17%), and 189 of 135,881 assault arrests (0.13%)." Davies also challenged the study's conclusion that approximately one-third of all drug arrests were rejected due to an illegal search, calling this number a "gross exaggeration." His examination of *statewide* statistics on drug arrests revealed that only a little over 2 percent (2.4 percent) were not pursued because of illegal police searches and seizures. Finally, in response to the study's conclusion that those who escape conviction posed significant risks to the community based on the fact that they were arrested for another felony within a two-year period, Davies remarked that not only did the research fail to take into account whether those arrested were convicted but that the study had stretched the definition of what constituted a "violent crime." His examination of the statewide data indicated that only approximately 7 percent of those released were rearrested for offenses against a person.

Another major study on the effects of illegal searches and the disposition of felony prosecutions was conducted by Peter Nardulli in 1983. He reviewed 7,500 criminal cases from nine politically, socially, and economically diverse counties to examine the incidence of suppression motions for physical evidence and, for comparative purposes, motions to suppress confessions and identifications. He found motions to suppress physical evidence filed in less than 5 percent of all felony cases, most often drug and weapons cases, and *successful* motions to suppress in a fraction of cases (0.69 percent). Of this percentage, weapons possessions and drug prosecutions were most likely to have evidence successfully suppressed (3.4 percent and 2.4 percent, respectively, with only 0.3 percent in other offense categories).

Taking a closer look at the small number of cases involving successful suppression motions, Nardulli found that most of the defendants were convicted in spite of the excluded evidence. And, of those forty defendants who were acquitted due to a successful defense motion to suppress illegally obtained evidence, he discovered that 80 percent involved "nonserious" crimes, including "drug or weapons possession, and non-violent offenses." In fact, he noted, most would have received only one or two months in jail, and only one of those forty defendants would have received more than a year in jail. "If the [exclusionary] rule were eliminated," Nardulli concluded, "we would be able to realize an increase in conviction rates of less than 0.5%."

Other studies have duplicated these findings. For example, the Institute for Law and Social Research investigated the effect of illegal searches on prosecutors' decisions to proceed with a case in the District of Columbia and within major cities in California, Georgia, Illinois, Louisiana, New York, and Utah. Three reports, published in 1977, 1979, and 1982, found that prosecutors in urban areas typically reject fewer than 1 percent of felony arrests because of potential challenges posed by illegal searches. In addition, a 1983 study by Floyd Feeney, Forrest Dill, and Adrianne Weir from the University of California–Davis concluded that approximately 0.5 percent of felony robbery, burglary, and assault arrests were dropped due to illegal searches.

There are two ways to interpret these empirical studies on the exclusionary rule's effect on nonprosecutions and nonconvictions of those accused of criminal acts. Critics of the exclusionary rule argue that, however slight, any percentage of "lost" cases due to exclusionary rule violations is too many, and that the price of these guilty criminals "going free" far outweighs any benefits of the rule because it imposes a substantial cost on society. Alternatively, there are those who counter that these are the "costs" of the Fourth Amendment. These exclusionary rule proponents also call attention to the immeasurable benefits of the rule in terms of its ability to protect individual privacy and command police respect for the Constitution.

———

A third approach to measuring the impact of the exclusionary rule is to examine its effect on police behavior. These studies operate under the assumption that the exclusionary rule is an effective deterrent to police misconduct if it forces police to change their behavior when conducting investigative activities in order to comply with the requirements of the Fourth Amendment. The rule's impact on police behavior has been evaluated by researchers who interview law enforcement officials and non–law enforcement personnel, and studies that attempt to measure whether law enforcement officers have a full understanding of search and seizure rules and appreciate these rules as restrictions on their conduct.

Several detailed qualitative studies shed light on police investigative behavior following *Mapp v. Ohio*. As noted in chapter 5, two early studies conducted by Stuart Nagel and Michael Katz discovered that those states that initiated the exclusionary rule immediately following *Mapp* were more likely to educate police officers in search and seizure law and to adhere more closely to search and seizure rules. Both scholars found successful implementation of *Mapp*, along with the negative side effects of a slight decrease in morale and a feeling, especially among law enforcement personnel, that the rule had hindered police work.

Other, more recent studies capture *Mapp*'s effect on law enforcement behavior in even greater detail. In 1987, Myron Orfield conducted extensive, structured interviews with twenty-six police officers in the Narcotics Section of the Organized Crime Division of the Chicago Police Department. He discovered that 85 percent of the officers interviewed stated that they knew when evidence was suppressed in a case they were working on and why, that they often found out the results of a suppression hearing "right away" or "immediately," and that they "generally understood" why the evidence had been suppressed. Sixty-one percent of the respondents stated that they learned something new "very frequently" or "every time" evidence was suppressed, and 39 percent noted that they learned something new "only occasionally" or "rarely." Orfield also found that more than 90 percent of the officers stated that their personal experience in a suppression hearing or seeing another officer's evidence suppressed helped them learn about the law of search and seizure, led them to use warrants "when at all possible," forced them to take care when engaging in warrantless searches, and made them more thorough in writing their case reports.

The study revealed that many of the officers were clearly concerned about the potential for lost convictions due to the exclusion of evidence. And, they indicated that they were unhappy if evidence was suppressed and that they did not enjoy having their behavior scrutinized. However, despite these concerns, all the officers interviewed approved of the exclusionary rule. Several added, however, that there should be a "good faith" exception to the rule. Orfield also discovered an unintended consequence of the exclusionary rule: police perjury. He noted that "virtually all of the officers admit that the police commit perjury, if infrequently, at suppression hearings," speculating that the incidence of police perjury is "greater than the police admit." However, he downplayed this finding by noting that the respondents assumed that judges had a tendency to discount what they believed to be perjured testimony.

Based on these interviews, Orfield concluded that the exclusionary rule had an "institutional deterrent effect" because the police department's response to the suppression of evidence was the design of programs and procedures to increase Fourth Amendment compliance, including improved training, internal review of "lost" cases, better record keeping, an increased use of search warrants, and greater interaction with local prosecutors. He also concluded that the rule specifically deterred individual police misconduct because it "has educated police officers in the requirements of the fourth amendment and has punished them when they have violated those requirements."

In 1992, Orfield conducted a second study based on forty-one interviews with judges, prosecutors, and public defenders in fourteen felony trial courtrooms in the Criminal Division of the Circuit Court of Cook County, Illinois. This study verified some of his earlier findings about the exclusionary rule's institutional and individual deterrent effect and also offered a more alarming perspective in regard to police perjury.

Orfield discovered that these non–law enforcement personnel, even more so than the law enforcement officers interviewed in the earlier study, believed in the exclusionary rule's institutional deterrent effect. The respondents, he noted, "uniformly believe that officers care about convictions and experience adverse personal reactions when they lose evidence." Seventy-eight percent remarked that experience with suppression motions "effectively educates officers in the law of search and seizure and that the law is not too complicated for police officers to do their job effectively." And 90 percent stated that they believed law enforcement officers understood search and seizure law well enough to do their job, with half of these respondents believing officers understood why evidence was suppressed in a particular case, and almost all believing officers understood why evidence was suppressed at least half of the time. Orfield also found that 85 percent of respondents agreed that the exclusionary rule led to an improvement in search and seizure techniques, including the increased use of search warrants. A majority responded that it contributed to a "closer working relationship between prosecutors and police." Based on these results, Orfield concluded that according to the non–law enforcement personnel interviewed, the exclusionary rule deterred illegal searches and contributed to police professionalism and greater observance of Fourth Amendment law.

However, he also discovered something more troubling. His interviewees discussed what they believed to be a pattern of "pervasive police perjury intended to avoid the requirements of the Fourth Amendment." Based on these interviews, Orfield observed that

> dishonesty occurs in both the investigative process and the courtroom. The respondents reported systematic fabrication in case reports and affidavits for search warrants, where officers created artificial probable cause which forms the basis of later testimony. Moreover, police keep dual sets of investigatory files; official files and "street files." Exculpatory material in the street files may be edited from the official record. Respondents, including prosecutors, estimate that police commit perjury between 20% and 50% of the time they testify on Fourth Amendment issues. This perjury may be tolerated, or even encouraged, by prosecutors at each step in the process in both direct and indirect ways.

The respondents also stated that judges frequently will accept as true police testimony even if they suspect possible perjury, especially in high-profile cases. According to Orfield, the respondents believed judges "purposefully ignore the law to prevent evidence from being suppressed, and even more often, knowingly accept police perjury as truthful. When the crime is serious, this judicial 'cheating' is more likely to occur." He was also told that "heater," or high-profile, cases, which would "arouse public ire if the defendant goes free for procedural or technical reasons," were more likely to be diverted to judges with high conviction rates. Orfield concluded that the judges and public defenders interviewed "perceive perjury to be *the* major factor limiting the deterrent effect of the rule." He observed, "The evidence presented thus far involves a powerful paradox. The deterrent effect of the exclusionary rule, though real to respondents, is seriously undercut by rampant police perjury which appears to be encouraged by judges' reluctance to protect rights in serious cases."

However, despite this unintended consequence of the rule, which the respondents conceded may undercut its deterrent effect, 90 percent of those surveyed believed that the exclusionary rule was the best remedy for Fourth Amendment violations. They stated that it had "dramatically improved police behavior" and that, compared with other possible remedies, it "is the only mechanism that injects any restraint in the system, or any respect for rights." Orfield also found no evidence, in either his own study or others that have explored the issue, that police perjury would disappear in the absence of the exclusionary rule. He concluded, based on these studies, that "the exclusionary rule — though far from perfect — must be judged a substantial success."

A similar methodological approach was employed by Milton Loewenthal, who conducted interviews with ninety New York police commanders and non–law enforcement personnel and participated in forty hours of "ride-alongs" with police officers. He concluded that the exclusionary rule helped command respect for the Fourth Amendment. Loewenthal found "strong evidence that, regardless of the effectiveness of direct sanctions, police officers could neither understand nor respect a Court which purported to impose constitutional standards on the police without excluding evidence obtained in violation of those standards." He also cautioned against discarding the exclusionary rule, which he believed would lead to increased police misconduct. "No matter what sanctions may be imposed in its stead, police officers are bound to view the elimination of the exclusionary rule as an indication that the fourth amendment is not a serious matter, if indeed it applies to them at all."

———

An alternative way of measuring the exclusionary rule's effect on police is to evaluate police knowledge of search and seizure law and to investigate whether police see application of the exclusionary rule as a learning experience that leads them to change their behavior to respect the Fourth Amendment. The premise of these studies is that the exclusionary rule cannot have a positive impact on behavior if law enforcement officials do not have a full understanding of how the Constitution constrains their behavior.

In 1991, William C. Heffernan and Richard Lovely surveyed four midsize northeastern police departments and held in-depth interviews with some department members to test the accuracy of police officers' knowledge of search and seizure rules and their predilection for engaging in illegal searches. For comparison purposes, they also surveyed a group of lawyers and a group of college students enrolled in an introductory criminal justice course. The questionnaire presented six scenarios of warrantless searches by police officers based on actual Supreme Court cases (respondents were not told that part) and asked a series of questions, including whether respondents believed the police conduct was lawful and how they would act in the same scenario. Each group was also given a series of multiple-choice questions about the Fourth Amendment.

The results revealed that in response to the hypothetical situations, officers were correct in their assessment about the lawfulness of the intrusion 57 percent of the time, which was slightly better than the college students (48 percent) and not as high as the lawyers (73 percent). Similarly, officers outperformed college students but did not score as high as the lawyers on the multiple-choice questions on search and seizure rules. Looking more closely at the survey responses of the law enforcement officers, Heffernan and Lovely found that those who had taken several law courses in addition to formal police training did almost as well as lawyers, as did those officers with some college preparation and those with nonpatrol assignments.

Interpreting these results, the researchers questioned whether *Mapp v. Ohio* and its imposition of the exclusionary rule on the states contributed to a greater understanding of the law. They concluded that "even if all police officers were disposed to adhere to the rules of search and seizure, there would nonetheless be substantial deviation from those rules as they are presently constituted because of police mistakes about what they require. Deterrence works efficiently only when the subjects of deterrence are relatively certain about what is expected of them. The rules of search and seizure, however, are sufficiently vague that even the best-informed officers are routinely mistaken about what they may and may not do."

In addition, Heffernan and Lovely discovered that 15 percent of the officers responding to the survey admitted that they knew that the scenario presented was "prohibited in a given setting," but that "they would nonetheless intrude in that setting," which demonstrated a knowing violation of the rule of law. If the exclusionary rule compelled respect for the law, they argued, police would not intentionally engage in an illegal search. Based on these overall results, they concluded that "with the complex body of rules of search and seizure now in place, officers' mistaken beliefs about the law are bound to frustrate the aims of any deterrence strategy" and offered that "exclusion offers only a weak deterrent safeguard against police illegality." However, they stopped short of dismissing the exclusionary rule's impact on police behavior, stating that "officers cannot disregard it altogether, in part because they can expect to be questioned by prosecutors and defense lawyers about their conduct and in part because it is hard to be wholly indifferent to the prospect of harming a case through the suppression of evidence." Its effectiveness, they concluded, "hinges on the institutional processes they can expect to confront when they carry out intrusions that lead to prosecution."

A look into a police department's "institutional process" to handle exclusionary rule violations was part of a 1998 study by Pepperdine law school faculty. Researchers surveyed law enforcement officers in five police departments and the Ventura County Sheriff's Department. The survey presented factual scenarios involving warrantless searches and seizures and police interrogations from recent Supreme Court decisions or from "well-recognized legal principles."

In regard to the hypothetical search and seizure scenarios presented, which the authors conceded "was not always a simple or straightforward exercise" and two of which "were the subject of some debate among the authors," the officers correctly responded two-thirds of the time, regardless of their rank, experience, or education, which led the researchers to conclude there was "a widespread inability to apply the law of search and seizure or police interrogation." When asked about their attitudes toward the exclusionary rule and its effect on their police work, 20 percent of the officers surveyed stated that they were "primarily concerned" with the risk of exclusion of evidence, 60 percent stated that it was an "important concern," and the remainder responded that it was of little or no concern.

As far as the respondents' direct experience with suppression motions, the researchers discovered that almost 80 percent of the respondents had testified on a motion to suppress evidence that they or their partner had seized, but that of this number, 60 percent noted they had never had evidence suppressed, and that more than 20 percent had only had evidence excluded a single time. However, responses to a follow-up question revealed that 55 percent of those surveyed had been involved in a successful suppression motion, which cast some doubt on the accuracy of the officers' recollections about successful suppression motions.

The study also investigated how officers learned about the outcome of a suppression motion. While more than two-thirds revealed that they heard the ruling in court or were told by the prosecutor, 10 percent stated that they found out from a fellow officer, and 5 percent never learned of the outcome. Oddly, their survey questions on police perjury revealed the opposite results from studies by Orfield and others. Eighty percent of the respondents in the Pepperdine study stated that they had not heard of instances of police deception or perjury within their agency, and those who did admit to some knowledge of police misconduct minimized its extent, noting perhaps one or two instances, with only a handful acknowledging significant misconduct. Finally, when asked about alternatives to the exclusionary rule, including criminal prosecution for violations, a civil tort remedy, internal discipline, or requiring additional schooling, 57 percent of respondents indicated that "the interests of the criminal justice system are well served by excluding unlawfully seized evidence" and that other alternatives were unnecessary. However, of those alternatives listed, one-third of the respondents indicated that requiring additional educational courses would be the most viable option.

Based on these results, the authors concluded that the exclusionary rule's ability to effectively deter police misconduct was a "failure" because the study revealed "the apparent absence of any formal procedure . . . for notifying officers when they have had evidence excluded by the court" and because officers who had previously experienced the exclusion of evidence did not "outperform" the other officers on the hypothetical questions. According to the researchers, "The exclusion of evidence, if it is to provide any specific deterrence, must be a learning experience for the officer. For that to happen, the prosecutor or the office's supervisor must ensure that the officer understands the reason for the exclusion and obtains the necessary education or training to avoid making the mistake again." They also concluded that the exclusionary rule lacked any general deterrent effect because one in five officers minimized its importance, and because the officers correctly answered the hypothetical situations "barely more than 50% of the time. . . . Officers cannot be deterred from engaging in illegal conduct if they don't understand what is illegal." At the end of the study, despite the fact that a strong majority of respondents called for maintaining the rule, the researchers concluded that it should be applied only in instances of intentional or willful misconduct by police, and in other instances, be replaced with a civil administrative remedy.

The Pepperdine study was criticized by several scholars in a symposium the following year. They questioned the researchers' methodology and interpretation of the data, particularly the confusing fact situations on which the questions were based, and their tendency to highlight the negative aspects of the exclusionary rule's impact on police behavior rather than its positive aspects. Several questioned the appropriateness of a civil administrative remedy, which was characterized as either inefficient or a worse alternative to the exclusionary rule because of the possibility that it would overdeter police officers, who would be personally liable for substantial Fourth Amendment violations.

Despite these limitations, the Pepperdine study and the research conducted by Heffernan and Lovely both demonstrate that one of the challenges with effective deterrence of police misconduct may be that the law governing police investigative activities is overly complicated. Of course, this leads one to question whether search and seizure rules are complicated because of *Mapp v. Ohio*, a Supreme Court decision that imposed the exclusionary rule on the states, or because of subsequent Court decisions that limited the exclusionary rule's reach, an issue further explained in chapters 7 and 8.

————

The full impact of *Mapp v. Ohio* cannot be assessed only by looking at how it influenced police behavior and the disposition of state criminal cases. The decision was also significant because it sparked the

CHAPTER 7

The Warren Court's Criminal Procedure Revolution and the Political Aftermath

As revolutionary as it seemed when it was decided, the Supreme Court decision in *Mapp v. Ohio* was just a precursor of what would come later in the Warren Court era. In what many have called the "criminal due process revolution," the Court handed down a series of decisions that significantly expanded constitutional protection for the criminally accused. This was accomplished through the incorporation of guarantees within the first eight amendments of the Bill of Rights into the due process clause of the Fourteenth Amendment. In the eight years between *Mapp v. Ohio* and 1969, Chief Justice Earl Warren's final year on the Court, the Supreme Court absorbed rights guaranteed in the Fifth, Sixth, and Eighth Amendments to apply against state governments, in addition to the federal government. This occurred at the same time the Supreme Court liberalized rules governing federal writs of habeas corpus, thereby ensuring a steady stream of appeals from state criminal defendants on federal constitutional grounds.

During this same period the Court also handed down decisions that elaborated upon *Mapp v. Ohio* and the exclusionary rule. By the end of Earl Warren's tenure as chief justice, intense criticism of the Court's criminal procedure decisions, aggravated by escalating crime rates and social and political unrest, contributed to the election of Richard Nixon and the appointment of conservative "strict constructionists" to the Supreme Court. This chapter reviews these developments.

Mapp v. Ohio marked the turning point for the Warren Court's expansion of constitutional protection for the rights of the accused. Within the next eight years the Court incorporated into the due process clause of the Fourteenth Amendment the Fifth Amendment privilege against self-incrimination and the protection against double jeopardy; Sixth

Amendment rights to the assistance of counsel, to confront witnesses, to a speedy trial, to an impartial jury, and to compulsory process; and the Eighth Amendment prohibition against cruel and unusual punishments. Some scholars have referred to this nationalization of the Bill of Rights as the "creation of a second bill of rights" because of the extensive scope of the Court's rulings. While some believe the Warren Court's incorporation decisions were its most important legacy, an equal number of critics assailed the Court for its judicial activism and disruption of the balance of power between the federal government and the states.

The Bill of Rights was added to the Constitution in 1791 in response to Anti-Federalist concerns that the federal government, whose powers were greatly expanded under the new Constitution, could become oppressive and abuse individual rights and liberties. At the time the amendments were not directed against the states because the consensus was that the federal government was the more likely threat. This conclusion was affirmed by the Supreme Court in *Barron v. Baltimore* (1833) and several cases prior to the Civil War. However, ratification of the Fourteenth Amendment opened the door to the possibility that its due process clause be utilized to incorporate the first eight amendments of the Bill of Rights as a limitation on the power of the states. Over the next several decades, several Supreme Court justices called for such an approach. Some justices urged "total incorporation" of all the rights embodied in the first eight amendments; others believed rights should be "selectively" incorporated depending on whether they were considered "fundamental." In the end, different majorities on the Court chose the latter approach. Beginning in 1925, the Supreme Court incorporated the right to freedom of speech into the due process clause of the Fourteenth Amendment (*Gitlow v. New York*), followed by the right to freedom of press (*Near v. Minnesota*, 1931) and freedom of peaceable assembly (*De Jonge v. Oregon*, 1937). However, the Court never fully explained its theory behind why these rights were fundamental and therefore meritorious of protection from both federal and state abuses of power.

The Court later articulated its approach to the absorption of Bill of Rights guarantees into the Fourteenth Amendment due process clause in its decision in *Palko v. Connecticut* (1937). Although the Court majority rejected the appellant's contention that the Fifth Amendment guarantee against double jeopardy should apply to the states, it used the case to articulate its selective incorporation doctrine. Justice Benjamin Cardozo, writing for the majority, explained that some, but not all, of the provisions in the Bill of Rights were in a "preferred position" and that the Court should incorporate only those rights that are "implicit in the concept of ordered liberty" and "so rooted in the traditions and conscience of our people as to be ranked as fundamental." He suggested that rights the Court had absorbed into the due process clause reflected "the belief that neither liberty nor justice would exist if they were sacrificed."

Cardozo contended that when considering whether a right should be incorporated, the Court should ask whether violation of the right would be "so shocking that our polity will not bear it" or whether it would contravene the "fundamental principles of liberty and justice which lie at the base of all our civil and political institutions." If a majority of the U.S. Supreme Court decided this was the case, then the right would be considered in a "preferred position," and thus worthy of absorption.

The next rights deemed fundamental and incorporated into the due process clause were the right to the free exercise of religion (*Cantwell v. Connecticut*, 1940), the right against the establishment of religion (*Everson v. Board of Education*, 1947), the right to be free from unreasonable search and seizure (*Wolf v. Colorado*, 1949), and the right to freedom of association (*NAACP v. Alabama*, 1958). With the First Amendment fully incorporated and the right against unreasonable searches and seizures incorporated through *Wolf* and, later, extended to the exclusionary rule in *Mapp v. Ohio*, consideration of other guarantees protecting the rights of criminal defendants seemed all but inevitable.

The Supreme Court had tackled criminal procedural rights before. However, it employed an alternative approach to incorporation. Rather than declaring, as it had in the First Amendment cases, that the actual guarantee was fully absorbed into the due process clause of the Fourteenth Amendment, the Court examined, on a case-by-case basis, whether a criminal defendant received a "fair hearing" as a requirement of due process. In so doing, however, it implicitly declared that Bill of Rights guarantees protecting criminal defendants were not fundamental and therefore not incorporated into the due process clause of the Fourteenth Amendment.

The Court's initial reluctance to use selective incorporation to apply criminal procedure rights against state action disappeared under the Warren Court. *Mapp v. Ohio* was the catalyst. The Warren Court's efforts have been described as the "criminal due process revolution" because the decisions significantly expanded the rights of criminal defendants in state courts. The impact of these criminal procedure decisions was widespread because law enforcement investigatory activities and the prosecution of criminal defendants are handled largely at the state and local level. Federalizing these guarantees would affect millions of cases each year. Many judicial scholars have observed that the Warren Court's due process revolution was its most important legacy.

––––––

A change in the Supreme Court's composition provided the means for the incorporation floodgates. In 1962, John F. Kennedy made two appointments to the Supreme Court; moderate Byron Raymond White replaced outgoing conservative Charles Whittaker, and Arthur Joseph Goldberg replaced the ailing Felix Frankfurter. Goldberg, a liberal judicial activist, quickly aligned himself with Chief Justice Earl Warren and Justices Hugo Black, William Brennan, and William O. Douglas, giving the chief justice a majority strongly in favor of using the due process clause to expand constitutional protection for the criminally accused. The remaining four justices opposed incorporation. John Marshall Harlan, as illustrated by his strong dissent in *Mapp v. Ohio*, endorsed a philosophy of judicial restraint and was most opposed to using the due process clause to incorporate Bill of Rights guarantees against the states. He was joined, but to a lesser degree, by Justice Potter Stewart and the recently seated White. Justice Tom C. Clark, who authored *Mapp*, was also reluctant to embrace the Court's march toward incorporation. However, as his dialogue with Justice Harlan in *Mapp* illustrated, he could be persuaded to join the liberal block in its effort to selectively incorporate certain fundamental guarantees.

Following *Mapp v. Ohio*, the next right declared fundamental and therefore absorbed into the Fourteenth Amendment due process clause was the Eighth Amendment ban against cruel and unusual punishment (*Robinson v. California*, 1962). The Warren Court's most celebrated decision, *Gideon v. Wainwright* (1963), which extended the right to the assistance of counsel to indigents charged with serious offenses in state courts, was delivered the following year. The Court also ruled that indigents convicted of a crime must be provided counsel in their first appeal (*Douglas v. California*, 1963). Next, the Court allowed the privilege against self-incrimination to be incorporated into the Fourteenth Amendment due process clause and applied to the states (*Malloy v. Hogan*, 1964), followed by one's Fifth Amendment "right of confrontation" (*Pointer v. Texas*, 1965).

The Warren Court's most controversial decision, *Miranda v. Arizona*, was decided in 1966. *Miranda* expanded upon two 1964 decisions, *Massiah v. United States* and *Escobedo v. Illinois*, regarding the nature of police custodial interrogation practices. In *Miranda*, the Court declared that, when evaluating the voluntariness of an individual's confession while in police custody, courts consider whether police used procedural safeguards "to secure the privilege against self-incrimination." The Court also detailed these safeguards, which are commonly referred to as "Miranda warnings." The Court then extended *Mapp*'s exclusionary rule to police interrogations and confessions, noting that illegally obtained confessions must be excluded from trial. Use of the exclusionary remedy, the majority reasoned, would force police to respect the accused's right to protection against self-incrimination while in police custody. If *Mapp* was the "Bunker Hill" of the due process revolution, then *Miranda* was its "Yorktown."

The following year the Warren Court turned to the Sixth Amendment and extended two guarantees to the states: the right to compulsory process (*Washington v. Texas*, 1967) and the right to a speedy trial (*Klopfer v. North Carolina*, 1967). In 1968, the Court extended the Sixth Amendment right to trial by jury in state criminal proceedings against the states (*Duncan v. Louisiana*). The Warren Court's nationalization of the Bill of Rights culminated the following year in a decision that overturned *Palko v. Connecticut* and applied the Fifth Amendment ban against double jeopardy to the states (*Benton v. Maryland*, 1969). Two years later the Eighth Amendment prohibition against excessive bail was assumed to be incorporated (*Schilb v. Kuebel*, 1971).

By the end of Warren's final term, most of the criminal procedure guarantees included in the Bill of Rights had been incorporated into the due process clause of the Fourteenth Amendment. The remaining one, which remains unincorporated today, is the Fifth Amendment requirement that one be prosecuted by grand jury indictment.

Other unincorporated guarantees outside of the criminal procedure realm include the Second Amendment right to bear arms, the Third Amendment prohibition of quartering soldiers, and the Seventh Amendment requirement of jury trials in civil suits involving twenty dollars or more. From 1925 until the end of Warren's term, shifting majorities on the Court had endorsed the selective incorporation doctrine, which, one observer noted, "possesses both the virtues of flexibility and compromise and the vices of selectivity and uncertainty."

———

The Warren Court's judicial activism, especially during the last several years of Warren's tenure, is undisputed. There are different theories as to why the Warren Court so aggressively focused on the rights of criminal defendants. Some observers saw the decisions as part of the Court's broader effort to ensure equal justice for all Americans, including criminal defendants. They note that its criminal procedure decisions should be read along with its opinions dealing with race because the Court aimed to address injustices felt primarily in communities of color. Others saw the criminal due process revolution as inevitable because of the inability of state legislatures to address law enforcement abuses in their own courts. Still others suggested that the federalization of criminal procedural rights was the result of the justices' personal experience with police misconduct and the inability of state courts to stop these abuses. Chief Justice Earl Warren, a former prosecutor, would himself characterize these decisions as an attempt to professionalize police and ensure more effective law enforcement. In his 1972 book, *A Republic, If You Can Keep It*, he explained that the decisions were aimed at ridding law enforcement of its coercive and unethical features and addressing procedural flaws in a system that disadvantaged criminal defendants. "We must have vigorous enforcement of the law, but that enforcement must be fair, equal in its application, and in accordance with our time-honored and loudly professed freedoms."

All revolutions attract their share of critics, and the Warren Court's criminal procedure revolution was no different. Some targeted the Court's use of the selective incorporation doctrine as inappropriate because it had no basis in history or law. Even those supportive of the decisions in principle called attention to the Court's undisciplined approach and its inability to justify its activism. Other critics suggested that incorporation of rights against the states was counterproductive because it frustrated state and local governments from serving as "laboratories of democracy" able to experiment and arrive at their own solutions to meet the challenges of enforcing their criminal law. Moreover, they added, the doctrine of incorporation erodes the principle of federalism, which also safeguards individual liberties.

The bulk of the criticism focused on the practical implications of the Court's rulings. As occurred in the aftermath of *Mapp v. Ohio*, these criminal procedure decisions, especially *Miranda v. Arizona*, were viewed as a threat to public safety. Because several of the Court's decisions were directed at police investigatory activities that take place at the pretrial stage of the criminal process, where police and prosecutors have the greatest amount of discretion, they were characterized as interfering with law enforcement's ability to effectively do its job. The decisions were also assailed for "handcuffing" the police and "coddling criminals" and transforming a trial from focusing on the guilt of the defendant into a "search for technical error."

Overall, the reaction to the Supreme Court's selective incorporation of Bill of Rights guarantees was mixed and, as often occurs, depended largely on one's personal political ideology. Those who believed criminal defendants needed additional constitutional protection, which they felt was unavailable in many states, were pleased with the Warren Court's activism, whereas those who believed the decision negatively affected law enforcement and interfered with state's rights opposed the Court.

With a great deal of the attention on the Warren Court's criminal procedure revolution following *Mapp v. Ohio*, it is easy to overlook the fact that the Court also handed down several decisions in these final years that clarified some questions left unanswered by *Mapp* and affected the exclusionary rule's reach. Moreover, the Court issued several important rulings on the substantive scope of the Fourth Amendment that would be used by future courts to restrict the exclusionary rule's application.

In addition to *Miranda v. Arizona*, which extended the exclusionary rule to illegally obtained confessions from suspects in police custody as a command of the Fifth Amendment, there were five major Warren Court exclusionary rule decisions following *Mapp v. Ohio*. In *Ker v. California* (1963), the Court clarified which standard should govern searches and seizures, declaring that while states have the general authority to determine what is reasonable, "the standard of reasonableness is the same under the Fourth and Fourteenth Amendments." The Court explicitly answered that states would now be governed by federal standards, which would make *Mapp*'s implementation easier.

Two decisions expanded the exclusionary rule's reach. In *Wong Sun v. United States* (1963), the exclusionary rule was extended to verbal evidence obtained in a warrantless search. The Court ruled that confessions following an arrest without probable cause were "fruits" of an unlawful search and therefore inadmissible. The Court also used the opportunity to clarify and uphold its "fruit of the poisonous tree" doctrine, which included the "independent source exception" and "attenuation" exception established under previous courts. And, in *One 1958 Plymouth Sedan v. Pennsylvania* (1965), a unanimous Court applied the exclusionary rule to forfeiture proceedings, reasoning that although this is a civil action, the penalty is as harsh as in a criminal proceeding, hence, such proceedings were, by nature, "criminal."

However, the Warren Court also limited *Mapp v. Ohio* by declining to apply the decision retrospectively. *Linkletter v. Walker* (1965) reflected the majority's concern with implementation of *Mapp* and the problem of a "jail delivery" — that retrospective application would open the door to thousands of cases, thereby taxing the administration of criminal justice. *Linkletter* is also noteworthy because the Court most clearly emphasized one rationale for the exclusionary rule — that it was targeted at deterring police misconduct — and ignored the rationales of the imperative of judicial integrity and healthy federalism. The majority construed the rule as not "a right or privilege accorded to the defendants charged with crime but as a sort of punishment against officers in order to keep them from depriving people of their constitutional rights." This focus on the deterrence rationale would resurface over the next several decades as the Supreme Court reinterpreted *Mapp* and the principles underlying the exclusionary rule.

Another important exclusionary rule decision was handed down in 1969, Warren's final year on the Court. In *Alderman v. United States*, the Supreme Court denied the exclusionary remedy to defendants who did not have standing. The majority held that suppression of illegally seized evidence can be "successfully urged only by those whose rights were violated in the search itself, not by those who are aggrieved solely by the introduction of damaging evidence. Coconspirators and codefendants have been accorded no special standing." The decision clarified that Fourth Amendment rights were "personal rights" of the accused that did not extend to third parties who were trying to challenge another's search that may have yielded evidence against them. The majority was unconvinced that the "benefits of extending the exclusionary rule to other defendants would justify further encroachment upon the public interest in prosecuting those accused of crime and having them acquitted or convicted on the basis of all the evidence which exposes the truth." The Court's use of this cost-benefit rationale for evaluating the applicability of the exclusionary rule would be used in later years when the Court was asked to apply the rule to other situations.

In addition to its exclusionary rule decisions, the Warren Court also both expanded and limited the substantive reach of the Fourth Amendment. These decisions are important to the exclusionary rule debate because the level of constitutional protection provided against unreasonable searches and seizures affects whether one can raise an exclusionary rule challenge.

The Warren Court handed down only a few decisions extending Fourth Amendment protection into new areas, such as wiretapping and electronic eavesdropping. For example, in *Katz v. United States* (1967), the Court adopted the modern "privacy" approach to the Fourth Amendment, holding that "the Fourth Amendment protects people, not places." The majority explained that it protects people in a place where they have a "reasonable expectation of privacy." Not protected, however, was what a person knowingly exposes to the public, a doctrine later known as "public exposure." Both the "reasonable expectation of privacy" standard and the "public exposure" doctrine announced in *Katz* would be used by future Supreme Courts to limit Fourth Amendment protection. *Katz* is also important because the Warren Court professed its preference that searches by law enforcement be made pursuant to a warrant. The Court also strengthened the standards necessary for issuance of search warrants based on hearsay evidence, ruling in *Aguillar v. Texas* (1964) and *Spinelli v. United States*

(1969) that information provided on a warrant affidavit be "reliable" and that it be "independently verified."

However, it is problematic to assume that the Warren Court only liberalized Fourth Amendment protection for criminal defendants. The Court also created a number of exceptions to the requirement that police officers obtain a warrant before conducting a search. Significantly, two rulings issued in the waning days of the Warren Court significantly limited the substantive reach of the Fourth Amendment and therefore the exclusionary rule. As one commentator observed, the "Warren Court sowed the seeds for the destruction of its own decisions."

In *Camara v. Municipal Court* (1967), despite noting that warrantless administrative searches were generally unprotected by the Fourth Amendment, the Court stated that some searches, such as those that would not lead to criminal prosecution, could be conducted without individualized suspicion of wrongdoing or a warrant as long as they were considered "reasonable." While at first blush *Camara* appeared to expand Fourth Amendment protection to administrative searches by reaffirming the warrant requirement, a closer look at the decision illustrates that the Court had actually lowered the threshold necessary for certain kinds of administrative searches. As long as a search was reasonable, the Court was stating, warrants based on the traditional probable cause standard were unnecessary.

Another class of warrantless searches declared "reasonable" and allowable under the Fourteenth Amendment was announced in *Terry v. Ohio* (1967). The case involved the constitutionality of so-called stop and frisk searches by law enforcement, where police detain a suspicious person for questioning and conduct a limited "pat down" search. Writing for an eight-justice majority, Chief Justice Warren ruled that these limited searches, conducted with "reasonable suspicion," were permissible in order to protect officer safety. Despite acknowledging that such searches were an "intrusion upon cherished personal security" and an "annoying, frightening and perhaps humiliating experience," the Court held that they should be governed "by the Fourth Amendment's general proscription against unreasonable searches and seizures." The Court also recognized that there were practical limitations to the exclusionary rule in these types of situations because police may not be interested in the arrest and prosecution of a person.

Terry v. Ohio was a landmark decision in its own right that would affect future developments in Fourth Amendment jurisprudence. As law professor Joshua Dressler explained, "*Terry* provided the impetus, as well as the framework, for a move by the Supreme Court away from the proposition that warrantless searches are per se unreasonable, to the competing view that the appropriate test of police conduct 'is not whether it is reasonable to procure a search warrant, but whether the search was reasonable.'" This "warrant preference construction" of the Fourth Amendment would give way to the "generalized reasonableness" construction of the Amendment.

The Warren Court's criminal procedure decisions were handed down in a time of social upheaval and rising crime rates. Although it is likely the crime rate would have increased regardless of the Court's decisions, the fact that the two occurred simultaneously practically ensured the public would associate the increase in crime with the Warren Court. This perception was aided by politicians willing to exploit the apparent link between the two. The public's growing discontent with a Court it believed was out of touch would shape presidential politics, lead to national legislative battles to reverse the Warren Court's criminal procedure decisions, and influence appointments to the U.S. Supreme Court.

Crime control became a national political issue for the very first time in the 1964 presidential contest between Republican Barry Goldwater and Democrat Lyndon Baines Johnson. It was Goldwater who first tapped into the public's fears. He made crime his primary domestic policy issue, arguing that because it had increased during Democratic administrations, the party's "soft on crime" approach was responsible. Although Goldwater would lose the election in a landslide, Johnson was a shrewd enough politician to realize the Republican was on to something. Capitalizing on the crime issue was also a political necessity; between 1964 and 1968, the incidences of reported crime would double, and public opinion polls consistently ranked crime as the dominant concern for most Americans. Upon taking the oath of office, Johnson placed considerable effort into finding ways to address the growing crime rate. His actions while in office ushered in a new era of federal involvement that has continued to this day.

On March 8, 1965, in his first speech to Congress, Johnson delivered his "Message on Law Enforcement on the Administration of Justice." He called for increased cooperation between the federal government and state and local governments to combat crime. His focus was on addressing root cause of crime, including poverty and lack of education. Several months later he signed Executive Order 11236, which created the President's Commission on Law Enforcement and the Administration of Justice. He charged the bipartisan commission with investigating the causes of crime and delinquency and providing recommendations on improving the administration of criminal justice.

In 1967 the commission forwarded to the president its report, *The Challenge of Crime in a Free Society*, which presented more than 200 recommendations on how to address the rising crime rate. While the report acknowledged that the Warren Court had issued landmark criminal procedure decisions that affected the administration of justice, it did not blame the Court for the increase in crime, nor did it call for a legislative or judicial strategy to combat these decisions. In regard to *Mapp v. Ohio's* exclusionary rule, the report noted that despite costs such as "complex and time-consuming court procedures" and the fact that "guilty criminals may be set free because the court's exclusionary rules prevent the introduction of a confession or of seized evidence," the exclusionary rule was "the product of two centuries of constitutional development in this country. They are integral parts of a system for balancing the interests of the individual and the state that has served the nation well."

Two weeks after receiving the report, President Johnson proposed Omnibus Crime Control and Safe Streets Act of 1967, which called for dedicated funding for improving criminal justice in the states. There was broad support for the proposal from the law enforcement community, as well as special interest organizations such as the American Civil Liberties Union. After it was sent to Congress, the House and Senate Judiciary Committees held hearings on the bill. While deliberation in the House was highly supportive of the administration's effort, it was a different story in the Senate.

Conservative southern senators used the opportunity to attack the Supreme Court's criminal procedure decisions, particularly *Miranda v. Arizona* and the *Miranda* rule of exclusion. Senators John L. McClellan (D-AR), Sam J. Ervin (D-NC), and Strom Thurmond (D-SC) led the effort. The trio found itself on familiar ground, having previously attacked the Court for its school desegregation and busing decisions.

In the first session of the Ninetieth Congress, Senators McClellan and Ervin introduced a number of bills to amend Johnson's proposed legislation. Senate Bill 676 was specifically directed at *Miranda*. The proposal would allow the admission of confessions into evidence if the trial judge alone determined it was voluntary. The trial court judge would have sole discretion in making this decision, regardless of the presence of *Miranda* warnings. Introducing the amendment, McClellan blamed the Supreme Court for the country's rising crime rate, remarking that with each Supreme Court decision expanding criminal procedure rights, the crime rate had increased. It was a powerful rhetorical device. The senator ominously warned, "This country is moving toward chaos. Just a few more Supreme Court decisions further to shackle law enforcement officials in their work and their responsibility, and we will finally reach the point that there will be no competent, legal, valid evidence which anyone can present against a criminal because it would infringe upon his rights if we expose his conduct."

In March 1967, hearings on S. 676 and twelve other amendments to Johnson's bill were held before the Senate Subcommittee on Criminal Laws and Procedure, chaired by McClellan. The proposal to modify *Miranda* dominated the proceedings. Testifying before the subcommittee were members of the law enforcement community, including chiefs of police, district attorneys, and conservative judges, all of whom called for the reversal of *Miranda* and other Warren Court criminal procedure decisions, including *Mapp*. In addition, dozens of letters from the law enforcement community and newspaper editorials regarding *Miranda*'s impact on crime were placed in the record. One was hard-pressed to find witnesses appearing in opposition to the amendment. Although the constitutionality of the bill was raised by several senators who argued that because *Miranda* was a constitutional ruling, it could be reversed only by a constitutional amendment, opposition to the decision was so great that the amendment passed handily.

Senate Bill 676 was included as Title II of the President's Omnibus Crime Control and Safe Streets Act. It amended Title 18 of the U.S.

Code to provide new standards for the admission of confessions and eyewitness testimony in federal courts. By giving the trial court judge sole discretion to determine the voluntariness of a confession, Title II circumvented the Supreme Court's ruling in *Miranda v. Arizona*. The revised Crime Control and Safe Streets Act was sent to the president, who faced a dilemma. Johnson knew the public expected presidential action addressing the increase in crime, which he promised, and the revised bill still included federal funding to the states. However, his administration strongly opposed the Senate's modifications. Ultimately, Johnson signed the bill because he understood a veto would have a negative political effect, and he wanted federal funding for state and local law enforcement.

Johnson later found a way to circumvent the implementation of Title II. Immediately after passage of the legislation, he instructed his attorney general, Ramsey Clark, Justice Tom C. Clark's son, that Title II not be invoked and that, instead, federal prosecutors only use evidence obtained under *Miranda*'s requirements. It would set a precedent for future presidential administrations, which also refused to call upon this portion of the legislation. And, several decades later the Supreme Court would rule on its constitutionality after conservative groups led an effort to force the federal government to implement the legislation.

———

At the same time President Lyndon Johnson was shepherding the Omnibus Crime Control and Safe Streets Act through Congress, he was embroiled in another, equally contentious battle with southern conservatives in the Senate. Once again, the Warren Court and its criminal procedure decisions would take center stage.

In the summer of 1968, Earl Warren announced his decision to retire from the bench. Johnson, who had announced earlier that year that he was not running for reelection, selected then Associate Justice Abe Fortas to succeed Warren as the next chief justice. To fill Fortas's seat, he nominated Homer Thornberry, a former member of Congress whom he previously elevated to a federal district court judgeship and, later, to the Fifth Circuit Court of Appeals. Although a lame-duck president, Johnson was confident his skill in working the Senate would lead to a successful confirmation of both jurists. The

Fortas nomination in particular did not appear to be a problem because he was unanimously confirmed as an associate justice only three years earlier. The choice of Thornberry, a friend of Johnson, appeared to be a greater challenge, as he expected charges of cronyism, but the president had carefully chosen the appellate court judge to appeal to southern senators.

But Johnson miscalculated. First, there was the expected criticism from Republicans unhappy that a lame-duck president was rushing the most important decision of who should lead the Supreme Court. Second was Fortas's decision to appear before the Senate Judiciary Committee. His appearance was unprecedented — he was the first nominee to the chief justiceship and only the second sitting justice to appear before the committee — and the hearing was a disaster. Fortas not only was intensely grilled about his personal relationship with Johnson and whether he had served as an informal adviser to the president; he also faced intensely hostile questions about the Warren Court's criminal procedure decisions. The questioning, led by Senator Strom Thurmond of South Carolina and Senator Sam Ervin of North Carolina, moved far beyond inquiring about Fortas's judicial philosophy and into a referendum on the Warren Court.

After several days of acrimonious debate, the Senate Judiciary Committee decided to delay its vote on the Fortas nomination until after the August recess. It was an effective strategy for those seeking to derail the nomination. Delay allows the opposition to organize and gather more information on the candidate. With the November election looming, there was every reason to stall.

When the Senate Judiciary Committee met in mid-September to vote on the nomination, Justice Fortas received a divided but favorable vote. In spite of this initial victory, however, his candidacy was doomed. Senators soon learned that Fortas had inappropriately received a fee for teaching a course at American University in Washington, D.C. It was enough fodder for the Republicans to organize a weeklong filibuster to stall the nomination. Attempts to end the filibuster failed, and Fortas eventually asked Johnson to withdraw his nomination. Fortas would remain on the bench as an associate justice, but his prospects for the center chair were now over. Thornberry's nomination was a moot point. It was early October, days before the Supreme Court's 1968 term was about to begin. Johnson took Fortas's name off the table and told the nation that Chief Justice Warren had decided to remain on the bench until a successor was chosen. At the same time, he announced that he would not be nominating another candidate for the chief justice position. That responsibility would fall to the thirty-seventh president of the United States.

The failed Fortas nomination ushered in a new era of the politics of judicial selection. Politicians from both sides of the aisle would thereafter seize Senate confirmation hearings as a way to challenge presidential nominations to the Court. Democratic senators would get their turn if a Republican was elected to the White House.

With domestic and international unrest, it was inevitable that the 1968 presidential campaign would focus on crime. Presidential candidate Richard Nixon duplicated Barry Goldwater's 1964 campaign strategy, running on a "law-and-order" platform and blaming previous Democratic administrations for being soft on crime. But Nixon also directly targeted the U.S. Supreme Court. He criticized it for its "liberal excesses" and, in particular, its criminal procedure rulings, the cumulative impact of which, he argued, "has been to set free patently guilty individuals on the basis of legal technicalities."

In his acceptance speech at the 1968 Republican National Convention, Nixon spoke of how the courts "have gone too far in weakening the peace forces against the criminal forces of this country," and he continued castigating the Warren Court on the general election campaign trail. One observer went so far as to say that Nixon campaigned against the Warren Court almost as much as he campaigned against his Democratic opponent, Senator Hubert Humphrey of Minnesota. Nixon vowed to restore balance to the Supreme Court through his judicial nominations. He promised to appoint strict constructionists to the bench, "men that try to interpret the law and don't try to make the law" and who would "not twist or bend the Constitution in order to perpetuate [their] personal, political and social values." It was a successful strategy. His attack on the Warren Court mirrored the concerns of a majority of Americans. A 1968 Harris poll revealed that 81 percent of Americans believed there was a breakdown in law and order, and a Gallup poll that same year revealed that almost two-thirds of Americans agreed with Nixon that the Warren Court was "soft on crime."

———

Once elected, Nixon had the chance to shape the Supreme Court in his own image. The opportunity to appoint justices varies considerably across presidential administrations. On average, a seat opens up roughly once every two to three years. Nixon had the rare opportunity to make four appointments during his first term in office. By 1971 the president successfully elevated four conservative justices, including a new chief justice, to the Supreme Court.

Nixon's first two appointments came within six months of his inauguration. After Chief Justice Warren announced his retirement for the second time, Nixon nominated Warren E. Burger to the center chair. Burger, a lifelong moderate Republican active in party politics, was an Eisenhower appointee to the U.S. Court of Appeals for the District of Columbia Circuit, where he served for thirteen years. He had a reputation as a "champion" of law and order and was known as an outspoken critic of the Warren Court's criminal procedure jurisprudence. In particular, Burger was a foe of the exclusionary rule. In a 1964 law review article, "Who Will Watch the Watchman?" Burger criticized *Mapp v. Ohio* as a product of judicial activism that intruded upon the power of the states. He suggested that the exclusionary rule was ineffective at deterring police practices, noting, "It is my belief that tested by the standard of practical consequences, by tangible results, by measurable improvement, this important doctrine of our jurisprudence has not been a notable success in achieving its stated objective." Burger also alleged that the exclusionary rule damaged the integrity of the criminal justice system. He suggested that "a vast number of people are losing respect for law and the administration of justice because they think that the Suppression Doctrine is *defeating* justice." In spite of Democratic control, there was little political opposition to Burger in the Senate, and the confirmation process was swift.

Nixon's second opportunity for a Supreme Court appointment came a short time later. That summer, the ethics controversy over Justice Abe Fortas grew after Nixon administration officials gave then Chief Justice Warren evidence Fortas had inappropriately accepted a consulting fee for a foundation under investigation. It was enough to force Fortas to resign from the bench. Nixon, committed to appointing a southerner, made two ill-advised nominations to fill the seat. Nominees Clement F. Haynsworth and G. Harrold Carswell came under fire for ethical lapses and inexperience, respectively, and Nixon became the first president since Grover Cleveland to have two successive nominees defeated in the Senate. After Nixon angrily denounced the Senate for its bias against southerners and vowed not to nominate another candidate from the South, only to subject that person to the "malicious character assassination" endured by his previous nominees, his nomination of Eighth Circuit Court of Appeals judge Harry A. Blackmun was confirmed. Blackmun, who would later refer to himself as "Old No. 3," acknowledging the path that brought him to the Court, was considered a moderate on civil rights issues and, most important to the president, a conservative on criminal defendants' issues. He endorsed a philosophy of judicial restraint and believed law enforcement officials should be provided deference so they could effectively do their job.

Nixon's next two opportunities to fill seats on the high bench came the following fall, in 1971, after the retirement of Justices Hugo Black and John Marshall Harlan. The president nominated Lewis F. Powell and William Hubbs Rehnquist, respectively, to the bench, and the confirmation process for the two candidates could not have been more different. Powell, an attorney for an elite law firm in Virginia with extensive public service experience, was widely respected in the legal and political community. He was regarded as a centrist with conservative leanings and was attractive to Nixon because he had been openly critical of some of the Warren Court's criminal procedure decisions, observing that the Court "may have gone too far." He was confirmed with ease. The Senate was saving its energy for Rehnquist.

Rehnquist was well known in legal and political circles as a partisan committed to a conservative political and judicial ideology. He was active in the Republican Party, having served as its attorney from 1958 to 1966, and he played a role in Barry Goldwater's 1964 presidential campaign. Rehnquist next served as the assistant attorney general in the Office of Legal Council in the Department of Justice from 1969 to 1971, during which time he supported abolishment of the exclusionary rule, habeas corpus proceedings, and *Miranda* warnings.

He also supported greater authority of law enforcement to engage in warrantless wiretapping and surveillance of criminal suspects, "no-knock" entry into homes of criminal suspects, and preventative detention of criminal suspects before trial. Naturally, he was an outspoken critic of the Warren Court.

The Rehnquist nomination concerned Senate Democrats, wary another Nixon appointee would tip the Court's balance firmly to the right. Civil liberties groups also expressed alarm about the candidate. Rehnquist was grilled intensely during the Senate Judiciary Committee hearing, and his nomination was almost derailed when, prior to the floor vote, senators learned that in 1952, while serving as a clerk for Justice Robert Jackson, Rehnquist had written a memo on a pending case, *Brown v. Board of Education*, in which he argued in favor of upholding *Plessy v. Ferguson* (1896) and the "separate but equal" doctrine. Rehnquist maintained that the memo was a rough draft of Jackson's views, a claim many found disingenuous, and Senate Democrats were able to filibuster against confirmation for several days. However, after almost a week of delay, several Senate Democrats joined Republicans in voting for "cloture," a sixty-vote majority necessary to end a filibuster, and Rehnquist was elevated to the Court in a divided vote.

With four conservative appointees on the bench, the Court's balance shifted just as Nixon desired and Warren Court supporters feared. The "conservative bloc" now consisted of Burger, Blackmun, and Powell, who replaced liberals Warren, Fortas, and Black, and Rehnquist, who replaced the equally conservative Harlan. The "liberal bloc" consisted of William O. Douglas, William J. Brennan, and Thurgood Marshall. The two swing votes were provided by Justice Potter Stewart, an Eisenhower appointee regarded as a moderate, and Byron R. White, a Kennedy appointee who frequently deferred to law enforcement and voted in favor of the government.

President Richard Nixon now had a solid conservative majority on the Supreme Court. However, appointments to the Court do not always turn out as presidents wish — approximately one in four eventually disappoint — so Nixon needed a backup plan. He focused his attention on working with Congress to legislatively address some of what he believed were the more egregious Warren Court decisions, including *Mapp v. Ohio* and its imposition of the exclusionary rule on the states. After President Lyndon Johnson successfully elevated crime as a major national domestic issue, there was an expectation that the executive branch would be involved in formulating public policy to address crime control. However, Nixon faced a problem, which had already manifested itself during his efforts to select individuals to the U.S. Supreme Court: a Congress controlled by the opposing party. Whether the administration would be successful in its efforts to legislatively address the Warren Court was an open question. And, to make matters worse, the crime rate continued to climb.

———

The Nixon administration worked with members of Congress from both political parties to legislatively attack the exclusionary rule in the same manner in which it addressed *Miranda v. Arizona* in the 1968 Crime Control and Safe Streets Act. The attempt would be unsuccessful, but the fact that the issue maintained its spot on the political agenda was a testament to the level of interest in using legislation to address unfavorable Supreme Court decisions.

In 1971, during the first session of the Ninety-second Congress, Senator Lloyd Bentsen (D-TX) introduced Senate Bill 2657, which would limit the federal exclusionary rule to apply only to those illegal searches and seizures that were considered "substantial." The bill was modeled after a draft proposal by the American Law Institute (ALI) released in 1971. The ALI, torn between members who wanted to discard the exclusionary rule altogether and those who wanted to keep it, proposed that the federal courts invoke a "substantiality test" for application of the exclusionary rule. To determine if the misconduct was substantial, the ALI proposal required the presiding judge to evaluate the importance of the interest violated, the extent of deviation from lawful conduct, the extent to which the violation was willful, and the extent to which the violation prejudiced the defendant. Regarding the "fruits" of an unlawful search, if the evidence would have been discovered eventually, then it would be admissible despite violations of the code.

There was criticism of the Bentsen bill. Most was directed at the fact that the proposal would not allow exclusion of evidence even if it was constitutionally required. Others expressed concern that the bill did not allow for a remedy for exclusionary rule violations. Consequently, the bill stalled. However, the exclusionary rule remained prominent on the political agenda, and the bill was reintroduced in February 1973. This version, Senate Bill 881, was also modeled after the ALI's substantiality test, but with one modification. Under this proposal, victims of an illegal search were provided a remedy. The proposal would amend the Federal Tort Claims Act to allow victims of illegal searches to sue the government for up to $25,000 in actual and punitive damages. If the person won the suit, he or she would then be precluded from suing the officer(s) who conducted the search. However, this bill also eventually died as Democratic senators, resistant to attempts to reverse the Warren Court's criminal procedure decisions, blocked the legislation.

After failing in its effort to legislatively address *Mapp v. Ohio* and the exclusionary rule, the Nixon administration looked to the newly constituted Burger Court. The president had successfully elevated four conservative justices critical of the Warren Court's criminal procedure decisions, and cases were now moving through the appellate process that presented opportunities to revisit these decisions. It would be only a matter of time before the Burger Court would put its own spin on the Warren Court's criminal procedure revolution.

CHAPTER 8

The Judicial and Political Effort to Undermine *Mapp v. Ohio* and the Future of the Exclusionary Rule

Over the years, the Burger Court has been denounced by civil libertarians for "eroding," "whittling down," or "chipping away" some of the Warren Court's landmark civil rights and civil liberties decisions. Although the extent to which the Burger Court's decisions resulted in the "counterrevolution" is open to interpretation — it stood by, and in fact elaborated upon, landmark decisions concerning women's rights and affirmative action — when it comes to the Court's criminal procedure decisions, these critics are on firmer ground.

The Burger Court's approach to the administration of criminal justice was markedly different from that of the Warren Court. In its criminal procedure decisions the Burger Court more clearly emphasized the "truth-seeking" function of the criminal justice system — placing greater importance on proving the guilt of the defendant rather than safeguarding constitutional rights. And, protection of constitutional rights was often evaluated by whether it negatively affected the law enforcement community's ability to do its job. This was particularly evident with the Burger Court's Fourth and Fifth Amendment exclusionary rule decisions. The Court expanded the number of exceptions to the exclusionary rule, it was unwilling to apply the rule outside of the prosecution's case in chief, and it restricted the situations where a defendant could raise an exclusionary rule challenge. Also significant was the fact that the Burger Court recast the Warren Court's exclusionary rule decisions, including *Mapp v. Ohio*, in a fashion that undermined its basic foundation. After President Ronald Reagan and George H. W. Bush elevated justices to the Supreme Court who embraced a conservative judicial philosophy, the Rehnquist Court then continued this tradition, relying on the Burger Court exclusionary rule decisions to further limit the rule's application.

The assault on the exclusionary rule was not limited to the courts. During President Reagan's two terms in office, his administration led the charge against the rule in the political arena, and there was a final attempt during the William Jefferson Clinton administration. Although these legislative attempts to modify the exclusionary rule would fail, the fact that the debate over its legitimacy continued to resonate in the political arena illustrates how the controversy over this landmark decision continued long after it was handed down by the Supreme Court.

This chapter details the Burger and Rehnquist Courts' major Fourth and Fifth Amendment exclusionary rule decisions. It describes how these Courts replaced the underlying principle in *Mapp v. Ohio* that the exclusionary rule was a constitutional necessity to realize the promise of the Fourth Amendment with the rationale that it was merely a judicially created remedy intended to deter police from Fourth Amendment violations, and explains how this limited the exclusionary rule's application. The chapter also reviews how the Warren Court's criminal procedure decisions, including *Mapp v. Ohio*, continued to affect presidential politics through appointments to the U.S. Supreme Court and federal initiatives to combat crime.

————

Chief Justice Warren Burger was elevated to the high court based on his law-and-order reputation and his outspoken criticism of the Warren Court. Once on the bench, he did not disappoint. In one of his earliest decisions, he criticized the exclusionary rule in a scathing dissenting opinion. The case, *Bivens v. Six Unknown Federal Narcotics Agents* (1971), concerned whether victims of an illegal search by federal agents could sue the federal government for damages. The majority ruled that they could. Dissenting, Burger used the opportunity to denounce the exclusionary rule, arguing that it was both ineffective and costly to society. The chief justice explained that because police did not have the training to understand the exclusionary rule or court decisions interpreting it, and because it was not a direct sanction against the offending officer, it did not provide the "educational value where it is most needed."

Burger criticized the exclusionary rule as a "single, monolithic, and drastic judicial response to all official violations of legal norms" and called for applying it only in situations where the illegal police conduct was "substantial." Burger also questioned whether the exclusionary rule fulfilled its stated objective — deterrence of police misconduct. He remarked that "some clear demonstration of the benefits and effectiveness of the exclusionary rule is required to justify it in view of the high price it exacts from society — the release of countless guilty criminals." Because such evidence did not exist, he concluded that the Court should abandon the exclusionary rule once a "meaningful alternative" was found.

In the mid-1970s, Burger was able to secure a majority to limit the exclusionary rule. The Court confronted several cases where it was asked to extend the exclusionary rule to "collateral settings." It declined to do so, ruling that the exclusionary rule should apply only to the prosecution's case in chief. In the course of deciding these cases, the Burger Court gradually redefined the Warren Court's *Mapp v. Ohio* decision by characterizing the exclusionary rule as a judicially created remedy subject to judicial modification rather than a personal constitutional right. It also emphasized that because the primary purpose of the rule was to deter future police misconduct, if such deterrence was unlikely, the Court should refuse its application. The imperative of judicial integrity and the need for healthy federalism, the two other rationales announced in *Mapp*, were ignored or given cursory attention. It was this evolution — the transformation of the way the exclusionary rule was cast to allow for its modification — that would be the Burger Court's legacy with regard to Fourth and Fifth Amendment exclusionary rule jurisprudence.

In *United States v. Calandra* (1974), the Burger Court considered whether a witness testifying before a grand jury could refuse to answer questions that were based upon information acquired from him in an illegal search. Justice Lewis F. Powell, writing for six members of the Court, reasoned that because the exclusionary rule was not constitutionally required as part of the Fourth Amendment, but was rather a "judicially created remedy designed to safeguard Fourth Amendment rights generally through its deterrent effects rather than a personal constitutional right of the party aggrieved," then the decision to apply the rule in a particular case "presents a question, not of rights, but of remedies." He next outlined how the Court should answer this question, stating that, "as with any remedial device, the application of the rule has been restricted to those areas where its remedial objectives are thought most efficaciously served."

To assess the rule's application, Powell proposed a utilitarian balancing approach — the weighing of the "costs" versus the "benefits" of the exclusionary rule — to answer whether it should be applied to grand jury testimony. Noting that the rule's "prime purpose is to deter future unlawful police conduct and thereby effectuate the guarantee of the Fourth Amendment against unreasonable search and seizure" and not "to redress the injury to the privacy of the search victim," he reasoned that it should be applied only in situations where its benefits outweighed the costs. Using this mechanical approach, Powell concluded that application of the exclusionary rule to grand jury proceedings would achieve only a "speculative and undoubtedly minimal advance in the deterrence of police misconduct" that was outweighed by the need to maintain the integrity of the grand jury's role.

The dissenting opinion by Justice William J. Brennan, joined by William O. Douglas and Thurgood Marshall, faulted the majority for its assertion that the rule was not constitutionally required. The dissent also chastised the Court majority for its sole focus on the deterrence rationale and for ignoring the fact that the exclusionary rule was essential to judicial integrity to ensure citizens "that the government would not profit from its lawless behavior, thus minimizing the risk of seriously undermining popular trust in government." It ended with Brennan's recognition that the exclusionary rule's days might be numbered. "I am left with the uneasy feeling that today's decision may signal that a majority of my colleagues have positioned themselves to . . . abandon altogether the exclusionary rule in search and seizure cases."

Calandra's impact was considerable. By characterizing the exclusionary rule as judicially created rather than constitutionally required, and by employing a utilitarian balancing scheme, the Court established a precedent that the rule should be applied only in situations where its "benefits" outweighed its "costs." Consequently, the application of the rule as a remedial device was limited to situations where it fulfilled its deterrent purpose.

The Burger Court used *Calandra*'s approach over the next several years. In each instance, a slim majority refused to extend the exclusionary rule to settings outside of the criminal trial, while dissenters complained bitterly about the majority's characterization of the exclusionary rule as judicially created rather than constitutionally required, and its "completely freewheeling" balancing of deterrence and the ability of law enforcement to effectively do its job.

In *United States v. Janis* (1976) the Court refused to apply the exclusionary rule to evidence illegally seized by state law enforcement officers in a federal civil proceeding. It reasoned that the deterrent effect of barring such evidence would be "insignificant to the cost of losing the evidence," and that there was not "sufficient justification for the drastic measure of an exclusionary rule." Later that year, in *Stone v. Powell*, the Court refused to apply the exclusionary rule to criminal defendants challenging the legality of their conviction in federal habeas corpus proceedings. The majority reasoned that if a state provided a criminal defendant a "full and fair" opportunity to litigate a claim of a Fourth Amendment violation in state court, then the federal government did not have to grant a state prisoner federal habeas corpus relief to relitigate the issue in federal courts. Deterrence of police misconduct, the majority explained, would not be furthered by expanding a state prisoner's habeas corpus relief on Fourth Amendment grounds.

In *United States v. Havens* (1980), the Court ruled that the government could use illegally obtained evidence to impeach the testimony of a criminal defendant who testified that he was not involved in a crime. The majority explained that while exclusion of evidence from the prosecution's case in chief fulfilled the deterrence objective, exclusion for impeachment would not further this objective and would instead impair "the fact-finding goals of the criminal trial." Four years later the Court refused to extend the exclusionary rule to civil deportation proceedings. In *INS v. Lopez-Mendoza* (1984), it allowed illegally seized evidence to be used against deportees unlawfully arrested by Immigration and Naturalization Service agents, reasoning that the costs of exclusion were too high and "might well result in the suppression of large amounts of information that had been obtained lawfully."

In addition to refusing to extend the exclusionary rule outside of criminal trials, the Burger Court also elaborated upon the exceptions to the "fruit of the poisonous tree doctrine." This doctrine allows the exclusion of "secondary" or "derivative" evidence that results from the primary evidence found in the unlawful police search. Two exceptions to the rule, the "independent source exception" and "attenuation," restricted the doctrine, and in *Nix v. Williams* (1984) the Burger Court recognized a third exception, known as the "inevitable discovery exception" or the "hypothetical independent source." While many lower courts already acknowledged this exception, the Supreme Court had yet to do so. The rationale for the exception was that if the illegally seized evidence would have inevitably been found legally, than the evidence should be admitted, regardless of the illegal search. To apply the exclusionary rule in such a situation, the Court reasoned, "would reject logic, experience, and common sense."

The Burger Court also limited the exclusionary rule's application by restricting who had "standing" to raise a Fourth Amendment challenge. In *Rakas v. Illinois* (1978), a case involving the arrest of passengers in a car that contained evidence which the passengers wanted suppressed, the majority ruled that persons charging a Fourth Amendment violation must have a privacy expectation and a personal property or possessory "interest" in the premise searched or items seized in order to invoke the exclusionary rule. The decision effectively overturned a Warren Court ruling, *Jones v. United States* (1960), where it had determined that if a person was "legitimately on the premises" or "in possession" of the items seized, he or she would automatically have standing to challenge the legality of a search. In *Rakas*, the Burger Court majority took a contrary view, announcing that the proper question was whether the "disputed search infringed an interest of the defendant which the Fourth Amendment was designed to protect." It answered by deciding that the search did not. By rejecting the possibility that a third party could raise a Fourth Amendment claim, the opportunity for an exclusionary rule challenge was voided.

Two years later, in *United States v. Salvucci* (1980) and a companion case, *Rawlings v. Kentucky* (1980), the Burger Court formalized its approach to whether one had standing to raise a Fourth Amendment challenge. It articulated a two-prong test that one have both a "possessory interest" and a "legitimate expectation of privacy" in the area searched. Later, in *United States v. Payner* (1980), the Court ruled that an individual could invoke the exclusionary rule only if the government conduct invaded that person's expectation of privacy and not that of a third party. In this case, the government had encouraged its agents to illegally search another individual in order to gather information ultimately used to prosecute and convict Payner for income tax violations. Despite the fact that Payner was the "target" of the search, the Court reasoned that he was not the actual victim of the illegal search because his personal privacy rights had not been infringed. The Court justified its decision using the cost-benefit analysis previously used to assess the appropriateness of the exclusionary rule in collateral settings, reasoning that when faced with a question of whether it should be applied in this instance, the intentional unlawful activity must be "weighed against the considerable harm that would flow from indiscriminate application of the exclusionary rule," and that "unbending application" of the exclusionary rule would "impede unacceptably the truth finding functions of judge and jury."

———

The Burger Court's refusal to extend the exclusionary rule into new settings such as grand jury testimony, civil tax proceedings, and federal habeas corpus proceedings because it reasoned that there would not be additional deterrence of police misconduct, and its new exception to the "fruit of the poisonous tree" doctrine and restrictions on standing all limited the application of the exclusionary rule yet did not affect the rule's primary application, the state's case against the victim of an unlawful search. This soon changed, however, when the Court decided to create the "good faith" or "reasonable mistake" exception to the exclusionary rule.

In 1984 the Burger Court addressed the good faith exception in two cases, *United States v. Leon* and *Massachusetts v. Sheppard*. *Leon* was a drug case prompted by an anonymous handwritten letter to police that a couple was selling drugs out of their home. The letter stated that the couple frequently traveled out of state and that they had no known source of income. The police placed the home under observation and saw behavior that resembled what was contained in the letter, but no actual evidence of a crime. They then used this information in their affidavit in support of a search warrant, which was granted. A search of the home produced contraband, and the suspects were arrested. In the lower courts, lawyers for the defense argued that police did not meet the threshold of probable cause necessary for the warrant, and that the evidence secured by the illegal search should be excluded from trial, while attorneys representing the United States argued that because the police were acting in "good faith," the Court should carve out a "good faith" exception to the exclusionary rule. The lower courts were unpersuaded, finding that the search warrant was faulty because it was not justified by the informant's tip, and suppressed the evidence.

The U.S. Supreme Court was more open to the government's argument. Writing for the majority, Justice White reaffirmed the point made in earlier cases that the exclusionary rule was judicially created to deter police misconduct and should be applied only in situations where deterrence was likely. He noted that there was "no evidence suggesting that judges and magistrates are inclined to ignore or subvert the Fourth Amendment or that lawlessness among these actors requires the application of the extreme sanction of exclusion." Application of the exclusionary rule, he explained, would be unwise; judges or magistrates responsible for a faulty search warrant would not be deterred because they "are not adjuncts to the law enforcement team; as neutral judicial officers, they have no stake in the outcome of particular criminal prosecutions. The threat of exclusion thus cannot be expected significantly to deter them."

To assess whether police would be deterred by exclusion of evidence in the case at hand, White employed the cost-benefit balancing approach the Court previously used to determine the rule's application in collateral settings. He identified the costs of the rule as interfering with the "criminal justice system's truth finding function," noting that "some guilty defendants may go free or receive reduced sentence as a result of favorable plea bargains." The benefit of deterrence of illegal police activity was characterized as "marginal or nonexistent." Part of the reason there would be no deterrence, White explained, was because "the deterrent purpose of the exclusionary rule necessarily assumes that the police have engaged in willful, or at the very least negligent conduct which has deprived the defendant of some right." In the case at hand, he stated, "there is no police illegality and thus nothing to deter." The opinion concluded with the Court's introduction of the good faith exception to the exclusionary rule: "The Fourth Amendment exclusionary rule should be modified so as not to bar the use in the prosecution's case in chief of evidence obtained by officers acting in reasonable reliance on a search warrant issued by a detached and neutral magistrate but ultimately found to be unsupported by probable cause."

Justice Brennan, joined by Marshall, dissented. He noted the Court's "gradual but determined strangulation of the rule" and denounced the Court's predilection for using the cost-benefit balancing approach to arrive at conclusions that seemed predetermined: "Although the Court's language in those cases suggests that some specific empirical basis may support its analyses, the reality is that the court's opinions represent inherently unstable compounds of intuition, hunches, and occasional pieces of partial and inconclusive data." Moreover, he added, "the language of deterrence and of cost/benefit analysis if used indiscriminately, can have a narcotic effect. It creates an illusion of technical precision and ineluctability. It suggests that not only constitutional principle but also empirical data supports the majority's result." Brennan castigated the majority for not honestly evaluating the benefits of the exclusionary rule using this balancing test. "We have not been treated to an honest assessment of the merits of the exclusionary rule, but have instead been drawn into a curious world where the 'costs' of excluding illegally obtained evidence loom to exaggerated heights and where the 'benefits' of such exclusion are made to disappear with a mere wave of the hand."

In a separate dissent, Justice John Paul Stevens adopted a different approach, reminding the majority that the Fourth Amendment had been violated in this case and that it offered no remedy to the victims of the illegal search. "Today, for the first time, this Court holds that although the Constitution has been violated, no court should do anything about it at any time in any proceeding."

In the companion case, *Massachusetts v. Sheppard,* the Court applied the good faith rule to arrive at a similar conclusion, stating that courts should not apply the exclusionary rule where the officer "acted in objectively reasonable reliance on a warrant issued by a detached and neutral magistrate that subsequently is determined to be invalid." Importantly, the exclusionary rule in both of these cases applied to situations where the police had obtained a search warrant. As such, the two decisions did not stand for the broader proposition that police, acting with good faith but without a warrant, could have illegally seized evidence admitted at trial.

———

The Burger Court's Fifth Amendment exclusionary rule decisions were also narrower than under the Warren Court. It was unwilling, as it had been under the Fourth Amendment, to exclude testimony obtained in violation of *Miranda v. Arizona* in collateral settings, and it limited application of the exclusionary rule by carving out a distinction between statements made in violation of the "core" of *Miranda* — those that violated the Fifth Amendment because they were coerced or compelled — and statements made in violation of *Miranda* warnings, which it characterized as "procedural safeguards" or "prophylactic rules." According to the Court, statements made in the absence or in violation of the *Miranda* warnings — the procedural safeguards designed to protect an individual from incriminating oneself in violation of the Fifth Amendment — may be admissible, while confessions that were coerced or compelled in violation of the Fifth Amendment would not.

For example, in *Harris v. New York* (1971), the Court ruled that statements made in violation of *Miranda* could still be used to impeach the credibility of a criminal defendant. It reasoned that exclusion of the evidence would not deter police misconduct and, using the same cost-benefit analysis employed in its Fourth Amendment exclusionary rule decisions, concluded that the cost of exclusion would be too high: "The impeachment process here undoubtedly provided valuable aid to the jury in assessing petitioner's credibility, and the benefits of this process should not be lost, in our view, because of the speculative possibility that impermissible police conduct will be encouraged thereby." *Harris* was reaffirmed several years later in *Oregon v. Hass* (1975). However, the Court later clarified that coerced statements, rather than those that were improper under *Miranda*, could not be used for impeachment purposes in *Mincey v. Arizona* (1978).

The distinction between confessions obtained in violation of one's *Miranda* warnings and those that were coerced or compelled in violation of the Fifth Amendment later dominated the Burger Court's Fifth Amendment exclusionary rule jurisprudence. For example, in *Michigan v. Tucker* (1974), a case involving information gathered from a comment made in the absence of full *Miranda* warnings that led to other incriminating evidence against a defendant, the Court ruled that the evidence could be admitted because the deterrent effect of exclusion would be minimal.

Tucker was later extended in *Oregon v. Elstad* (1985), a case where the defendant made an incriminating statement in the absence of *Miranda*, was arrested based upon that statement, *then* read his *Miranda* warnings, whereupon he confessed to the crime. The defendant challenged the second confession as "tainted" because the initial incriminating statement was made without his *Miranda* warnings. The Court interpreted *Miranda* as recognizing that the warnings "were not themselves rights protected by the Constitution but were instead measures to insure the right against compulsory self-incrimination was protected." Based on this reasoning, it determined that the second confession was admissible because it had not been "coerced" from the defendant in violation of the Fifth Amendment; rather, the police had merely failed to provide "the full measure of procedural safeguards associated with this right." The reason for the *Miranda* warnings, the majority explained, was to deter police from coercing the defendant, which had not occurred in this case because the defendant still had a choice regarding whether to make the second confession. The majority noted, "Once warned, the suspect is free to exercise his own volition in deciding whether or not to make a statement to the authorities."

The Fifth Amendment exclusionary rule was also at issue in *New York v. Quarles* (1984), a case concerning whether physical evidence obtained due to a confession made in the absence of *Miranda* warnings should still be accepted because prompt questioning was necessary to protect public safety. The majority reasoned that "the need for answers to questions in a situation posing a threat to the public safety outweighs the need for the prophylactic rule protecting the Fifth Amendment's privilege against self-incrimination."

———

The Burger Court's Fourth Amendment exclusionary rule decisions were a significant departure from the Warren Court's landmark *Mapp v. Ohio* ruling. In almost every exclusionary rule decision during this period, the rule was characterized as "judicially created" rather than a personal constitutional right. This weakened the foundation provided in *Weeks v. United States* and *Mapp* where the Supreme Court concluded that the exclusionary rule was constitutionally required. The significance of this development lies in the fact that by characterizing the rule as merely a remedy, the Court empowered itself to pick and choose its application.

The Court's emphasis on the deterrence rationale was also a departure from *Mapp*. This not only ignored the two other rationales offered to justify the exclusionary rule — the imperative of judicial integrity and healthy federalism — but also set up a situation where the Court could avoid application of the rule to situations where it concluded that deterrence of police misconduct could not be achieved, such as collateral settings or situations where police acted in good faith or had a "reasonable belief" that their actions were constitutional. Ironically, by limiting the instances when the exclusionary rule could be imposed, these exceptions potentially undermine the rule's ability to deter police misconduct.

The Court's use of the utilitarian cost-benefit balancing approach to determine if the exclusionary rule should be applied in a particular case is also problematic. The difficulty lies in the complexity it takes to accurately measure the costs and benefits of the exclusionary rule. It is nearly impossible to quantitatively measure the benefits of the Fourth Amendment and deterrence of police misconduct, while the costs of the exclusionary rule seem spectacular, despite the fact that studies illustrate that imposition of the rule rarely results in lost prosecutions and lost convictions.

The Court's Fifth Amendment decisions were also a departure from the Warren Court and its landmark *Miranda v. Arizona* ruling. The Court declared that the exclusionary rule applied only to coerced statements in violation of the Fifth Amendment, whereas "un-Mirandized" statements could still be admitted because the Court's *Miranda* warnings were only prophylactic rules that helped protect one from incriminating oneself. As with its Fourth Amendment exclusionary rule decisions, such an approach limited application of the exclusionary rule and therefore its ability to deter police misconduct and protect the Fifth Amendment rights of those accused of a crime.

The Burger Court's exclusionary rule decisions were also part of its broader effort to limit the substantive reach of the Fourth Amendment. The Court narrowed its scope in three major ways: by increasing exceptions to the warrant requirement, by elaborating upon the public exposure doctrine, and by expanding the circumstances where warrantless searches were considered "reasonable" and, therefore, constitutional.

New exceptions to the warrant requirement included allowing third parties to grant consent to a search, full-body searches incident to arrest for a minor traffic or petty offense, and searches of impounded cars and closed containers. The "public exposure" doctrine was expanded in decisions where the Court ruled that police need not obtain a warrant for certain types of searches because they took place in a setting where an individual did not enjoy a "legitimate expectation of privacy" and were therefore not considered searches within the meaning of the Fourth Amendment. This included searches of one's bank records, numbers dialed from one's phone, goods shipped through the mail, fenced land, and aerial surveillance of one's private backyard. All were allowed as permissible under the Fourth Amendment.

The Court also expanded the types of warrantless searches it considered "reasonable" and therefore allowable under the Fourth Amendment. These included more intrusive stop and frisk searches, including those for "crimes of possession" such as drugs, searches of pervasively regulated businesses, searches of secondary school students, and searches of suspects at airports and international borders. All were considered reasonable and allowable without a warrant under the Fourth Amendment. In the end, while there were several Burger Court decisions that could be interpreted as offering a more expansive reading of constitutional protection from unreasonable searches and seizures under the Fourth Amendment, the vast majority of its decisions were a noticeable trend away from the high-water mark provided under the Warren Court.

By the mid-1980s, the Burger Court had limited the application of the exclusionary rule by refusing to extend it to collateral settings, by introducing a new exception to the fruit of the poisonous tree doctrine, and by limiting who had standing to raise a Fourth Amendment challenge. While the Court did not reverse *Mapp v. Ohio* outright, these decisions substantially affected the way the exclusionary rule would be used by the courts for victims of illegal searches and seizures.

Throughout Burger's tenure, the Warren Court's criminal procedure decisions also remained on the political agenda. Although the Ford and Carter presidencies would be consumed with other pressing matters, President Ronald Reagan seized upon crime as a major domestic policy issue. He was impatient with the Burger Court's inability to limit or reverse the Warren Court's criminal procedure revolution, and his administration worked with conservative members of Congress to legislatively address some of its most controversial decisions, including *Mapp v. Ohio.*

Soon after taking the oath of office, Reagan directed his attorney general, William French Smith, to look into the issue of violent crime. The Attorney General's Task Force on Violent Crime later published a report that included recommendations on how to combat the rising crime rate. While the bulk of the report focused on punishment and incarceration of offenders, it also directly attacked the Warren Court. Its criminal procedure decisions were blamed for negatively affecting the "truth-seeking" function of the criminal justice system and for favoring the rights of criminal defendants over the need to protect public safety. The exclusionary rule was one of its main targets.

The task force faulted the exclusionary rule for "barring evidence of the truth, however important, if there is any investigative error, however unintended or trivial." The costs of the rule were characterized as "unacceptably high." The report concluded that in its "present application the exclusionary rule not only depresses police morale and allows criminals to go free when constables unwittingly blunder, but it diminishes public respect for the courts and our judicial process." The report advised a legislative effort to modify the exclusionary rule, so the Reagan administration reached out to members of the Senate.

In 1982, three bills were introduced in the Senate that targeted the exclusionary bill directly. Senate Bill 101, introduced by Dennis DeConcini (D-AZ), was similar to the 1971 and 1973 Bentsen bills; it would modify the exclusionary rule to apply only in situations where law enforcement's transgressions were "intentional or substantial." Senate Bill 751, introduced by Strom Thurmond (R-SC) and Orrin Hatch (R-UT), was even more radical; it called for abolishing the exclusionary rule in federal proceedings altogether and replacing it with a civil tort remedy for victims of an illegal search. The senators explained that the proposed legislation made more logical sense than the exclusionary rule because it would punish the individual officer and provide a remedy for the victim of the illegal search rather than exclude evidence, which may result in guilty defendants going free. A third proposal, Senate Bill 1995, sponsored by Robert Dole (R-KS), would create a reasonable, *good faith* exception to the exclusionary rule. The senator introduced the bill because by 1982 the Supreme Court had yet to make a ruling on the constitutionality of such an exception.

Over the next two years the Senate Judiciary Committee held, according to committee chair Senator Charles Mc.C. Mathias (R-MD), "the first congressional hearings that have been devoted solely to an examination of the rule itself." The hearings explored, among other things, whether the exclusionary rule was required by the Constitution or was a judicially created remedy that could be abrogated by Congress, and whether there were viable alternatives to the exclusionary rule.

Testifying before the Senate in favor of one or all of the legislative modifications were representatives from the U.S. Department of Justice; the Crime Victims Legal Advocacy Institute; Steven Schlesinger, a professor from the Department of Politics of Catholic University; and Judge Malcolm Wilkey from the U.S. Court of Appeals for the Fifth Circuit. Both Schlesinger and Wilkey had published articles calling for the abolition of the rule. Also appearing were representatives from Americans for Effective Law Enforcement, the International Association of Chiefs of Police, and the Police Executive Research Forum. The bills' advocates testified to the high costs of the exclusionary rule in terms of lost prosecutions and convictions. The proposals were appropriate, they argued, because the exclusionary rule was a judicially created remedy and not constitutionally required.

Appearing in opposition were Professor William W. Greenhalgh, from Georgetown University and chair of the Criminal Justice Section of the Legislative Committee of the American Bar Association; Professor Leon Friedman, from Hofstra University, representing the American Civil Liberties Union; and a panel of individuals testifying on behalf of the National Association of Criminal Defense lawyers. Scholars Wayne LaFave, from the University of Illinois, and Yale Kamisar, from the University of Michigan, both of whom had written extensively on the exclusionary rule and the Fourth Amendment, also appeared in opposition to the three bills. The witnesses opposed the proposed legislation on constitutional grounds, arguing that Congress did not have the authority to modify the exclusionary rule, which, they argued, was mandated by the Constitution. They also raised concerns that determining what was a substantial exclusionary rule violation or a reasonable, good faith effort by police was an inherently subjective exercise.

Senate opinion about the three bills split along ideological lines, with Republicans generally supporting the effort and Democrats opposing it. Republicans were more likely to criticize the Supreme Court and its "liberal excesses," which included giving too much power to criminal defendants at the expense of law enforcement, while Democrats were more willing to support Supreme Court decisions limiting government and less likely to give police and prosecutors more power at the risk of defendants' rights.

Several months later, in June 1982, the Subcommittee on Criminal Justice under the House Judiciary Committee opened its own set of hearings. Because specific legislation had yet to be introduced, the hearings were more general in nature. Many of the witnesses appearing before the Senate Judiciary Committee also appeared before the House subcommittee. It was close to the end of the session, and House Democrats signaled that they would likely kill any proposed legislation. None was introduced, and the Senate bills died at the end of the session.

There was a second attempt at exclusionary rule legislation at the end of President Reagan's first term of office. This time, the rule took center stage in a wide-ranging anticrime package proposed by the president. Because the Burger Court had yet to rule on the constitutionality of the good faith exception to the exclusionary rule, the administration included this modification in the crime package. In a speech introducing the proposed legislation, Reagan highlighted the costs of the exclusionary rule and explained how the good faith exception was necessary to "restore a proper balance between the forces of law and the forces of lawlessness."

Reagan's effort to fold the exclusionary rule measure into the omnibus bill proved to be too politically volatile. But the issue remained on the agenda, and Senator Strom Thurmond, a longtime critic of the rule, introduced the good faith exception in a separate measure, Senate Bill 1764, the Exclusionary Rule Limitation Act. The bill would amend the federal code to allow evidence seized in a search or seizure in a federal criminal proceeding "if the seizure was undertaken in a reasonable good faith belief in its conformity with the fourth amendment to the constitution." The Senate Judiciary Committee later approved the bill by a ten-to-six vote, and it was enacted on the floor of the Senate by a vote of sixty-three to twenty-four. A similar measure was introduced in the House in September 1984, but after two weeks of debate, Democratic House members were able to kill the proposal. Later that year, legislative efforts to modify the exclusionary rule stalled as the Burger Court carved out a good faith exception to the exclusionary rule in *United States v. Leon* and *Massachusetts v. Sheppard* (1984).

At the conclusion of his first term in office, President Ronald Reagan was dissatisfied with Congress's inability to legislatively address some of the Warren Court's more controversial decisions, including *Mapp v. Ohio* and the exclusionary rule. And, despite the Burger Court's ability to carve out a good faith exception to the exclusionary rule and halt the rule's expansion into collateral settings, Reagan was displeased the Court had not reversed the decision outright. He stepped up his attack.

At the beginning of his second term, President Ronald Reagan asked his new attorney general, Edwin Meese III, to find a way to address the Warren Court's "liberal excesses." Meese shared Reagan's criticism of the Warren Court and disappointment with the Burger Court's inability to halt the trend, and he vigorously pursued his mandate. He ordered the Office of Legal Policy, the research component of the U.S. Department of Justice, to study the "current status of the truth-seeking function of the criminal justice system." The research yielded eight reports, released over the next year, titled the "Truth in Criminal Justice Series." The reports explored some of the more controversial issues regarding the law of criminal procedure and evidence, and all were critical of the Warren Court for its judicial activism. Each recommended that the Office of Legal Policy embark on legal and political strategies to reverse the Court's criminal procedure decisions.

In prefatory statements to each report, Meese described how the Warren Court had placed the criminal justice system in peril: "Over the past thirty years . . . a variety of new rules have emerged that impede the discovery of reliable evidence at the investigative stages of the criminal justice process and that require the concealment of relevant facts at trial." He explained that these rules have "been a cause of grave concern to many Americans, who perceive such rules as being at odds with the goals of the criminal justice system." Steven Markmun, the assistant attorney general for legal policy who oversaw the writing of the eight reports, reiterated this theme in a law review comment where he also alleged that, taken as a whole, the reports "suggest a significant relationship between the jurisprudential revolution in criminal justice during the past twenty-five years and the sharp increase in violent crime."

The report titled "The Search and Seizure Exclusionary Rule" characterized *Mapp v. Ohio* as created by "judicial fiat" and not supported in the "original intent or meaning" of the Constitution. To support this proposition, it approvingly cited Burger Court decisions stating that the exclusionary rule was merely a remedy intended to deter law enforcement, and that if deterrence was unlikely, the rule should not be invoked. Going further, the report questioned the deterrence rationale. Although it cited recent studies indicating that the "costs" of the rule constituted only a small percentage of lost felony prosecutions, it added that these costs may very well be significant in absolute terms; "losing that many convictions certainly poses serious dangers to the community, and there is evidence that the number of lost convictions is concentrated particularly among certain crimes generally perceived as serious, e.g., weapons and drug offenses." The report also suggested that lost convictions would lead to other costs in terms of "public anger and the heightened fear of crime that may result from the release or truncated prosecution of serious criminals even in a small number of cases."

The report concluded with a recommendation that the administration pursue both a legal and a political strategy to abolish the exclusionary rule and replace it with alternatives such as criminal penalties and constitutional torts to help deter police illegality. The legal strategy was characterized as having the most potential for success because the state of the exclusionary rule was "precarious" given the jurisprudential developments under Chief Justice Warren Burger. It urged the administration to pursue a litigation campaign to encourage the Supreme Court to reverse the exclusionary rule: "It is important to take advantage of the Court's increasing lack of confidence in the exclusionary rule as a deterrent to police misconduct, to highlight the costs of continued reliance on the rule, and to persuade the court that alternatives exist that effectively redress and deter violations." The exclusionary rules of *Miranda v. Arizona* and *Massiah v. United States* were also heavily criticized in two reports, "The Law of Pretrial Interrogation" and "The Sixth Amendment Right to Counsel under the Massiah Line of Cases."

And, two other documents published in 1988, *The Constitution in the Year 2000: Choices ahead in Constitutional Interpretation* and *Guidelines on Constitutional Litigation*, also targeted *Mapp, Miranda*, and *Massiah*, which were described as "inconsistent" with the administration's positions on criminal procedure and dangerous to "the search for truth in criminal investigations and prosecution."

Given the Reagan administration's inability to enact legislation to alter the exclusionary rule in his first term, the president's strategy switched from a legislative to a judicial one. If he could put the right people on the bench, as had Nixon, perhaps the newly constituted Court could correct the excesses of the old.

———

In June 1986, Chief Justice Warren Burger announced he would step down from the Court, giving Ronald Reagan the opportunity to nominate a new chief justice. It was Reagan's second Supreme Court appointment. In 1981, he fulfilled a campaign promise when he nominated the first woman, Sandra Day O'Connor, a judge on the Arizona State Court of Appeals, to replace retiring Justice Potter Stewart. A moderate conservative, especially on criminal justice issues, O'Connor consistently voted in favor of the state and against the expansion of criminal procedure rights. She was easily confirmed by the Senate. For his second appointment, Reagan selected Associate Justice William Rehnquist to replace Chief Justice Burger. Antonin Scalia, a judge he appointed to the Court of Appeals for the District of Columbia Circuit in 1982, was nominated to fill Rehnquist's seat.

The president followed the strategy employed by Nixon when considering whom to elevate to the Court. He was concerned primarily with appointing judicial and political conservatives with track records ideologically consistent with his administration. And, as was Nixon before him, he was concerned about crime and the Warren Court's criminal procedure decisions. As judicial nominees, Rehnquist and Scalia fit the bill. Despite another politically charged Senate hearing,

Rehnquist was confirmed by a two-thirds majority. The Senate then unanimously approved the Scalia nomination.

Reagan was given another opportunity to leave his legacy on the Court eleven months later when Lewis Powell announced his resignation. After the failed nominations of U.S. Court of Appeals judges Robert Bork and Douglas Ginsberg, Reagan's third choice, Anthony M. Kennedy, a judge on the Ninth Circuit Court of Appeals, was confirmed. Although Kennedy's record suggested that he might be as conservative as the previous nominees, he was a low-profile candidate who was unanimously backed in the Senate.

By the end of the Reagan administration, the Rehnquist Court was fairly evenly divided on both ends of the ideological spectrum. The four Supreme Court appointments during the Bush and Clinton administrations would change the character of the Court, but not the conservative majority. In 1990, President Bush successfully elevated David Souter, a moderate from the First Circuit Court of Appeals, to replace William Brennan and Clarence Thomas, a judge on the U.S. Court of Appeals for the DC Circuit, to replace Thurgood Marshall. While Souter has grown more moderate, Thomas is regarded as a safe conservative vote, often aligning himself with Scalia and Rehnquist.

President Clinton's two appointments to the Court made little headway with the Rehnquist conservative majority. Ruth Bader Ginsberg, from the U.S. Court of Appeals for the DC Circuit was easily confirmed in 1993 to replace Byron White, and Stephen G. Breyer, a former judge on the U.S. Court of Appeals for the First Circuit, replaced Harry Blackmun in 1994. Both consistently vote liberally, although like all justices, they display streaks of independence.

The Rehnquist Court that examined the Warren Court's criminal procedure decisions consisted of a solid four-justice majority with the chief justice and Justices Scalia, Kennedy, and Thomas. O'Connor and Souter constituted the moderate bloc, which leaned toward the conservative end of the spectrum. The liberal minority consisted of Stevens, Ginsberg, and Breyer. *Mapp v. Ohio* and the exclusionary rule, still a subject of much criticism, was considered by the Rehnquist Court, but the conservative majority was unable to reverse the decision outright. It was, however, able to continue the trend started under the Burger Court to limit the exclusionary rule.

The Rehnquist Court has decided only a handful of major exclusionary rule cases, and each advanced the Burger Court's exclusionary rule jurisprudence. The rulings were based upon the foundation established by the Burger Court that the exclusionary rule was judicially created rather than a constitutional imperative and that its sole justification was the deterrence of police misconduct. To evaluate the application of the rule in a particular setting, the Rehnquist Court also applied the utilitarian balancing test employed under Burger's tenure: that it be applied only in situations where the "benefits" of the rule outweighed the "costs."

The Rehnquist Court first addressed the exclusionary rule in two decisions extending the good faith or reasonable mistake exception established in *United States v. Leon* and *Massachusetts v. Sheppard* (1984). In *Illinois v. Krull* (1987), the Rehnquist Court applied the good faith exception to situations where "officers act in objectively reasonable reliance upon a statute [authorizing the search] but where the statute is ultimately found to violate the Fourth Amendment." *Krull* was a five-to-four decision, reflecting the divisiveness on the Court. Relying on *Leon* and *Sheppard*, the majority ruled that if an officer acted in "objectively reasonable reliance" on a statute he believed to be constitutional, then unless the law was clearly unconstitutional, the officer "cannot be expected to question the judgment of the legislature that passed the law." The Court observed that because the exclusionary rule was designed to deter police misconduct, application in this context would be futile because it would be targeted at legislators, who, like judicial officers, "are not the focus of the rule" and would not be deterred by exclusion of the evidence. Nor did the majority find any evidence that legislators were prone to violate the Fourth Amendment, which might justify the exclusionary rule's application in this case.

Eight years later, in *Arizona v. Evans* (1995), the Court considered a case involving a warrantless search incident to arrest. Although such searches are a common exception to the warrant requirement, it was later learned that the information from the computer database that the accused had an outstanding warrant was the result of a clerical error — it had in fact been quashed — which meant that the arrest and therefore the search and seizure of the evidence was inappropriate. This was the ruling of the Arizona Supreme Court, which noted that it was "repugnant to the principles of a free society" to place a person "into police custody because of a computer error precipitated by government carelessness."

The Supreme Court majority disagreed, ruling that the search was constitutional because police had a "reasonable belief" their actions were constitutional at the time of the search. In reasoning similar to that in *Leon*, *Sheppard*, and *Krull*, the majority explained that the purpose of the exclusionary rule was to deter police misconduct rather than misconduct by court clerks, and that neither the police nor the court clerk who made the error would be deterred if the rule was applied in this instance because "court clerks are not adjuncts to the law enforcement team engaged in the often competitive enterprise of ferreting out crime, they have no stake in the outcome of particular criminal prosecutions."

The Rehnquist Court also continued the trend, originating under Burger, of refusing to extend the exclusionary rule beyond the prosecution's case in chief in criminal trials. In *Pennsylvania Board of Probation and Parole v. Scott* (1998), a five-justice majority ruled that the Fourth Amendment exclusionary rule did not apply to parole revocation proceedings. The majority reviewed the Burger Court's decisions refusing to extend the exclusionary rule to collateral settings and noted that the same conditions applied in the case at hand — that it should be applied only in those situations "where its remedial objectives are thought most efficaciously served." It characterized the state's interest in making sure parolees complied with the terms of their probation as "overwhelming" and concluded that "application of the exclusionary rule would both hinder the functioning of state parole systems and alter the traditionally flexible, administrative nature of parole revocation proceedings." The majority determined that the benefits of the exclusionary rule in this setting were "minimal" because it would not deter police misconduct in that parole proceedings fall outside their "zone of primary interest" and would not effectively deter parole officers' misconduct because they are not directly involved in "ferreting out crime."

The Rehnquist Court sent mixed messages regarding *Miranda v. Arizona* and the *Miranda* rule of exclusion. Two early decisions continued the trend started under Burger to differentiate confessions that were coerced and in violation of the Fifth Amendment and those in violation of one's Miranda warnings. In *Pennsylvania v. Muniz* (1990), the Court considered whether questions asked of a suspect who had not been informed of his *Miranda* rights during booking were admissible. And, in *Illinois v. Perkins* (1990), the Court considered whether an un-Mirandized confession made by a jail inmate to an undercover police officer "planted" in an adjacent cell could be admitted in a criminal trial. In both instances the Court concluded that despite the absence of *Miranda* warnings, the defendants had not been coerced during the questioning, hence there was no Fifth Amendment violation, and the statements were admissible.

However, the Court's distinction between un-Mirandized involuntary confessions and those that were coerced in violation of the Fifth Amendment was called into question in *Dickerson v. United States* (2000). The case, which involved a defendant's challenge to the admission of incriminating statements made to police in the absence of *Miranda* warnings, received a great deal of attention in the press because it was used by outside conservative interest groups to request the Court to reconsider *Miranda v. Arizona* and the constitutionality of section 3501 of the U.S. Code, which was the codification of Title II of the 1968 Omnibus Crime Control and Safe Streets Act, which statutorily reversed *Miranda v. Arizona* and gave the trial court judge sole discretion to determine whether a confession should be admitted.

Former law school professor Paul Cassell, a vocal critic of *Miranda*, represented the conservative Washington Legal Foundation and the Safe Streets Coalition before the Supreme Court. Cassell argued that the Warren Court's *Miranda v. Arizona* decision requiring the exclusion of involuntary confessions was not required by the Constitution and that the *Miranda* warnings were "prophylactic" rules that could be modified by Congress. He reasoned that if the sole purpose of *Miranda*'s exclusionary rule was to deter police from misconduct during custodial interrogations rather than ensure a constitutional right, then the federal courts did not have the authority to impose such procedural rules on state courts. Cassell contended that section 3501 of the U.S. Code, which allowed the trial court judge to determine the voluntariness of a confession, rather than whether one received *Miranda* warnings, should govern the admissibility of confessions.

Cassell's litigation strategy was motivated by the fact that the Supreme Court under Burger and Rehnquist had frequently criticized

Miranda and might use this opportunity to overrule it by invoking section 3501 of the U.S. Code. He also believed the Rehnquist Court would be motivated by principles of federalism and resist forcing prophylactic rules on state courts.

However, when faced with opportunity to overrule *Miranda*, seven members of the Court declined to do so. Without commenting on the merits of *Miranda*, Chief Justice Rehnquist, writing for the majority, found no justification for overruling the decision, stating that "the principles of *stare decisis* weigh heavily against overruling it now." He explained that "*Miranda* has become embedded in routine police practice to the point where the warnings have become part of our national culture." Despite conceding that the Court had handed down decisions in the past that supported the view that *Miranda* was not constitutionally based, Rehnquist characterized *Miranda v. Arizona* as a "constitutional decision of this Court," citing language in the decision which "indicated that the majority thought it was announcing a constitutional rule." And, as a constitutional ruling, it could not be overruled by an act of Congress, which Congress clearly intended to do in Title II of the 1968 Omnibus Crime Control and Safe Streets Act.

The full impact of *Dickerson* has yet to be realized; Ohio State University law professor Joshua Dressler, who has written extensively on criminal procedure, questions whether the Court's declaration that *Miranda* is constitutionally based implicitly reverses other decisions where the Court has suggested otherwise. And, he suggests that *Dickerson* may stand for a more far-reaching proposition; that procedural rules created by the Supreme Court may not be subject to revision by Congress. "To the extent that *Dickerson* stands for the proposition that *Miranda* announced a prophylactic rule (the requirement of *Miranda* warnings) to protect a constitutional right — *and that this makes the case a constitutional decision* — this seems to mean that prophylactic rules have nearly as much power as constitutional rights. *Dickerson* may teach — although it never speaks to the question explicitly — that states and Congress cannot tamper with prophylactic rules except to devise alternative rules that are as or more effective in guarding against unconstitutional violations." If Dressler is correct, then despite proclamations by the Burger and Rehnquist Courts that the Fourth Amendment exclusionary rule is merely a judicially created remedy rather than constitutionally required, it may also be safe from legislation affecting its application.

With the exception of *Dickerson*, the Rehnquist Court's Fourth and Fifth Amendment exclusionary rule jurisprudence has been little different than that decided under Chief Justice Warren Burger. The decisions continued trends started several years previously to limit the exclusionary rule's application, and, while the central holding in *Mapp v. Ohio* still remained, its foundation continued to be undermined because of the Court's insistence that the exclusionary rule was judicially created and thus subject to modification. Deterrence of police misconduct continued to be invoked as the sole reason for the exclusionary rule, and the Court applied it only in those situations where the benefits outweighed the costs.

The Rehnquist Court also continued the trend, started during the Burger Court, of cutting back on the substantive nature of the Fourth Amendment. This was accomplished by more exceptions to the Fourth Amendment warrant requirement and an expansive reading of the public exposure doctrine. For example, in decisions regarding exceptions to the warrant requirement of the Fourth Amendment, the Court allowed former roommates to give consent to a search of an apartment; it relaxed the definition of what constituted a voluntary search to allow brief questioning of individuals in a bus during routine drug and weapons interdiction; it expanded searches incident to arrest to include searches of an entire home and automobile searches to include the search of closed containers and of passengers' belongings; and it redefined the "plain view" exception to also include what is known as "plain touch" or "plain feel." The Court also continued with a liberal construction of the public exposure doctrine, ruling that people had no expectation of privacy in buildings on one's property outside of their residence or in garbage bags left on the street, and no expectation of privacy in publicly navigable airspace and other public thoroughfares.

The Rehnquist Court's most significant contribution to Fourth Amendment jurisprudence has been its expansion of permissible searches based on the lesser standard of "reasonableness" rather than probable cause. The Court has embraced the "generalized reasonableness" construction of the Fourth Amendment, suggesting that searches made without a warrant be only reasonable to withstand constitutional scrutiny. These cases fall into two categories: those involving situations where police reasonably believed individuals were involved in criminal activity, and those classified as "special needs" cases involving administrative inspections and regulatory searches, where the primary purpose of the government's activity was to protect the general public, rather than prosecute individuals for violating criminal laws. For example, the Court allowed warrantless "pretext" traffic stops in high-crime areas, and warrantless drug testing of secondary school students wishing to participate in any extracurricular activities.

While significant, these developments were not unexpected. The Warren Court's more liberal construction of the Fourth Amendment had been gradually eroding since 1968. These Rehnquist Court decisions expanded upon a line of reasoning established under Burger and reflected the Reagan and Bush administration's Supreme Court appointments, which emphasized "law and order" and a conservative judicial ideology.

———

Despite Rehnquist Court decisions limiting the reach of *Mapp v. Ohio* and the exclusionary rule, legislative reform of the rule remained on the political agenda during the Bush and Clinton presidencies. Throughout these two administrations, there were efforts, led either by the White House or by conservative Republicans in Congress, to legislatively modify the exclusionary rule. While the efforts were ultimately unsuccessful, the fact that the issue remained on the political agenda is a testament to how much *Mapp* resonated with politicians and the public decades after it was decided.

The closest Republicans came to success was in 1994, when the GOP gained control of the House of Representatives after serving as a minority party for more than forty years. Under the stewardship of Newt Gingrich, the newly elected Speaker of the House, the 1994 "Contract with America" included a provision recommending abolition of the exclusionary rule. It was now at the top of the political agenda.

During the first hundred days of the session, the time period House Republicans pledged to enact the contract, hearings were held on House Bill 666, the Exclusionary Rule Reform Act. The proposed legislation would codify *Leon* with the "reasonable good faith" exception that evidence be included in trial, but with a significant modification. It would also extend the good faith exception to allow federal prosecutors to use evidence seized during *warrantless* searches as long as the police conducting the search had reason to believe the search was legal. Bill McCollum (R-FL), who introduced the bill, reduced the exclusionary rule to a technicality. He argued that the rule was responsible for "killing a lot of our police officers' efforts and the prosecutors' efforts to get convictions." Because of the Republicans' rush to push the bill through the legislative process, there was insufficient time for hearings on the exclusionary rule. In late January 1995, H.R. 666 was voted favorably out of committee in a nineteen-to-fourteen vote that, not unexpectedly, broke along party lines.

In the Senate, there were similar efforts to limit the exclusionary rule. Orrin Hatch (R-UT), chair of the Senate Judiciary Committee, along with majority leader Robert Dole (R-KS), wrote the Senate version of the exclusionary bill. Senate Bill 3 was similar in form to Hatch's previous legislative efforts during the Nixon administration; it would eliminate the exclusionary rule and replace it with a civil action as the exclusive remedy for Fourth Amendment violations.

As the House and Senate exclusionary rules were pending, an unusual coalition of liberal and conservative groups came together to oppose the proposed legislation. The coalition, which included groups from the Left such as the American Civil Liberties Union and the National Association of Criminal Defense Lawyers joined groups from the Right such as the Citizens' Committee for the Right to Keep and Bear Arms, the Gun Owners of America, and the National Rifle Association in an effort to ask Congress to reconsider the proposed legislation. The coalition wrote a letter calling upon members of Congress and the administration to "adopt a plan to halt the abuse of power by federal law enforcement agencies" and urged that H.R. 666 and S. 3 be rejected. Remarkably, the coalition called upon congressional leaders to actually strengthen the exclusionary rule, which reflected a policy shift for the conservative interest groups. The shift was motivated by concern that some federal agencies had gone "too far" in infringing upon individuals' right to be protected from unreasonable searches and seizures under the Fourth Amendment. The letter concluded that "Congress should certainly preserve, and indeed strengthen the Exclusionary Rule to safeguard citizen rights and curb police misconduct."

The coalition's efforts were partially successful. House Republicans were persuaded that recent actions by the Bureau of Alcohol, Tobacco and Firearms (ATF) at Ruby Ridge, Idaho, and the Branch Davidian complex in Waco, Texas, illustrated a predilection for abuse of federal authority. An amendment excepting the ATF and the Internal Revenue Service from the legislation attracted Republican support and passed, 228 to 198. Although liberal Democrats and members of the Congressional Black Caucus led the fight to oppose H.R. 666 as amended, it ultimately passed the House in this revised form, 289 to 142.

The Senate held Judiciary Committee hearings on the exclusionary rule in March 1995. As occurred with the proposed legislation in the early eighties, a number of academics appeared before the Senate Judiciary Committee, offering their insight into the constitutionality of the proposed changes. The debate between these scholars did not end with the committee hearing; included in the published report were almost 200 pages of additional testimony in response to questions posed by senators and additional submissions for the record. A review of the testimony illustrates scholars' widely divergent views on the issues, which in many ways reflected the differing views in Congress and on the Supreme Court with regard to *Mapp v. Ohio*'s and *Miranda v. Arizona*'s exlusionary rule. However, in the end, despite the fact that the House was able to move quickly, modification of the exclusionary rule stalled in the Senate as Democrats were able to kill the proposed legislation.

———

Today, as the crime rate has declined, the controversy over *Mapp v. Ohio* and the exclusionary rule has moved to the bottom of the political agenda. The heated debate over the rule has also diminished as people have become accustomed to it as a restriction on police conduct. Acceptance of the rule even extends to the law enforcement community. One of the most comprehensive recent studies on the exclusionary rule's effect on law enforcement was conducted by the American Bar Association in 1988. Researchers gathered testimony from hundreds of judges, prosecutors, defense attorneys, and police officers over a two-year period and conducted a random survey of 800 individuals involved in the criminal justice system. The 1988 report, *Criminal Justice in Crisis*, concluded that "the exclusionary rule neither causes serious malfunctioning of the criminal justice system nor promotes crime." It also revealed that law enforcement officials, "toward whom the deterrent force of the exclusionary rule is primarily directed," reported that the exclusionary rule was not a "serious obstacle" to their job. Rather, many believed "the demands of the exclusionary rule and resulting police training on Fourth Amendment requirements have promoted professionalism in police departments across the country."

The study concluded that the "exclusionary rule appears to be providing a significant safeguard of Fourth Amendment protections for individuals at modest cost in terms of either crime control or effective prosecution. This 'cost,' for the most part, reflects the values expressed in the Fourth Amendment itself, for the Amendment manifests a preference for privacy and freedom over that level of law enforcement efficiency which could be achieved if police were permitted to arrest and search without probable cause or judicial authorization." The real problem facing the system, it summarized, was the inadequacy of resources available to detect and address crime.

———

The debate over the exclusionary rule is now taking place in the state courts. In several jurisdictions, state supreme courts, dissatisfied with Burger and Rehnquist Court decisions that limit constitutional protection under the Fourth Amendment, are looking to their state constitutions to protect their citizens against unreasonable searches and seizures. This "new judicial federalism" is part of an overall trend that began in the mid-1970s which emphasized reliance on state constitutions for protection of rights and liberties. The reliance on state constitutions presents state courts with the opportunity to interpret state constitutional rights and liberties independent of the U.S. Supreme Court's interpretation of analogous rights.

New judicial federalism provides criminal defendants who are victims of an illegal police search a more welcoming forum in which to litigate their claim. State courts, which were previously seen as a threat to individual rights, are now a haven as an increasingly conservative Supreme Court has eroded criminal procedure rights created by the Warren Court. As law professor David A. Harris observed, "Between 1970 and 1989, state courts published more than 450 opinions that interpreted state constitutional provisions as exceeding what federal constitutional guarantees required. More than a third of these cases concerned fundamental aspects of the judicial process." In regard to the exclusionary rule, this was most often seen in a state court's refusal to read a "good faith" or "reasonable mistake" exception into the exclusionary rule. State supreme courts in New York, New Jersey, New Hampshire, Massachusetts, and Mississippi have refused to carve out such an exception to their state constitutional provisions protecting citizens from unreasonable searches and seizures. Other state supreme courts are offering a more expansive interpretation of who has standing to raise a claim against police misconduct. For example, the Louisiana Supreme Court has interpreted its state constitution to allow third parties to raise an exclusionary rule challenge.

It is ironic that today, forty-five years after *Mapp v. Ohio* federalized the exclusionary rule so that evidence seized illegally could be excluded from all state criminal trials, state criminal procedure threatens to become as fragmented as it was prior to *Mapp*. However, in light of the U.S. Supreme Court's increasingly conservative interpretation of the Fourth Amendment, these state courts have found it necessary to revert to their state constitutions to ensure what *Mapp v. Ohio* promised in the first place: that Americans be fully protected against unreasonable searches and seizures.

Epilogue

In 1968, at age forty, Dollree Mapp moved from Cleveland, Ohio, to New York. She did not tell anyone she was leaving. "I was bored because I am constantly searching for improvement," she says. "I wanted a different environment." Mapp purchased a two-story brick home in Cambria Heights in Queens County and a used furniture store in Harlem. To manage the store, Mapp hired Alan Lyons, a young man she met after moving to New York. It did not take long for Mapp to find herself on the wrong side of the law. In October 1969 a confidential informant told New York City police officers that Mapp and Lyons were packaging and selling narcotics out of a Queens, New York, apartment and that drugs were being stored in Mapp's home.

Based on the tip, which the police admitted came from "a confidential informant who has not proven reliable in the past," police officers placed Mapp and Lyons under surveillance for several weeks. They noted that Mapp traveled between her home and the apartment in Queens, and a person at the Queens apartment complex identified Mapp as the person who paid the rental fee for the apartment. The lead detective on the case, John Bergersen, who oversaw the surveillance, also said that he overheard Mapp and Lyons discuss packaging the drugs. The evidence that the two were involved in criminal activity was enough for police to secure a warrant to search the Queens apartment and Mapp's home for "heroin and other narcotic drugs."

Several days later, police, armed with the warrant, searched the apartment. They found drug paraphernalia and more than a pound of heroin with an estimated street value of $1 million. Lyons, who was at the apartment, was arrested. Police then searched Mapp's home. Although they did not find any narcotics, they did find rent receipts that linked her to the Queens apartment. For the officers, it was sufficient evidence that Mapp was involved with criminal activity, and she was arrested. After posting $5,000 bail, Mapp and Lyons were released.

In late October, several months after Mapp's release, police received a tip from an informant that Mapp was a receiver of stolen property. Once again, they placed her home under surveillance and, armed with a warrant, searched her home on November 2. They found 50,000 envelopes of heroin with a $150,000 street value and stolen property, including television sets, typewriters, portable radios, and antiques worth approximately $100,000. Mapp was arrested and charged with possession of narcotics and stolen property.

On April 23, 1971, Mapp and Lyons were convicted in state supreme court in Queens County for possession of narcotics. The following month they were each sentenced to a mandatory prison sentence of twenty years to life. In 1969, Governor Nelson Rockefeller of New York had worked with the state legislature to amend its criminal code to institute such a mandatory sentence for class A felonies such as murder, kidnapping, and possession of dangerous drugs. It was one of the harshest sentencing laws in the country, and the governor would continue his efforts to strengthen the state's mandatory sentences for drug possession as he contemplated a campaign for the presidency.

Mapp appealed her conviction, and on June 26, 1972, the New York Appellate Division reversed the judgment based on its assessment that the trial court made four errors regarding the admission of the state's testimony. Four of the five judges determined that at trial, when Mapp and Lyons took the stand in their own defense, the state attempted to impeach their credibility on collateral issues, which violated two long-standing rules of evidence. However, Mapp's reprieve was short-lived. Several weeks later she and Lyons were retried, reconvicted, and resentenced to twenty years to life. Mapp was sent to the State Correctional Institution for Women at Bedford Hills, New York.

Mapp went to Bedford Hills furious with herself. "I ran around with the wrong guy," she explains. "He was a friend of mine." She was also angry at the system, but was determined not to let life in prison beat her. "I went in as a bitch," she says. "I was angry every day I was there." Mapp's name was familiar to the other inmates as well as prison employees. "I was arrogant," she admits. "The guards didn't want to deal with me. I never smiled and I never talked to them. I didn't ask any favors from anyone." She went to prison with her head held high and demanded to be treated respectfully. She made an impression on one corrections officer early into her sentence. "He called me Dollree," she recalls. "I said to him, 'Who are you? I don't know you from the street. You can call me Ms. Mapp.'"

––––––

From an early age Mapp had looked for ways to better herself, and she chose to use her time at Bedford Hills to learn the law. She familiarized herself with the law library and taught herself about postconviction appeals in the federal system. Mapp also provided legal assistance to other inmates. "I would help out other female inmates and work with them in the law library," Mapp explains. "This would command a level of respect from the other inmates and the guards." Mapp was aware of how her original conviction was reversed due to legal errors committed by the trial court judge, so she reviewed her case in search of other mistakes that might lead to a reversal.

In 1975, Mapp's family hired civil liberties lawyer Eleanor Jackson Piel to represent her in a petition for a writ of habeas corpus in U.S. District Court for the Southern District of New York. The basis of the writ was that the police search of the apartment and home was unconstitutional. Piel argued that, among other things, the confidential informant's hearsay evidence did not establish sufficient probable cause for the issuance of the warrant because the informant did not have a reliable track record. However, the district court judge, Walter Bruchhausen, dismissed the petition after determining that the police's independent investigation of the appellants provided sufficient evidence of the informant's trustworthiness. Piel appealed the decision to the Court of Appeals for the Second Circuit, which affirmed the ruling. There was one last option for Mapp — an appeal to the U.S. Supreme Court. This time, Mapp would not get a hearing before the justices. Mapp's petition for a writ of certiorari requesting review was denied.

Mapp continued looking for a way to win her freedom. In 1977, Piel filed a second petition for a writ of habeas corpus in federal district court. She argued that Mapp's rights were denied at trial because she and Lyons were represented by the same law firm, and that because of this conflict of interest, she was not provided adequate counsel. Piel also contended that Mapp was denied due process because police falsified evidence against her client. Although the latter claim was a long shot, the charge was bolstered by the fact that several years after Mapp's conviction, the lead detective in the case, John Bergersen, was dismissed from the New York Police Department for taking a bribe from a narcotics dealer.

However, district court judge Kevin Thomas was unpersuaded by Mapp's claim that she was unaware that sharing counsel with her co-defendant, which she had authorized, may have compromised her legal representation. He explained, "Ms. Mapp is an intelligent woman who is no stranger to legal proceedings and the appellate process. Indeed, it appears that she in no small degree participated in the conduct of her own appeal." Mapp's legal savvy worked against her. Thomas also dismissed Mapp's claim that Bergersen may have falsified evidence, finding that his dismissal at a departmental hearing after Mapp's conviction "does not mean that he was dishonest at the time of petitioner's trial." The writ was denied. Mapp decided not to appeal the decision.

Resigned to her fate, Mapp continued learning about the law while at Bedford Hills. However, her fortunes turned in her favor when on New Year's Eve, 1980, Mapp and fifteen other prisoners convicted under the state's strict drug laws had their sentences commuted by Governor Hugh Carey. She was eligible for parole the next day and, after her parole board hearing on January 19, was released from prison shortly thereafter. Her anger had not dissipated. As she was leaving the prison, one of the guards said to her, "Do you know what, Ms. Mapp? We will never forget you." Her reply? "Do you know something? I've forgotten you already." She was already looking forward to a new chapter in her life.

After Mapp was paroled, she went "looking for a way to even out my life." She went to work for a New York not-for-profit group, the Voluntary Attorney Service Team (VAST), which went into the prisons and provided legal assistance for inmates. The group was led by Tom Higgins, whom Mapp sought out after her release. She believed that her experience with the criminal justice system could be of help to others in need. "There are many cries for help coming from prison," Mapp explains. "You meet people, and you know a little about their story. You have empathy for them." She worked as a legal aid. "I would help the inmates contact lawyers, write letters, and teach them how to use the law library." In some cases, Mapp helped inmates craft petitions for writs of habeas corpus and legal briefs. "These services were needed," she observes, recalling her own legal struggle. "They were crucial because, often, prisoners' families desert them. When a family deserts you and doesn't support you, you are vulnerable in the system. This is what often happens in prison. VAST would reach out and help people."

After working for VAST for several years, Mapp earned her real estate license and sold property in Queens County, where she currently resides. While her license is now expired, at eighty-two years old she continues to invest in property and look for new opportunities.

—————

Today, Mapp is circumspect about her experiences with the law. She is still angry about her treatment at the hands of Sergeant Carl Delau and Cleveland's Bureau of Special Investigation, which she believes unfairly targeted her because of her race and her associates. However, Mapp also accepts full responsibility for her ill-fated friendship with Alan Lyons and the arrest in New York. "I have no regrets," she says simply. "I have lived my life as I saw fit. Fit for myself, not anyone else." She is also quick to remind people that her legal troubles in New York had nothing to do with the incident in Cleveland, Ohio.

Today Mapp is living comfortably in Cambria Heights, New York. She does not think often about the landmark Supreme Court decision that bears her name, and while she is pleased that the Court ruling in *Mapp v. Ohio* helps protect Americans from unreasonable searches and seizures, she always considered her early court struggle a personal one. "Any time someone is abused by the system, they have a right to stand up for themselves," she explains. "I fought to the end to see what would happen because I believed in my honesty and innocence." Mapp is also a bit amused by the whole experience. "They write about this decision all of the time," she says. "To the Supreme Court I was just the girl with those dirty books." And, she adds, with a twinkle in her eye, "They never returned those books. I guess they are having a good time with them."

CHRONOLOGY

1914	The U.S. Supreme Court decides *Weeks v. United States*, a unanimous decision declaring the exclusionary rule as constitutionally required under the Fourth Amendment.
1936	The Ohio Supreme Court decides *State v. Lindway*, which allows illegally seized evidence to be admitted in criminal trials.
1949	The U.S. Supreme Court decides *Wolf v. Colorado*, where it incorporates the Fourth Amendment to apply against state action. However, it declines to extend the exclusionary rule to the states.
May 20, 1957	Bombing at the home of Donald "the Kid" King.
May 23, 1957	Dollree Mapp is arrested for possession of gambling paraphernalia found during an illegal search of her home.
May 26, 1957	Mapp is rearrested and charged with possession of obscene materials in violation of Ohio state's antiobscenity law.
September 3, 1958	*Ohio v. Mapp* is heard in the Cuyahoga County Court of Common Pleas.
September 4, 1958	Mapp is convicted of violating the state antiobscenity law and sentenced to seven years in the Ohio Reformatory for Women. She remains free on bail as her case is appealed.
September 6, 1958	Mapp's attorneys file a motion for a new trial, which is denied.
September 26, 1958	Mapp's attorneys file a notice of appeal in the Ohio State Eighth District Court of Appeals.
March 28, 1959	The Ohio State Eighth District Court of Appeals affirms Mapp's conviction.
April 24, 1959	Mapp's attorneys file a motion of appeal to the Ohio State Supreme Court.
May 27, 1959	Mapp's attorneys file their brief on "behalf of defendant-appellant" in *Ohio v. Mapp*.
June 11, 1959	The prosecuting office files a "motion to dismiss as a matter of right" in *Ohio v. Mapp*.

October 12, 1959	Mapp's attorneys file a "brief of defendant-appellant in reply and opposing motion to dismiss" in *Ohio v. Mapp*.
October 24, 1959	The Ohio Civil Liberties Union requests permission to file an amicus curiae brief on behalf of Mapp's case, which is later granted.
October 26, 1959	The Ohio Civil Liberties Union and the American Civil Liberties Union file an amicus curiae brief on behalf of Mapp's case.
March 23, 1960	The Ohio Supreme Court affirms Mapp's conviction; four of the seven justices determine the state antiobscenity law is unconstitutional, but a supermajority is necessary for invalidating state laws under the state constitution.
June 15, 1960	Mapp's attorneys file a notice of appeal to the U.S. Supreme Court.
October 24, 1960	The U.S. Supreme Court notes probable jurisdiction and agrees to review Mapp's case.
March 29, 1961	The Supreme Court hears oral arguments in *Mapp v. Ohio*.
June 19, 1961	The Supreme Court decides *Mapp v. Ohio*, ruling that evidence seized in violation of the Fourth Amendment must be excluded from state criminal trials.
October 1961	The National District Attorneys Association files a petition to the Supreme Court requesting that it rehear *Mapp v. Ohio*, which is denied.
March 1965	In his first speech to Congress, President Lyndon Baines Johnson delivers his "Message on Law Enforcement on the Administration of Justice."
September 1967	President Johnson proposes the Crime Control and Safe Streets Act of 1967.
March 1968	Congress holds hearings on the proposed Crime Control and Safe Streets Act.
1968	The Omnibus Crime Control and Safe Streets Act is signed into law. Title II of the act legislatively reverses the Supreme Court *Miranda v. Arizona* decision.

February 18, 1970	Dollree Mapp is arrested after being linked to an apartment that contained narcotics. She is released on bail pending trial.
November 2, 1970	Mapp is arrested for possession of narcotics and stolen goods found in her home.
January 1971	Senator Lloyd Bentsen (D-TX) introduces Senate Bill 2657 to limit the exclusionary rule to only situations involving "a substantial" violation. The bill dies.
April 23, 1971	Mapp is convicted in New York Supreme Court in Queens County for possession of narcotics.
June 26, 1972	The New York Appellate Division reverses Mapp's conviction in the state supreme court in Queens County. Mapp is reconvicted five weeks later.
February 1973	Senator Lloyd Bentsen (D-TX) introduces Senate Bill 881, which limits the exclusionary rule to "substantial" violations and replaces it with a tort remedy. The bill dies.
March 1975	The U.S. District Court for the Southern District of New York dismisses Mapp's first petition for a writ of habeas corpus.
March 16, 1976	The U.S. Court of Appeals for the Second Circuit affirms the district court's dismissal for a petition for a writ of habeas corpus.
November 15, 1976	The U.S. Supreme Court denies Mapp's petition for a writ of certiorari.
March 15, 1978	The U.S. District Court for the Southern District of New York dismisses Mapp's second petition for a writ of habeas corpus.
October 1981	The Senate Subcommittee on Criminal Law, the Committee on the Judiciary, holds hearings on "The Exclusionary Rule Bills."
February 1982	Dennis DeConcini (D-AZ) introduces Senate Bill 101 to limit the exclusionary rule to substantial violations. Strom Thurmond (R-SC) and Orrin Hatch (R-UT) introduce Senate Bill 751, which would abolish the exclusionary rule in and replace it with a civil tort remedy. Senate Bill 1995, introduced by Robert Dole (R-KS), would create

	a reasonable, good faith exception to the exclusionary rule.
June 1982	The Subcommittee on Criminal Justice under the House Judiciary Committee holds hearings on the exclusionary rule.
January 1984	Senator Strom Thurmond (R-SC) introduces Senate Bill 1764, which would create a "reasonable, good faith" exception to the exclusionary rule. The Senate Judiciary Committee approves the bill, and it passes on the floor of the Senate. A similar measure is introduced in the House in September 1984, but after two weeks of debate, the bill dies.
January 1995	Representative Bill McCollum (R-FL) introduces House Bill 666, "The Exclusionary Rule Reform Act." The proposed legislation would codify *Leon* with the "reasonable good faith" exception and would extend the good faith exception to allow federal prosecutors to use evidence seized during *warrantless* searches as long as the police conducting the search had reason to believe the search was legal.
January 1995	The House Subcommittee on Criminal Justice under the House Judiciary Committee holds hearings on the exclusionary rule legislation. The bill is voted favorably out of committee and passed on the House floor. However, it later dies due to Senate inaction.
January 1995	Senator Orrin Hatch (R-UT) introduces Senate Bill 3, which would abolish the exclusionary rule in federal proceedings and replace it with a federal tort remedy.
March 1995	The Senate Subcommittee on Criminal Law, the Committee on the Judiciary, holds hearings on Senate Bill 3. Eventually, the bill dies in committee.

RELEVANT CASES

Adams v. New York 192 U.S. 585 (1904)
Adamson v. California 332 U.S. 46 (1947)
Agnello v. United States 269 U.S. 20 (1925)
Aguillar v. Texas 378 U.S. 108 (1964)
Alderman v. United States 394 U.S. 165 (1969)
Amos v. United States 255 U.S. 313 (1921)
Arizona v. Evans 514 U.S. 1 (1995)
Barron v. Baltimore 32 U.S. 243 (1833)
Benton v. Maryland 395 U.S. 784 (1969)
Bivens v. Six Unknown Federal Narcotics Agents 403 U.S. 388 (1971)
Boyd v. United States 116 U.S. 616 (1886)
Briethaup v. Abram 352 U.S. 423 (1957)
Byars v. United States 273 U.S. 28 (1927)
Camara v. Municipal Court 387 U.S. 523 (1967)
Cantwell v. Connecticut 310 U.S. 296 (1940)
De Jonge v. Oregon 299 U.S. 353 (1937)
Dickerson v. United States 530 U.S. 428 (2000)
Douglas v. California 372 U.S. 353 (1962)
Duncan v. Louisiana 391 U.S. 145 (1968)
Elkins v. United States 364 U.S. 306 (1960)
Escobedo v. Illinois 378 U.S. 478 (1964)
Everson v. Board of Education 330 U.S. 1 (1947)
Gambino v. United States 275 U.S. 310 (1927)
Gideon v. Wainwright 372 U.S. 335 (1963)
Gitlow v. New York 268 U.S. 652 (1925)
Gouled v. United States 225 U.S. 298 (1921)
Harris v. New York 401 U.S. 222 (1971)
Illinois v. Gates 462 U.S. 213 (1982)
Illinois v. Krull 480 U.S. 340 (1987)
Illinois v. Perkins 496 U.S. 292 (1990)
INS v. Lopez-Mendoza 468 U.S. 1032 (1984)
Irvine v. California 347 U.S. 128 (1954)
Jones v. United States 362 U.S. 257 (1960)
Katz v. United States 389 U.S. 347 (1967)
Ker v. California 374 U.S. 23 (1963)
Klopfer v. North Carolina 386 U.S. 213 (1967)
Linkletter v. Walker 381 U.S. 618 (1965)
Lustig v. United States 338 U.S. 74 (1949)
Malloy v. Hogan 378 U.S. 1 (1964)

Mapp v. Ohio 367 U.S. 643 (1961)

Mapp v. Clement 451 F. Supp. 505 (1978)

Mapp and Lyons v. Warden, N.Y. Correctional Institute 531 F.2d 1167 (2d Cir. 1976)

Mapp and Lyons v. Warden, N.Y. Correctional Institute 429 U.S. 982 (1976)

Massachusetts v. Sheppard 468 U.S. 981 (1984)

Massiah v. United States 377 U.S. 201 (1964)

McDonald v. United States 335 U.S. 451 (1948)

McNabb v. United States 318 U.S. 332 (1943)

Michigan v. Tucker 417 U.S. 433 (1974)

Mincey v. Arizona 437 U.S. 385 (1978)

Miranda v. Arizona 384 U.S. 436 (1966)

NAACP v. Alabama 337 U.S. 445 (1958)

Nardone v. United States 308 U.S. 338 (1939)

Near v. Minnesota 283 U.S. 697 (1931)

New York v. Mapp and Lyons 333 N.Y.S.2d 539 (1972)

New York v. Quarles 467 U.S. 649 (1984)

Nix v. Williams 467 U.S. 431 (1984)

Ohio v. Mapp 170 Ohio St. 427 (1960)

Olmstead v. United States 277 U.S. 438 (1928)

One Plymouth Sedan v. Pennsylvania 380 U.S. 693 (1965)

Oregon v. Elstad 470 U.S. 298 (1985)

Oregon v. Hass 420 U.S. 714 (1975)

Palko v. Connecticut 302 U.S. 319 (1937)

Pennsylvania Board of Probation and Parole v. Scott 524 U.S. 357 (1998)

Pennsylvania v. Muniz 496 U.S. 582 (1990)

People v. Cahan 44 Cal. 2d 434 (N.Y. 1955)

People v. Defore 150 N.E. 585 (N.Y. 1926)

People v. Gonzales 20 Cal. 2d 165 (N.Y. 1942)

Pointer v. Texas 380 U.S. 400 (1965)

Rakas v. Illinois 439 U.S. 128 (1978)

Rawlings v. Kentucky 448 U.S. 98 (1980)

Rios v. United States 364 U.S. 253 (1960)

Robinson v. California 370 U.S. 660 (1962)

Rochin v. California 342 U.S. 165 (1952)

Roth v. United States 354 U.S. 476 (1957)

Schilb v. Kuebel 404 U.S. 357 (1971)

Sibron v. New York 392 U.S. 40 (1968)

Silverthorne Lumber Co. v. United States 251 U.S. 385 (1920)

Smith v. California 361 U.S. 147 (1959)

Spinelli v. United States 393 U.S. 410 (1969)

State v. Lindway 2 N.E.2d 490 (Ohio, 1936)

Stefanelli v. Minard 342 U.S. 199 (1952)
Stone v. Powell 428 U.S. 465 (1976)
Terry v. Ohio 392 U.S. 1 (1967)
Trupinao v. United States 344 U.S. 699 (1948)
Twining v. New Jersey 211 U.S. 78 (1908)
United States v. Calandra 414 U.S. 338 (1974)
United States v. Havens 446 U.S. 620 (1980)
United States v. Janis 428 U.S. 433 (1976)
United States v. Jeffers 352 U.S. 48 (1951)
United States v. Leon 468 U.S. 897 (1984)
United States v. Payner 447 U.S. 727 (1980)
United States v. Rabinowitz 399 U.S. 56 (1950)
United States v. Salvucci 448 U.S. 83 (1980)
United States v. Wallace and Tiernan Co. 336 U.S. 793 (1949)
Warden v. Hayden 387 U.S. 294 (1967)
Washington v. Texas 388 U.S. 14 (1967)
Weeks v. United States 232 U.S. 383 (1914)
Wilkinson v. United States 365 U.S. 399 (1961)
Wolf v. Colorado 338 U.S. 25 (1949)
Wong Sun v. United States 371 U.S. 471 (1963)

BIBLIOGRAPHICAL ESSAY

Note from the series editors: The following bibliographical essay contains the primary and secondary sources the author consulted for this volume. We have asked all authors in the series to omit formal citations in order to make our volumes more readable, inexpensive, and appealing for students and general readers. In adopting this format, Landmark Law Cases and American Society follows the precedent of a number of highly regarded and widely consulted series.

Several dozen books and hundreds of articles have been written on the Fourth Amendment and the exclusionary rule. This bibliographical essay focuses on the history of the Fourth Amendment and the debate over its warrant clause, the merits of the exclusionary rule, studies on the exclusionary rule's effect on law enforcement behavior, the implementation and impact of the rule in nonexclusionary rule states, the Warren, Burger, and Rehnquist Courts and criminal procedure, the executive and legislative branch response to *Mapp*, and new judicial federalism. Readers interested in a more comprehensive look at these subjects will find the following book and journal citations useful for conducting further research. What follows is not intended to be exhaustive; rather, I highlight several of the more useful books or articles in each category. This essay also provides a review of the primary and secondary sources used for this book.

Professor Wayne LaFave once noted that the Fourth Amendment was the most litigated provision in the Bill of Rights. He should know; he authored a five-volume treatise on the subject. Those interested are encouraged to review LaFave's *Search and Seizure: A Treatise on the Fourth Amendment*, 5th ed. (Eagan, Minn.: Thomson/West, 2004). The series provides a comprehensive review of Fourth Amendment case law and analysis of its evolution over time. His treatment of the exclusionary rule is particularly impressive. Volume 1 dedicates more than 300 pages to the rule's development, and volume 5 more than 400 pages to its administration. Also useful is his article "Search and Seizure: 'The Course of True Law . . . Has Not . . . Run Smooth,'" 1966 *Illinois Law Forum* 255. The title comes from a quotation from Justice Felix Frankfurter, who aptly observed that "the course of true law pertaining to searches and seizures, has not — to put it mildly — run smooth" (*Chapman v. United States*, 1961). Review of the history and development of the Fourth Amendment can be found in Jacob W. Landynski's *Search and Seizure and the Supreme Court: A Study in Constitutional Interpretation* (Baltimore: Johns Hopkins University Press, 1966); Nelson B. Lasson, *The History and Development of the Fourth Amendment to the United States Constitution* (Baltimore: Johns Hopkins University Press, 1937); and Telford Taylor, *Two Studies in Constitutional Interpretation* (Columbus: Ohio State University Press,

1969). Each book provides a unique perspective on the Fourth Amendment's historical roots. Insight can also be found in several dozen law review articles. I found the following useful: Anthony G. Amsterdam, "Perspectives on the Fourth Amendment," 58 *Minnesota Law Review* 349 (1974); William Cuddihy and B. Carmon Hardy, "A Man's House Was Not His Castle: Origins of the Fourth Amendment to the United States Constitution," 37 *William and Mary Quarterly* 371 (1980); Tracey Maclin, "The Central Meaning of the Fourth Amendment," 35 *William and Mary Law Review* 197 (1993); Bob Redemann, "Historical and Philosophical Foundations of the Exclusionary Rule," 12 *Tulsa Law Journal* 323 (1977); and Silas J. Wasserstrom and Louis Michael Seidman, "The Fourth Amendment as Constitutional Theory," 77 *Georgetown Law Journal* 19 (1988). While each author offers a different perspective on the Fourth Amendment, each work is thoroughly researched and extensively cited.

Those wishing insight into the debate over the Fourth Amendment's warrant requirement will appreciate the following citations. In addition to Taylor, noted earlier, scholars endorsing the "generalized reasonableness construction" of the Fourth Amendment include Akhil Reed Amar in *The Constitution and Criminal Procedure: First Principles* (New Haven, Conn.: Yale University Press, 1997), a book based on his earlier article "Fourth Amendment First Principles," 107 *Harvard Law Review* 757 (1994). Amar is joined by Thomas K. Clancy, "The Role of Individualized Suspicion in Assessing the Reasonableness of Searches and Seizures," 25 *University of Memphis Law Review* 483 (1994); and Joseph D. Grano, "Rethinking the Fourth Amendment Warrant Requirement," 19 *American Criminal Law Review* 603 (1982). Those endorsing the "warrant preference construction," which emphasizes the primacy of the warrant requirement, include Phyllis T. Bookspan, "Reworking the Warrant Requirement: Resuscitating the Fourth Amendment," 44 *Vanderbilt Law Review* 473 (1991); Donald Dripps, "Akhil Amar on Criminal Procedure and Constitutional Law: 'Here I Go Down That Wrong Road Again,'" 74 *North Carolina Law Review* 1559 (1996); Tracey Maclin, "When the Cure for the Fourth Amendment Is Worse than the Disease," 68 *Southern California Law Review* 1 (1994); Carol S. Steiker, "Second Thoughts about First Principles," 107 *Harvard Law Review* 820 (1994); and Silas J. Wasserstrom, "The Court's Turn toward a General Reasonableness Interpretation of the Fourth Amendment," 27 *American Criminal Law Review* 119 (1989). If readers are interested in only one scholarly treatment of this debate, I highly recommend Thomas Davis, "Recovering the Original Fourth Amendment," 98 *Michigan Law Review* 547 (1999).

Hundreds of articles have been written on the exclusionary rule. A general examination of its historical basis can be found in Francis Allen, "Federalism and the Fourth Amendment: A Requiem for Wolf," 1961 *Supreme Court Review*, 1; Gerald V. Bradley, "Present at the Creation? A Critical Guide to

Weeks v. United States and Its Progeny," 30 *Saint Louis University Law Journal* 1031 (1986); Bradford Wilson, "The Origin and Development of the Federal Rule of Exclusion," 18 *Wake Forest Law Review* 1073 (1982); and Note, The Historical and Philosophical Foundations of the Exclusionary Rule, 12 *Tulsa Law Journal* 323 (1976). Scholars who discuss a constitutional basis for the exclusionary rule include Steven Cann and Bob Egbert, "The Exclusionary Rule: Its Necessity in a Constitutional Democracy," 23 *Howard Law Journal* 299 (1980); William C. Heffernan, "On Justifying Fourth Amendment Exclusion," 1989 *Wisconsin Law Review* 1193, and "The Fourth Amendment Exclusionary Rule as a Constitutional Remedy," 88 *Georgetown Law Journal,* 799 (2000); and Thomas S. Shrock and Robert C. Welsh, "Up from *Calandra:* The Exclusionary Rule as a Constitutional Requirement," 59 *Minnesota Law Review* 251 (1974).

There are a wealth of articles that discuss the merits of the exclusionary rule. Early commentary in support of the rule before it was extended to states in *Mapp v. Ohio* can be found in Thomas S. Atkinson, "Admissibility of Evidence Obtained through Unreasonable Searches and Seizures," 25 *Columbia Law Review* 11 (1925); and Francis Allen, "The *Wolf* Case: Search and Seizure, Federalism, and the Civil Liberties," 45 *Illinois Law Review* 1 (1950). An opposing perspective is offered in Virgil W. Peterson, "Law and Police Practice: Restrictions in the Law of Search and Seizure," 52 *Northwestern University Law Review* 46 (1957–1958); William T. Plumb, "Illegal Enforcement of the Law," 24 *Cornell Law Quarterly* 337 (1939); John Barker Waite, "Police Regulation by Rules of Evidence," 42 *Michigan Law Review* 679 (1944); and Dean John Wigmore, "Evidence — Fourth Amendment — Documents Illegally Seized," 9 *Illinois Law Review* 43 (1915), and "Using Evidence Obtained by Illegal Search and Seizure," 8 *American Bar Association Journal* (1922).

More recent articles on the exclusionary rule detail its evolution since the Supreme Court ruling in *Mapp v. Ohio.* A leading exclusionary rule scholar, Yale Kamisar, has written more than a dozen on the subject. His seminal work, "Does (Did) (Should) the Exclusionary Rule Rest on a 'Principled Basis' Rather Than an 'Empirical Proposition'?" 16 *Creighton Law Review* 565 (1983), provides an impassioned defense of the exclusionary rule. Also worthwhile are "On the Tactics of Police-Prosecution Oriented Critics of the Courts," 49 *Cornell Law Quarterly* 437 (1964); "Public Safety v. Individual Liberties: Some 'Facts' and 'Theories,'" 53 *Journal of Criminal Law, Criminology and Police Society* 171 (1962); "Some Reflections on Criticizing the Courts, and 'Policing the Police,'" 53 *Journal of Criminal Law, Criminology and Police Society,* 453 (1962); and "In Defense of the Search and Seizure Exclusionary Rule," 26 *Harvard Journal of Law and Public Policy* 119 (2003). Other articles offering a favorable view of the exclusionary rule include Jack G. Day and Bernard A. Berkman, "Search and Seizure and the Exclusionary Rule: A Re-examination in the Wake of *Mapp v. Ohio*," 56 *Western Reserve Law Review* (1961); Donald Dripps, "Beyond the Warren Court and Its Conservative Critics: Toward a Unified Theory of Constitutional Criminal Procedure," 23 *University of Michigan Journal of Law Reform* 591 (1990), "Living with *Leon*," 95 *Yale Law Journal* 906 (1986), and "The Case for the Contingent Exclusionary Rule," 38 *American Criminal Law Review* 1 (2001); John Kaplan, "Search and Seizure: A No-Man's Land in the Criminal Law," 49 *California Law Review* 474 (1961), and "The Limits of the Exclusionary Rule," 26 *Stanford Law Review* 1027 (1974); Lewis R. Katz, "*Mapp* after Forty Years: Its Impact on Race in America," 52 *Case Western Law Review* 471 (2001); Stanley Ingber, "Defending the Citadel: The Dangerous Attack of 'Reasonable Good Faith,'" 36 *Vanderbilt Law Review* 1511 (1983); Wayne LaFave, "The Fourth Amendment in an Imperfect World: On Drawing 'Bright Lines' and 'Good Faith,'" 43 *University of Pittsburgh Law Review* 307 (1982); Arnold H. Loewy, "The Fourth Amendment as a Device for Protecting the Innocent," 81 *Michigan Law Review* 1229 (1983); Timothy Lynch, "In Defense of the Exclusionary Rule," 23 *Harvard Journal of Law and Public Policy* (2000); William J. Mertens and Silas Wasserstrom, "The Good Faith Exception to the Exclusionary Rule: Deregulating the Police and Derailing the Law," 88 *Columbia Law Review* 247 (1981); and Roger Traynor, "*Mapp v. Ohio* at Large in the Fifty States," 1962 *Duke Law Journal* 319. These works also lament the demise of the exclusionary rule under the Supreme Court during the Burger and Rehnquist Courts.

There are, however, an equal number of contemporary critics of the exclusionary rule. They include Akhil Reed Amar, "Against Exclusion (Except to Protect Truth or Prevent Privacy Violations)," 20 *Harvard Journal of Law and Public Policy* 457 (1997); Robert Burns, "*Mapp v. Ohio*: An All American Mistake," 19 *DePaul Law Review* 80 (1969); Fred Inbau, "Public Safety v. Individual Civil Liberties: The Prosecutor's Stand," 53 *Journal of Criminal Law, Criminology and Police Society* 85 (1962), and "More about Public Safety v. Individual Civil Liberties," 53 *Journal of Criminal Law, Criminology and Police Society* 329 (1962); Steve Schlesinger, *Exclusionary Injustice: The Problem of Illegally Obtained Evidence* (New York: M. Dekker, 1977); and Christopher Slobogin, "Why Liberals Should Chuck the Exclusionary Rule," 1999 *University of Illinois Law Review* 363. A number of state and federal judges have publicly commented on problems with the exclusionary rule, including Warren Burger, "Who Will Watch the Watchman?" 14 *American University Law Review* 1 (1964); Henry J. Friendly, "The Bill of Rights as a Code of Criminal Procedure," 53 *California Law Review* 929 (1965); Harold J. Rothwax, *Guilty: The Collapse of the Criminal Justice System* (New York: Random House, 1996); and Malcolm Richard Wilkey, *Enforcing the Fourth Amendment by Alternatives to the Exclusionary Rule* (Washington, D.C.: National Legal Center for the Public Interest, 1982), and "The Exclusionary Rule: Costs and Viable Alternatives," 1

Criminal Justice Ethics 16 (1982). Exclusionary rule opponents suggest that the rule be replaced by alternatives, including civil damage actions, criminal penalties, or nonjudicial devices such as review boards. Insight into these alternative solutions can be found in William A. Schroeder, "Deterring Fourth Amendment Violations: Alternatives to the Exclusionary Rule," 69 *Georgetown Law Journal* 1361 (1981); William Geller, "Enforcing the Fourth Amendment: The Exclusionary Rule and Its Alternatives," 1975 *Washington University Law Quarterly* 621 (1975); and Donald V. MacDougall, "Criminal Law: The Exclusionary Rule and Its Alternatives — Remedies for Constitutional Violations in Canada and the United States," 76 *Journal of Criminal Law and Criminology* 608 (1985). Those interested in an accessible discussion of the advantages and disadvantages of the exclusionary rule by leading scholars will enjoy "The Exclusionary Rule Debate" in *Judicature* (special reprint, 1979).

A number of studies have been published on the exclusionary rule's effect on law enforcement behavior. Early empirical studies evaluated whether the rule deterred police misconduct. They include "Effect of *Mapp v. Ohio* on Police Search-and-Seizure Practices in Narcotics Cases," a study by Columbia law school students in 4 *Columbia Law Journal and Social Problems* 87 (1968); Dallin H. Oaks, "Studying the Exclusionary Rule in Search and Seizure," 37 *University of Chicago Law Review* 665 (1970); and James E. Spiotto, "Search and Seizure: An Empirical Study of the Exclusionary Rule and Its Alternatives," 2 *Journal Legal Studies* 243 (1973). For an excellent critique of these early studies, see Thomas Y. Davies, "On the Limitations of Empirical Evaluation of the Exclusionary Rule: A Critique of the Spiotto Research and *United States v. Calandra*," 69 *Northwest University Law Review* 40 (1974). Another critique and presentation of original research on the deterrent effect of the exclusionary rule is provided in Bradley Canon, "Is the Exclusionary Rule in Failing Health? Some New Data and a Plea against a Precipitous Conclusion," 62 *Kentucky Law Journal* 681 (1974), and "Testing the Effectiveness of Civil Liberties Policies at the State and Federal Levels: The Case of the Exclusionary Rule," 5 *American Politics Quarterly* 57 (1977).

Later studies examine the exclusionary rule's effect on "lost" cases — those prosecutors declined to pursue or those that resulted in nonconvictions. They include *The Impact of the Exclusionary Rule on Federal Criminal Prosecutions* (Comptroller General of the United States, Rep. No. GGD-79-45, 1979); *The Effects of the Exclusionary Rule: A Study of California* (National Institute of Justice, 1982); Peter Nardulli, "The Societal Cost of the Exclusionary Rule: An Empirical Assessment," 1983 *American Bar Foundation Research Journal* 585; and Craig D. Uchida and Timothy S. Bynum, "Search Warrants, Motions to Suppress and 'Lost Cases': The Effects of the Exclusionary Rule in Seven Jurisdictions," 81 *Journal of Criminal Law and Criminology* 1034 (1991). For a critical assessment of these early studies, Thomas Y. Davies's "A

Hard Look at What We Know (and Still Need to Learn) about the 'Costs' of the Exclusionary Rule: The NIJ Study and Other Studies of 'Lost' Arrests," 1983 *American Bar Foundation Research Journal* 611, provides what Wayne LaFave has called "the most careful and balanced assessment conducted to date of all available empirical data."

In-depth qualitative studies that provide insight into police attitudes toward the exclusionary rule based on interviews with law enforcement and non–law enforcement can be found in Myron W. Orfield Jr. "Comment, The Exclusionary Rule and Deterrence: An Empirical Study of Chicago Narcotics Officers," 54 *University of Chicago Law Review* 1016 (1987), and "Deterrence, Perjury, and the Heater Factor: An Exclusionary Rule in Chicago Criminal Courts," 63 *University of Colorado Law Review* 75 (1992). Milton Loewenthal uses a similar methodology in his detailed study, "Evaluating the Exclusionary Rule in Search and Seizure," 49 *UMKC Law Review* 24 (1980).

The exclusionary rule's effect in deterring police misconduct can also be measured by examining whether it contributes to greater police knowledge of the rules of search and seizure. Studies in this category include William C. Heffernan and Richard W. Lovely, "Evaluating the Fourth Amendment Exclusionary Rule: The Problem of Police Compliance with the Law," 24 *University of Michigan Journal of Law Reform* 311 (1991); and L. Timothy Perrin et al., "If It's Broken, Fix It: Moving beyond the Exclusionary Rule," 83 *Iowa Law Review* 669 (1998).

Another way of examining *Mapp*'s impact is to study how the decision was implemented in states without the exclusionary rule prior to *Mapp* in order to evaluate compliance with Supreme Court decisions. The framework for such an examination is provided in Bradley C. Canon and Charles A. Johnson's *Judicial Policies: Implementation and Impact* (Washington, D.C.: CQ Press, 1999). Additional studies on the problems encountered in the communication of Supreme Court decisions to law enforcement have been conducted by sociologists and criminologists. An early general study is provided in Jerome H. Skolnick, *Justice without Trial: Law Enforcement in a Democratic Society* (New York: Wiley, 1966). A general discussion of the problems encountered in the implementation of *Mapp v. Ohio* and other Supreme Court criminal procedure decisions can be found in Harry M. Caldwell and Carol A. Chase, "The Unruly Exclusionary Rule: Heeding Justice Blackmun's Call to Examine the Rule in Light of Changing Judicial Understanding about Its Effects Outside the Courtroom," 78 *Marquette Law Review* 45 (1994); Wayne LaFave, "Improving Police Performance through the Exclusionary Rule — Part I: Current Police and Local Court Practices," 30 *Montana Law Review* 391 (1965), and "Improving Police Performance through the Exclusionary Rule — Part II: Defining the Norms and Training the Police," 30 *Montana Law Review* 566 (1965); Daniel Meltzer, "Deterring Constitutional Violations by Law Enforcement Officers," 88 *Columbia Law Review* 247 (1988); Neil Milner, "Supreme Court Effectiveness and the Police Organization," 36 *Law and Contemporary Problems* 467 (1971); Monrad G. Paulsen, "Safeguards in the Law of Search and Seizure," 52 *Northwest University Law Review* 65 (1957), and "The Exclusionary Rule and Misconduct by the Police," 52 *Journal of Criminal Law Criminology and Police Science* 255 (1961); Albert Quick, "Attitudinal Aspects of Police Compliance with Procedural Due Process," 6 *American Journal of Criminal Law* 25 (1978); and Jack Weinstein, "Local Responsibility for Improvement of Search and Seizure Practices," 34 *Rocky Mountain Law Review* 150 (1962).

More specific case studies of *Mapp*'s implementation can be found in Michael Katz, "The Supreme Court and the States: An Inquiry into *Mapp v. Ohio* in North Carolina: The Study and the Implications," 45 *North Carolina Law Review* 119 (1966); Stuart S. Nagel, "Law and Society: Testing the Effects of Excluding Illegally Seized Evidence," 1965 *Wisconsin Law Review* 283; David Horowitz, "*Mapp v. Ohio*: Police Behavior and the Courts," in *The Courts and Social Policy* (Washington, D.C.: Brookings Institute, 1977); and Stephen Wasby, *The Impact of the United States Supreme Court: Some Perspectives* (Homewood, Ill.: Dorsey Press, 1970). And, while it primarily involves *Miranda v. Arizona*, an excellent discussion of implementation of the Supreme Court's criminal procedure decisions is discussed in Neal Milner, *The Court and Local Law Enforcement: The Impact of Miranda* (Beverly Hills, Calif.: Sage, 1971), and Stephen Wasby, "The Communication of the Supreme Court's Criminal Procedure Decisions: A Preliminary Mapping," 18 *Villanova Law Review* 1086 (1973). Firsthand accounts of how *Mapp* affected police behavior can be found in Michael Murphy, "Judicial Review of Police Methods Law Enforcement: The Problem of Compliance by Police Departments," 44 *Texas Law Review* 939 (1966); Eugene Hyman, "In Pursuit of a More Workable Exclusionary Rule: A Police Officer's Perspective," 10 *Pacific Law Journal* 33 (1978); Stephen H. Sachs, "The Exclusionary Rule: A Prosecutor's Defense," 28 *Criminal Justice Ethics* (1982); and Arlen Specter, "*Mapp v. Ohio*: Pandora's Problems for the Prosecutor," 111 *University* of *Pennsylvania Law Review* 4 (1962).

There are hundreds of books and articles on law enforcement that are relevant to a discussion of *Mapp v. Ohio*. For instance, a thorough discussion of the process of obtaining search warrants, the challenges encountered, and perspectives on search warrants from police, prosecutors, and judges can be found in Richard Van Duizend, L. Paul Sutton, and Charlotte A. Carter, *The Search Warrant Process: Preconceptions, Perceptions, Practices* (Williamsburg, Va.: National Center for Courts, 1985), and William J. Stuntz, "Warrants and Fourth Amendment Remedies," 77 *Virginia Law Review* 881 (1991). More specifically, Michael Ban presented two academic papers based on his doctoral dissertation on warrant use in Boston and Cincinnati to evaluate whether

Mapp v. Ohio led to an increase in warrant use: "Local Courts v. The Supreme Court: The Impact of *Mapp v. Ohio*" (American Political Science Association meeting, September 1973) and "The Impact of *Mapp v. Ohio* on Police Behavior" (Midwest Political Science Association, Chicago, May 1973). Police perjury is reviewed in Orfield, noted previously, and Gabriel J. Chin and Scott C. Wells, "The 'Blue Wall of Silence' as Evidence of Bias and Motive to Lie: A New Approach to Police Perjury," 59 *University of Pittsburgh Law Review* 233 (1998).

To understand *Mapp*'s full impact, it is useful to place it in the context of the Warren Court's criminal procedure revolution. An excellent description of this period in the Court's history is provided in Richard C. Cortner's *The Supreme Court and the Second Bill of Rights: The Fourteenth Amendment and the Nationalization of Civil Liberties* (Madison: University of Wisconsin Press, 1981). There are a number of excellent treatments of the Warren and Burger Courts' contribution to criminal procedure, including Albert W. Alschuler, "Failed Pragmatism: Reflections on the Burger Court," 100 *Harvard Law Review* 1436 (1987); Francis Allen, "The Judicial Quest for Penal Justice: The Warren Court and the Criminal Cases," 1975 *Law Forum* 518; Peter Arenella, "Rethinking the Functions of Criminal Procedure: The Warren and Burger Courts' Competing Ideologies," 72 *Georgetown Law Journal* 185 (1983); Vincent Blasi, ed., *The Burger Court: The Counter-revolution That Wasn't* (New Haven, Conn.: Yale University Press, 1983); Donald A. Dripps, "Beyond the Warren Court and Its Conservative Critics: Toward a Unified Theory of Constitutional Criminal Procedure," 23 *University of Michigan Journal of Law Reform* 591 (1990); Jerold H. Israel, "Criminal Procedure: The Burger Court, and the Legacy of the Warren Court," 75 *Michigan Law Review* 1319 (1977); Yale Kamisar, "The Warren Court and Criminal Justice: A Quarter-Century Retrospective," 31 *Tulsa Law Journal* 1 (1995); A. Kenneth Pye, "The Warren Court and Criminal Procedure," 67 *Michigan Law Review* 249 (1968); Stephen A. Saltzburg, "Foreword: The Flow and Ebb of Constitutional Criminal Procedure in the Warren and Burger Courts," 69 *Georgetown Law Journal* 151 (1980); Bernard Schwartz, ed., *The Burger Court: Counter-Revolution or Confirmation* (New York: Oxford University Press, 1988); and Tinsley Yarbrough, *The Burger Court: Justices, Rulings and Legacy* (Santa Barbara, Calif.: ABC-CLIO, 2000). The exclusionary rule's reach has also been limited under the Rehnquist Court. Works worth consulting include Laurence A. Benner, "Diminishing Expectations of Privacy in the Rehnquist Court," 22 *John Marshall Law Review* 825 (1989); Martin H. Belsky, *The Rehnquist Court: A Retrospective* (New York: Oxford University Press, 2002); John F. Decker, *Revolution to the Right: Criminal Procedure Jurisprudence during the Burger-Rehnquist Court Era* (New York: Garland, 1992); Stanley Friedelbaum, *The Rehnquist Court: In Pursuit of Judicial Conservatism* (Westport, Conn.: Greenwood Press, 1994);

Herman Schwartz, ed., *The Rehnquist Court: Judicial Activism on the Right* (New York: Hill and Wang, 2002); and Tinsley Yarbrough, *The Rehnquist Court and the Constitution* (New York: Oxford University Press, 2000).

The Warren Court's criminal procedure revolution, including its decision in *Mapp v. Ohio*, has been criticized in the executive and legislative branches of government for contributing to an increase in crime. Information on the debate over the exclusionary rule during the Johnson administration can be found in *The Challenge of Crime in a Free Society: A Report by the President's Commission on Law Enforcement and the Administration of Justice* (Washington D.C.: U.S. Government Printing Office, 1967), and *The President's Commission on Law Enforcement and the Administration of Justice Task Force Report: The Police* (Washington, D.C.: U.S. Government Printing Office, 1967). Insight into the Reagan administration's perspective is provided in *The Attorney General's Task Force on Violent Crimes, Final Report* (Washington, D.C.: U.S. Department of Justice, 1981), and its Truth in Criminal Justice Series. Of the latter, the *Report to the Attorney General: The Search and Seizure Exclusionary Rule* (Washington, D.C.: Office of Legal Policy, 1986) offers a detailed account of the administration's critique of the exclusionary rule and its suggestions for judicial and legislative strategies to reverse *Mapp v. Ohio*. The Justice Department's eight-report Truth in Criminal Justice Series is also reprinted in 22 *University of Michigan Journal of Law Reform* (1989). Also useful are the Office of Legal Policy's *Report to the Attorney General: The Constitution in the Year 2000: Choices ahead in Constitutional Interpretations* (Washington, D.C.: Government Printing Office, 1988); and *Report to the Attorney General: Guidelines on Constitutional Interpretations* (Washington, D.C.: Government Printing Office, 1988). Information on Congress's investigation of the exclusionary rule is provided in several congressional committee hearings, including *The Exclusionary Rule Bills: Hearings before the Subcommittee On Criminal Law of the Senate Comm. On the Judiciary*, 97th Cong., 1st and 2nd sess. (1982); U.S. Senate Judiciary Subcommittee on Criminal Law, March 25, 1982; *Exclusionary Rule in Criminal Trials: Oversight Hearings before the Subcommittee on Criminal Justice of the House Committee. On the Judiciary*, 98th Cong., 1st sess. (1983); *Taking Back Our Streets Act of 1995:* Hearings before the Subcommittee on Crime of the Committee on the Judiciary, House of Representatives, 104th Cong., 1st sess., on H.R. 3 January 19 and 20, 1995; *The Jury and the Search for Truth: The Case against Excluding Relevant Evidence at Trial: Hearing on S. 3 before the Senate Committee on the Judiciary*, 104th Cong. (1995). Also useful were the floor debates in both the House and the Senate, which are reprinted in the *Congressional Record* and weekly synopses of congressional action in *Congressional Digest*. A review of congressional attempts to reverse Warren Court criminal procedure decisions can be found in "Title II of the Omnibus Crime Bill: A Study of the Interaction of Law and Politics," 48 *Nebraska Law*

Review 193 (1968), and "Excluding the Exclusionary Rule: Congressional Assault on *Mapp v. Ohio*," 61 *Georgetown Law Journal* 1453 (1973).

Although it is reviewed only briefly in this volume, scholarship on the battle taking place in the states over criminal procedure rights is provided in the literature on new judicial federalism. This relatively recent trend of litigants pursuing protection under state constitutions is explained in William J. Brennan Jr. "State Constitutions and the Protection of the Individual," 90 *Harvard Law Review* 489 (1977), and "The Bill of Rights and the States: The Revival of State Constitutions as Guardians of Individual Rights," 61 *New York University Law Review* 535 (1986). More specifically, information on new federalism's impact on criminal procedure is offered in Timothy A. Baughman, "*Mapp v. Ohio* and the End of Federalism — A 'New' Federalism on the Way?" 64 *Michigan Bar Journal* 108 (1985); James W. Diehm, "New Federalism and Constitutional Criminal Procedure: Are We Repeating the Mistakes of the Past?" 55 *Maryland Law Review* 223 (1996); Mary Jane Morrison, "Choice of Law for Unlawful Searches," 41 *Oklahoma Law Review* 579 (1988); and Donald E. Wilkes Jr., "The New Federalism in Criminal Procedure: State Court Evasion of the Burger Court," 62 *Kentucky Law Journal* 421 (1974).

Primary research on *Mapp v. Ohio* as it moved through the state and federal judicial systems can be found in law school libraries or through Lexis-Nexis. *Ohio v. Mapp*, 170 Ohio St. 427 (1960), includes records of all the state court activity, including all attorneys' briefs and the amicus curiae brief from the American Civil Liberties Union. These records are available in the records of Ohio Supreme Court, Case No. 36,091, and at the Supreme Court Library for the State of Ohio in Columbus, Ohio. The decision of the U.S. Supreme Court in *Mapp v. Ohio* is at 367 U.S. 643 (1961). Mapp's grand jury indictment and the trial transcripts of the Court of Common Pleas, County of Cuyahoga, proceedings can be found in Tom C. Clark's private papers, as well as Record No. 236 of the Supreme Court of the United States. The petitions in favor of and in opposition to review by the Supreme Court, the briefs of the attorneys representing Mapp and the state of Ohio, and the amicus curiae brief from the American Civil Liberties Union are available in microfiche form at most law school and state law libraries. Oral arguments in *Mapp v. Ohio* are available on audiotape and can be found at the National Archives in College Park, Maryland. A transcript of the oral arguments is on file with the author. These official reports were supplemented with information provided from the private papers of former Justice Tom C. Clark. His papers include original votes on the petition for review, notes from Court conferences, and internal Court memoranda. Clark's papers also include all the drafts of the majority, concurring and dissenting opinions. Materials from other relevant Fourth Amendment cases used for this project can also be found in Clark's papers. Justice Clark's papers are open and available to the public for scholarly research at the Special Archives in the Tarlton Law Library at the University of Texas at Austin School of Law. The private papers of Chief Justice Earl Warren, also used for this project, can be found at the Library of Congress in Washington, D.C. In addition to these primary sources, several secondary sources provide insight into this case. An excellent analysis of the Court's *Mapp* deliberations is provided in Dennis D. Dorin, "'Seize the Time': Justice Tom Clark's Role in *Mapp v. Ohio*," in *Law and Legal Process*, Victoria L. Swigert, ed. (Beverly Hills, Calif.: Sage, 1982), and "Marshaling Mapp: Justice Tom Clark's Role in *Mapp v. Ohio*'s Extension of the Exclusionary Rule to State Searches and Seizures," 52 *Case Western Reserve Law Review* 401 (2001). Secondhand accounts of what occurred during the *Mapp* deliberations are provided in Paul R. Baier, "Justice Clark, the Voice of the Past, and the Exclusionary Rule," 64 *Texas Law Review* 415 (1985); Fred Graham's *The Self-Inflicted Wound* (New York: Macmillan, 1970); and Bernard Schwartz's *Super Chief: Earl Warren and His Supreme Court — A Judicial Biography* (New York: New York University Press, 1983). In addition, several Supreme Court justices have publicly commented on the case. An excellent account of the decision and its aftermath can be found in Justice Potter Stewart's "The Road to *Mapp v. Ohio* and Beyond: The Origins, Development and Future of the Exclusionary Rule in Search-and-Seizure Cases," 93 *Columbia Law Review* 1365 (1983).

The bulk of the background information on this case was obtained by in-depth personal interviews with Ms. Dollree Mapp. The information provided from these interviews is present throughout the text of the manuscript. These interviews are available in transcribed form in the author's personal files. Sergeant Carl Delau's perspective is drawn from a telephone interview and several secondary sources, including "A Knock at the Door: How the Supreme Court Created a Rule to Enforce the Fourth Amendment," in *The Constitution: That Delicate Balance* by Fred W. Friendly and Martha J. H. Elliott (New York: Random House, 1984), and a passage in Joel Samaha's textbook, *Criminal Procedure*, 5th ed. (Belmont, Calif.: Wadsworth/Thomson Learning, 2002). I was only able to conduct one telephone conversation with Mr. Delau. He was unable to speak to me beyond this because he is working with another scholar on a book project on this case. In addition, an early book on this decision, *Trespass! The People's Privacy vs. the Power of the Police, Great Constitutional Issues: The Fourth Amendment* (New York: Coward, McCann and Geoghegan, 1977), by Leonard A. Stevens, offers a description of the case and Delau's perspective.

News reports on the police search of Mapp's home and her subsequent court battle can be found in the local newspaper, the *Cleveland Plain Dealer*. Also useful were articles from the *Cleveland Call and Post*. Twenty years later, an account of Mapp's arrest in New York City can be found in the *New York Times*.

INDEX